9.00

PRAEGER LIBRARY OF U.S. GOVERNMENT DEPARTMENTS
AND AGENCIES

The
Government
Printing Office

The Government Printing Office

ROBERT E. KLING, JR.

FOREWORD BY
JAMES L. HARRISON

PRAEGER PUBLISHERS
New York · Washington · London

To my wife and sons

PRAEGER PUBLISHERS
111 Fourth Avenue, New York, N.Y. 10003, U.S.A.
5, Cromwell Place, London S.W.7, England

Published in the United States of America in 1970
by Praeger Publishers, Inc.

© 1970 by Praeger Publishers, Inc.

Library of Congress Catalog Card Number: 73–76791

This book is No. 26 in the series
Praeger Library of U.S. Government Departments and Agencies

Printed in the United States of America

Foreword

by JAMES L. HARRISON
Fourteenth Public Printer of the United States

Many years ago, gaslight etched the faces of a rank of printers as they plucked leaden characters, one by one, from a wooden case. These men concentrated sadly on the work at hand, composing eulogies to an assassinated President. A hundred years later, fluorescent lighting bathed the faces of a new rank of printers at work at the keyboards of modern typesetting machines. These men, too, were wrapped in sadness as they, too, composed eulogies for a martyred President. The first death, Abraham Lincoln's, and the second, John F. Kennedy's, roughly frame the chronology of this book. It not only traces the more-than-hundred-year history of the world's largest general printing plant, but also provides the first really comprehensive view of the U.S. Government Printing Office (GPO).

It would seem reasonable that information on a federal activity with the responsibility for manufacturing and distributing billions of pieces of public printing annually would be simple to find. Such is not the case. Almost every text on the organization and functions of our government discusses the legislature, the judicial system, and the many departments, bureaus, and offices of the executive branch in great detail. The Government Printing Office, if mentioned at all, is dismissed in a sentence or two. Except for an official history written nearly a decade ago, a monograph more than four times as old, and a thin volume prepared twenty years before the turn of the century (and now almost in the rare book category), nothing exists. This book attempts to fill this information gap. It contains a touch of history and a few speculations on its future.

The author, who was my assistant for a number of years and now serves my successor in the same capacity, is well qualified to report on both the history and current activities of this agency, and to make some prognostigations about it, having moved through its ranks from apprentice to top adviser. I think both the serious student of government, and the casual reader will find his story of the GPO informative and immensely rewarding.

Preface

Change has come slowly to the Government Printing Office. Some ascribe this to bureaucratic inertia or to the sheer size of the operation. Others explain it by pointing to the sluggish progress of the commercial industry. Whatever the reasons, it is a fact that, from the GPO's opening in Civil War times to a point almost in the 1960's, few changes took place. But, in the last decade or so, what was once a rather ponderous, reactionary, craft-oriented enterprise has been transmuted into a lean, progressive, business-oriented activity whose mission just happens to be supplying printing and binding to the U.S. Government.

With this transition, the tempo of change has quickened. Administrative streamlining, long overdue, has started. The policies of the congressional Joint Committee on Printing, chiefly in connection with the regional procurement of printing, are being vigorously implemented and are certain to reorder the structure of the organization and the mission priorities of the GPO as well. And there have been other dramatic developments.

Not long after I completed the manuscript for this book, Adolphus Nichols Spence II was appointed Public Printer by President Richard M. Nixon. The new Public Printer, former head of the Defense Printing Service and Naval Printing and Publications Service and a career federal employee, experienced a stormy period of initiation. No sooner had he taken office than a long-standing labor issue—the formula used to set journeyman wages—flared into full flame.

Drawing courage from the success of the postal workers' strike and the air traffic controllers' slowdown, GPO compositors mounted an offensive designed to force the Joint Committee on Printing and the Public Printer to accept a new method of computation. The initial volley was a refusal to work overtime at a period when congressional work choked the office. Following this, a surprisingly effective "sick-out" developed, and, for the first time in over a century, the GPO was picketed. (An early-day strike is described in Chapter II.) Copy piled up. The pace of meetings and discussions built rapidly. Then, at the height of the strife, Public Printer Spence made an unprecedented personal appeal to more than a thousand GPO compositors gathered at nearby St. Aloysius Church. On Spence's assurances that the wage formula and other demands would be given a full review, the sick-out stopped as abruptly as it had begun.

The new Public Printer has also canceled out the historic controversy on relocation, stating that the GPO's "growing pains" would be resolved by means not requiring movement to another site.

That the future will bring new surprises there is no doubt. Fortunately, the GPO seems strong enough to endure the stresses that accompany change.

Writing this modest volume about the GPO has been no one-man project. Although it is not an official history and does not pretend to tell the GPO's whole story from any single point of view, in its preparation I found it necessary to draw upon the talents and energies of many others and to borrow heavily from the people with whom I have worked. I took freely from *100 GPO Years,* the Office's centennial history, published in 1961 and chiefly the labor of Harry Schechter, now retired as Chairman of the GPO Style Board. I also relied upon the lively intellect of my predecessor as Special Assistant to the Public Printer, Eustis Morsberger, to check my attitudes and catch my literary shortcomings. Finally, I leaned unashamedly on my imperturbable, indefatigable amanuensis, who deserves most of the credit for this manuscript having seen the light of day. To all of these friends and colleagues, I want to express my gratitude.

ROBERT E. KLING, JR.

Washington, D.C.
August, 1970

Contents

The
Government
Printing Office

I

"Publick" Printing in America

From almost the moment of its invention, printing has served as an important adjunct of government—at least in the Western world. Ruling factions soon recognized the power that accrued to those who controlled what was printed. As this power grew in direct proportion to the literacy level of the people, printing in turn served further to raise that level. Both the strength of government and the people's ability to comprehend rose concurrently. Printing created a new relationship between people and their governments, involving the individual to a far greater extent in his national destiny than ever before. Nowhere did this relationship find more fertile ground in which to grow and flower than in the English colonies. One result was the establishment in most English-speaking nations of regularized forms of government printing. In England and Canada today, there exist agencies known as "The Queen's Printer." Similar facilities provide similar services for all governments—either within their bureaucratic structures or by arrangement with privately owned plants. In the United States, the tradition led to the establishment of what since 1861 has been designated the Government Printing Office, or more familiarly, the GPO. By 1970, this agency was responsible for printing billions of books, pamphlets, and forms that explained, implemented, or catalyzed government action.

Progenitor of the GPO

Printing was already more than two centuries old when it came to America.

There was no brisk demand for printed matter in the colonies at first. Children were taught to read, write, and "sum" at home, and reading was generally confined to the Bible, almanacs, and the classics. The need for additional books and other printed materials increased only gradually, receiving renewed impetus when the first university in the New World was founded with the help of John Harvard's legacy of £800 and his library of 320 books. Recognizing that any institute of learning must be abundantly supplied with texts, the founders of Harvard College arranged for a press, type, and other necessary equipment to be sent from England, and in 1638 the first press in America was set up in Cambridge.

The first three efforts of the new press were "The Freeman's Oath," consisting of 222 words, an *Almanack for the Year 1639,* and *The Whole Booke of Psalmes,* a collection of psalms "newly turned into metre," otherwise known as *The Bay Psalm Book.* No copies of the first two items have survived, but a number of copies of *The Bay Psalm Book* have been preserved and today are among the most treasured items of Americana. The book was a major undertaking. It required about a year to produce and was a very creditable accomplishment measured by the standards then prevailing.

In 1643, the press at Cambridge printed "The Capital Laws of Massachusetts," the first clearly identifiable "publick" printing in the United States—that is, printing for a duly constituted government. Most early printing, however, must in one sense be designated as public printing, since much of the printing equipment was purchased and transported to the New World with public funds. Until the colonies developed a commercial and social structure, presses were kept busy by the government and were true public agencies filling specific requirements for the community.

EARLY COLONIAL PRESSES

The generally official nature of printing in the seventeenth century helps to explain the attitude of the authorities toward purely commercial printing, as evidenced by their efforts to regulate and control all presses. In 1682, William Nuthead and his partner were roundly chastised for printing the acts of the Virginia Assembly without a license. Earlier, in 1665, Marmaduke Jones had brought a printing press and equipment from England, intending to set up business in Boston, only to find that the General Court of Massachusetts had passed an order preventing the establishing of printing presses anywhere but in Cambridge. This act was perhaps the first effort at governmental control of printing in the New World.

But printing flourished wherever a colony was established. The need and demand for printing grew along with the colonies, touching nearly every facet of colonial life—government, business, and religion. Newspapers appeared and disappeared with regularity. Nearly every town had a *Gazette,* and there were other titles designed to appeal to colonists of all persuasions: *The Scourge of Aristocracy* and *The Tree of Liberty* for revolutionaries; *The Olive Branch* and *The Missionary* for peacemakers; later there was even an *Idiot*—for Bostonians of 1810!

One of the earliest of the successful newspapers was the *New England Courant,* published in Boston by James Franklin. Not the least of its attractions were the articles submitted by "Silence Dogood," James's thirteen-year-old brother, Benjamin, who slipped his articles under the printshop door late at night to conceal his identity from his brother. In 1772, the *Courant* ran headlong into government interference when it suggested that the government authorities had not been overly assiduous in safeguarding the colony from pirates. The government reacted by clapping James in jail. After his release, he was "strictly forbidden" to print or publish the *New England Courant* "or any Pamphlet or Paper of Like Nature" without supervision of the Provincial Secretary.

James Franklin managed to circumvent this restriction by publishing the *Courant* with his young brother listed as "the printer thereof." But the ruse boomeranged, and Ben, who was indentured to his brother, declared himself publicly freed of his indenture. When James attempted to hold his brother until he was of age, Ben let him know that their business relations were at an end, whereupon James, piqued at Ben's fractiousness, obtained promises from all local printers not to hire the young man. With employment thus closed to him in Boston, Ben Franklin embarked on his well-known adventures in Philadelphia and his subsequent rise to great honors in America—and in the world.

James Franklin's brush with the authorities was not an isolated instance. Although printing had proved to be one of mankind's greatest boons, governments had found that the press had an unlimited potential for mischief. In England, as in most European countries, the press was licensed by the state. Sir William Berkeley, Governor of the colony of Virginia, summed up the position of the English monarchy:

> I thank God, there are no free schools nor printing, and I hope we shall not have these hundred years; for learning has brought disobedience, and heresy, and sects into the world, and printing has divulged them, and libels against the best government. God keep us from both.*

* *The Statutes at Large; being a collection of all the laws of Virginia, from the first session of the legislature, in the year 1619.* William Waller Hening (New York, 1823), vol. 2, p. 517.

There was good reason for the king's agents to be wary of the power of the press. Freedom from England was advocated in print; war was encouraged by the self-reliant and intrepid colonial printers; and on July 6, 1776, Dunlap & Claypoole of Philadelphia printed the Declaration of Independence.

Printing for the Continental Congress

Independence brought with it new and unfamiliar responsibilities. The Continental Congress, which had been prosecuting the war with England and developing a framework of federation under which the states could operate, also had to organize and establish the services needed to conduct the public business at a national level. Printing for the Congress was one of these services.

It is not surprising that arranging to have its acts and proceedings set down on paper proved very difficult. Printing was still an infant art. Two or three pages of composition was a day's work for an expert printer. Type itself was scarce since most of it was imported from Europe, and vessels plying the Atlantic had more important cargo to transport. It was not unusual for a Revolutionary printer, possessing a meager amount of type, to print one page at a time and redistribute the types into his type case so that he would have type enough to set the next page. Printshop problems of this period would have seemed familiar even to Johann Gutenburg, since presses were virtual replicas of the crude winepress he used, and the paper produced by the infant papermaking industry was of poor quality and often unobtainable. The Continental Congress, under pressure from the British forces, was constantly moving the provisional capital from place to place, thereby aggravating the problem of getting congressional printing needs promptly and properly filled. Moreover, since the Congress was habitually short of funds, some printers were reluctant to give freely of their services and materials. Not until after the peace treaty was signed in Paris in 1783, and the new nation had established itself on a firm footing, did printers begin to vie for the privilege and prestige of government printing.

Most of the proceedings of the Continental Congress were shrouded in the greatest secrecy, undoubtedly firing the intense interest of the public in the business being conducted. The Secretary of the Congress kept minutes of the deliberations in longhand. Notes covering the period 1774–89 were published as the *Rough and Secret Journals* only in 1821. However, that portion of the proceedings released to the public as the *Journal of Congress,* as well as the other legislative printing, was done by William and Thomas Bradford of Philadelphia from 1774–76. But their work failed to satisfy delegates. When an enterprising Scots publisher, bookbinder, and printer, Robert Aitken, reprinted a satisfactory sample copy of the *Journal,* the Continental Congress appointed him its official printer. Aitken's firm lasted about two years before being replaced by John Dunlap, who set the *Journal of Congress* for 1777 in type but failed to complete the work until 1779. Dunlap was accordingly replaced by David C. Claypoole of Philadelphia, who proved the best of the Continental Congress printers but whose costs were something of a shock to the body. From October to December, 1779, his charges were $20,000. In 1783, Dunlap, who had taken David Claypoole as his partner in 1780 and set up a plant in Annapolis, was hired again, continuing this time as official printer until 1789.

Printing for the U.S. Congress, 1789–1818

The First Session of the First U.S. Congress was called to order in New York City on March 4, 1789. The new lawmakers adopted such an unwieldy system of providing for the printing of bills and documents that a special joint committee was formed to study the whole matter of printing, including the printing of the acts and proceedings of the Congress. As a result, the House *Journal* for the First Session of the First Congress, comprising 177 folio* pages, was printed by Thomas Greenleaf, the proprietor of the New York *Advertiser*.

As for the verbatim proceedings and debates of Congress (as distinct from the matter released in the *Journal*), no official reports were made. When Congress moved to its new home in Washington, D.C., in December, 1801, a number of senators and congressmen questioned the worth of printing any congressional documents whatsoever. No local printing facility of any consequence existed in the raw town. John Randolph, a member of the Ways and Means Committee—later Minister to Russia and a dueling opponent of Henry Clay—informed the House of Representatives that documents could not be printed in less than twenty days, "owing to the state of machinery in this place."

In 1803, President Thomas Jefferson sent a message to Congress in his own handwriting. A heated debate ensued, in which the merits of the President's proposals were lost in the violent colloquy over whether the message and supporting documents should or should not be printed. The proprinting faction prevailed, and the message and documents were printed in an octavo† volume of 100 pages. Five hundred copies were ordered at a cost of $520.75—an extravagance to which James Bayard, Sr., of Delaware objected.

By and large, the august legislature of the United States depended upon local newspapers to advise the public of the proceedings and fiery debates that characterized this early

* Folio indicates numbering on one side only.
† A page size of roughly six by nine inches, which derived its name from the number of pages (eight) printed in one impression on a standard sheet.

period. Accuracy, appearance, and form left much to be desired, and members of Congress constantly complained. In 1796, a committee reported favorably on a proposal to employ stenographers for accurate, official recording of proceedings, but the matter died—not, however, before Samuel Harrison Smith's Philadelphia *Gazette* had offered to pay $1,500 of the $4,000 price tag placed on the hiring of stenographers to record the House proceedings.

Five years later, in 1801, Smith, at President Thomas Jefferson's urging, moved his establishment to Washington and began to publish reports of congressional debates in the *National Intelligencer*. The premise upon which the *Intelligencer* published was lofty but virtually impossible to fulfill. Issued three times a week, the paper submitted handwritten reports of congressional proceedings to concerned members for revision or alteration at their convenience. This procedure was doomed insofar as timeliness was concerned, and debates printed in an abridged form in the *National Intelligencer* were habitually far in arrears.

In the meantime, other printing firms, sensing opportunities in the nation's capital, began moving to the area. Congressional printing contains the imprints of at least six printing establishments for this period. Among these was the firm of Gales and Seaton, which was to dominate the printing of congressional proceedings for nearly a quarter of a century. Joseph Gales became Smith's partner in the *Intelligencer* in 1809 and a year later the sole owner. On October 8, 1812, he made an announcement in his paper that was to signal the entry of a highly resourceful printer-stenographer-businessman combination into the work of reporting the proceedings of Congress:

The editor of this paper, finding its extensive concerns too multifarious for the superintendence of any individual though possessed of more industry and assiduity than he can lay claim to, has taken in connection with him in business Mr. William Seaton. . . . This arrangement whilst it will leave the editor at liberty to devote more particular attention to the Congressional Reports . . . will, he hopes, ensure greater correctness and better typographical execution than heretofore.

Both Joseph Gales and William Seaton were skilled stenographers and as such received preferential treatment by both houses of the legislature. Places were reserved for them at the side of the Speaker of the House. They reported the debates of Congress with considerable accuracy and speed, compared to former reporting.

In 1818, Congress appointed a joint committee to "consider and report whether any further provisions of law are necessary to insure dispatch, accuracy, and neatness in the printing done for the two Houses of Congress." The committee's report—issued on February 19, 1819, and known as the Wilson-Rogers Report, after its authors, General James J. Wilson, Senator from New Jersey, and General T. J. Rogers, Representative from New Jersey—contained several worthwhile observations on the economics of government printing. It was the first to suggest a government printing office. The report stated, in part:

How far it is reputable for Congress to endeavor to get their work done below a fair and reasonable price may be a matter of doubt, but it does not admit of a question that compensation ought to be adequate to the object of procuring that work to be done at a proper time and in a suitable manner. A second mode suggested to and considered by the committee was the establishment of a national printing office (with a bindery and stationery annexed), which should execute the work of Congress while in session and that of the various Departments of Government during the recess. . . . The Committee are of the opinion that such an establishment . . . would be likely to produce promptitude, uniformity, accuracy, and elegance in the execution of the public printing, and . . . be found the most economical.

Half a century would pass before these words would be implemented by action.

THE PROFITEERING YEARS, 1819–60

In 1819, a second committee made its report, which led to the passage of a joint resolution known as the Printing Act of 1819. Basically, the Act attempted to bring some semblance of order out of the chaotic situation that had developed under the low-bid system. It established rates for congressional printing and introduced a system by which the House and Senate selected an official printer for each session of Congress. Unfortunately, specifying prices to be paid for typesetting and presswork proved to be a grave error. Technological improvements in printing equipment soon enabled printers to increase their incomes from typesetting and printing far beyond those of 1819. Since the rates remained unchanged until 1846, Congress laid the groundwork for twenty-seven years of unprecedented profit for printers fortunate enough to be supplying government printing.

Gales and Seaton were the first beneficiaries of the law in 1819. Their firm was elected printer to both houses the day the joint resolution was passed. They remained House printers until 1827 and were elected again from 1833 to 1843. Duff Green supplanted the firm as Senate printer between 1828 and 1835, when Gales and Seaton were again awarded the contract, only to be replaced by the firm of Blair and Rives in 1838.

Senatorial fireworks erupted at the executive session of the Senate following the inauguration of President William Henry Harrison in 1833, when Senator Willie P. Mangum of North Carolina presented a resolution aimed at removing Blair and Rives as Senate printers. The colloquy that ensued involved Senators William R. King of Alabama and fiery Henry Clay of Kentucky. King challenged Clay to a duel, but before the gentlemen could engage in mortal combat, friends interceded, and the bitter and offensive language that had precipitated the exchange was mutually excused. Despite the oratory of the Senator from Kentucky, Blair and Rives, both Kentuckians, were dismissed as Senate printers and Gales and Seaton once more appointed.

Under the law of 1819, profiteering was inevitable. The attractive scale of rates set by the Act became ever more desirable as technology improved. Printing costs for the five years following the passage of the law more than doubled those of the preceding five years.

There were periodic investigations. In 1828, the *House Hearings on Printing* revealed that

> Large documents are directed to be printed which in fact are altogether useless, and the evil is greatly increased when numerous copies are ordered, which in many cases swell the profits of the printer without corresponding benefits to the country. The size of the public documents is unnecessarily large, which arises from the habit of prolixity and detail into which the departments are all liable to fall, more especially as a new practice has been introduced by the secretaries of the departments sending reports of their clerks or heads of bureaus instead of condensing them to make their own communications.

In 1840, the House, smarting under the growing clamor against the obvious abuses of the public trust in connection with printing, appointed a Select Committee on Public Printing to study the whole state of government printing. The committee was explicitly instructed to explore the feasibility of a "national printing office." The outcome was anticlimactic. The Democratic majority members recommended a reduction of 15 per cent in current rates, compared to the 20 per cent reduction recommended by the Whig minority, although it had been clearly established that the rates paid were almost double the going rate for commercial printers. The Whigs later introduced a bill for the erection of a public printing office, but the bill failed by a sizable margin in the House. The same committee issued another report in 1842, as a result of which rates paid for printing were reduced 20 per cent below the 1819 scale. But the following year Congress obligingly added funds to compensate Gales and Seaton for the difference between the new and old rates. By that time, public printing had become a full-blown patronage item bestowed by the party in power on firms sympathetic to its programs. House and Senate printers continued to be changed with regularity, the choice falling on the firm favored at the moment by the majority party.

In 1846, the Democratic majority and the Whig minority united in passing the Joint Resolution of 1846, which overturned the system of electing public printers and substituted for it the contract method that had been in effect before 1819. As a matter of fact, between 1840 and 1846, the system of awarding printing contracts to the lowest bidder had been restored by law for various executive and judicial agencies of the government. The resolution of 1846 also created a congressional committee on printing, consisting of three members from each house, empowered to adopt measures "deemed necessary to remedy any neglect, delay, or waste" on the part of government printing contractors—language still used in those sections of the U.S. Code pertaining to the present Joint Committee on Printing.

The impact of the Resolution of 1846 on Washington printers was deadly. When an Albany, New York, firm underbid local firms and moved men and equipment to Pennsylvania Avenue, Washington printers, stripped of lucrative government work, fell on hard times.

The contract system worked no better than it had several decades before. Exorbitant prices were charged. Plates of government publications were not preserved, with the result that the entire publication had to be reset in type when additional copies were required. Engravings made for the Senate and used afterward in House publications were charged to the House as original engravings. Excessive prices were paid for paper. The cost of printing to the government during the six long years of competitive bidding was equal to the cost of printing for the entire twenty-seven years over which the law of 1819 had been in effect.

In 1852, Congress reversed itself, and the fixed rate system was reinstituted. Once again, printers were elected directly by Congress. There was one substantial difference in the provisions of the Act of 1852, however. It provided for the appointment of a Superintendent of Public Printing by the President. He was to keep records of all material printed at the public expense and was to be responsible for the quality and timeliness of public printing. He was empowered to advertise and award contracts for the paper required for printing and to render accounts of paper transactions annually to Congress. The Superintendent of Public Printing was also authorized to penalize public printers who failed to perform according to contract by deducting up to 10 per cent of the standard costs fixed by the 1852 law.

On the surface, the new law seemed eminently workable, but it had several shortcomings. First, it contained fixed rates for various types of work, a provision already proved to be unworkable. Second, these rates failed to anticipate technological advances. Third, the specified rates made the posts of Public Printer for the House and Senate so financially attractive that abuses were certain. Since election as Public Printer by either house was a political plum, and those elected were expected to make liberal donations to party chests, politicians got the posts, and the work was farmed out to practical printers for a percentage of the receipts. Binding, engraving, and paper were obtained in much the same fashion, with percentages taken at several levels by suppliers who, in turn, fed the party coffers. Printing costs continued to soar under the system, and the huge profits were systematically skimmed to promote partisan activities. The cost of the Thirty-fourth Congress's printing totaled $2.25 million dollars. When the House ordered the Select Committee on Public Printing to investigate, the Committee reported overcharges of three-quarters of a million dollars.

The figure of Cornelius Wendell now emerged as the pivotal force in government printing. Upon his election as House Printer in 1855, Wendell built and equipped a large printing plant on H and North Capitol streets. In 1857, General George W. Bowman took office as Superintendent of Public Printing, introducing a number of far-reaching reforms that produced annual savings of about $200,000. Wendell, of course, began to feel the pinch and moved to get Bowman out of the way. He offered him free of charge the *Washington Union,* which he himself had purchased not long before. Wendell also promised Bowman $20,000 per year so long as Wendell performed public printing and assured Bowman that he would be awarded the Senate printing. Unable to refuse such a liberal offer, Bowman resigned as Superintendent of Public Printing and took over the *Union.*

When summoned by a congressional committee looking into these transactions in 1860, Bowman produced a "bill of sale" signed by Wendell that stated in part:

> Know all men by these presents that I, Cornelius Wendell, . . . for a valuable consideration to me paid by Geo. W. Bowman, . . . now Superintendent of Public Printing, the receipt whereof I hereby acknowledge, do hereby give, grant, bargain, sell, and convey unto the said Bowman, his heirs and assigns forever, the newspaper establishment . . . known as the *Washington Union.*

The Bowman-Wendell agreement soon developed snags. Bowman claimed he was paid only $3,000 of the $20,000 promised by Wendell. After his hotly contested election as Senate Printer for the Thirty-sixth Congress, Bowman promptly transferred the Senate printing to another establishment. Wendell, meanwhile, had turned over his printing plant to his employees, who were to repay him from profits. Without the Senate printing contract the new firm, known as Larcombe and English, would be hard pressed. It happened, however, that Governor Tom Ford of Ohio was elected House Printer after a lengthy debate, corresponding in bitterness to that in the Senate. Being a politician, not a printer, Ford upon his election disposed of a one-third interest in House printing to John W. Defrees, who *was* a printer and had been Ford's chief competitor for the post. Both Ford and Defrees agreed that Larcombe and English should be subcontractor for House printing, and Wendell's former firm was saved.

As the government printing situation continued to deteriorate, the opposition press called for scrapping the existing printing system. Within Congress itself, criticism reached such a crescendo that three committees launched simultaneous inquiries into every facet of public printing. Hot debate was triggered in both houses. Proponents of a national printing office claimed that significant savings could be realized by the establishment of a government plant to do all government printing. Some suggested that savings would amount to 50 per cent of the cost. Opponents claimed that Congress had suffered long enough under the various public printing systems, and the fact that the abuses and excesses of these systems were common knowledge did much to spur Congress to action.

On June 16, 1860, H.R. 22, providing for the acquisition of a government printing plant, passed the Senate by a vote of 31 to 14. The House had passed essentially the same bill by a vote of 120 to 56. Differences between the House and Senate versions were quickly settled, and Joint Resolution No. 25 was signed by President James Buchanan on June 23, 1860. Under this Act, the Superintendent of Public Printing was given authority "to contract for the erection or purchase of the necessary buildings, machinery, and materials" to do the printing for Congress, the executive and judicial departments, and the Court of Claims.

Superintendent of Public Printing John Heart made an agreement with Joseph T. Crowell on December 1, 1860, to purchase the former plant of Cornelius Wendell at North Capitol and H Streets. The Joint Committee on Public Printing approved the contract, and on January 17, 1861, Congress provided the funds. The resolution stated:

> To enable the Superintendent of the Public Printing to carry into effect the provisions of the joint resolution in relation to the public printing, approved June 23, 1860, $135,000: *Provided,* That no part of this appropriation shall be expended until the title to the property purchased shall have been examined and approved by the Attorney General of the United States.

After nearly three-quarters of a century, Congress had finally seen fit to provide for a printing facility that would be totally responsive to its printing and binding needs. The Government Printing Office was about to be established.

II

The GPO's First Hundred Years

The man to whom fell the task of organizing the new Government Printing Office was John D. Defrees of Indiana. He was appointed Superintendent of Public Printing by Abraham Lincoln in March, 1861. Although his selection had definite political overtones, he did have the advantage of being both a successful printer and lawyer. At the time of his selection, he was publisher of the *Indiana State Journal* and a power in the Whig Party.

THE NEW GOVERNMENT PRINTING OFFICE

The physical plant into which Superintendent Defrees moved was a four-story brick building, designed by Architect of the Capitol Edward Clark and erected five years earlier for Cornelius Wendell, surrounded by auxiliary buildings comprising a paper warehouse, a machine shop, a boiler house, a coal house, a wagon shed, and stables. The main building, topped with a single cupola equipped with a fire bell, contained about 60,000 square feet of floor space and stretched west along H Street from the corner of North Capitol almost 250 feet. The $135,000 purchase price included all equipment, materials, and machinery, and must be considered quite a bargain, even for 1861. The full value of the property, including buildings, land, and machinery, was placed at $146,000.

Passersby could hear the rumble of the steam engine that drove the plant's twenty-six power presses. But passersby were few and negotiated the neighborhood only when business demanded their presence, for "Swampoodle," as the area was known, was hardly a scenic place. Tiber Creek, little more than an open sewer, ran about half a block away on its course southeast to the Potomac. Periodically, when rains fell heavily, the Tiber overflowed its banks and deposited refuse and silt near the new GPO. Pigs, geese, and goats shared the neighborhood. Only a single residence lay in the entire square to the north of the printing office, although farther along North Capitol Street stood St. Aloysius "noisy with a chime of bells," as Dr. John B. Ellis described it in the *Sights and Secrets of the National Capital,* a book published in Philadelphia in 1869. The inhabited part of the city rose well to the west of the Government Printing Office, which was decidedly on the outskirts of Washington although quite near the Capitol.

The new office employed about 350 persons. Hours were from 8 to 5 for both day and night shifts. An "intermission" of one hour from 1 P.M. to 2 P.M. was authorized for "dinner." Each year, when Congress adjourned, the night force was abolished. Employee strength varied as work fluctuated. Pay for compositors was $12 per week. The Superintendent of Public Printing was paid $2,500 per year and was also expected to provide a $20,000 bond for the "faithful performance of duties." In 1861, office salaries amounted to $56,000 for "persons employed in the public printing" and $7,900 for "persons employed in the public binding." (This was for slightly under eight months, March 4 to October 31, 1861.)

The inventory of equipment included with the purchase of the Wendell plant contained some interesting items—5 dozen spitoons for the composing room, "chairs, tables, counters, shelving, etc., for 200 girls," 2 wheelbarrows, 1 black horse, and 1 bobtail bay horse.

Defrees's first annual report submitted to the Speaker of

the House, Galusha A. Grow, December 12, 1861, claimed savings of "at least $60,000" over the costs estimated in accordance with the Act of 1852 and went to great pains to establish the savings attributable to the new system of printing for the government. In his words, "This establishment has been under my charge since the 23d day of March last, and the result has been such as to indicate the wisdom of Congress in making the change." To all intents and purposes, Congress was either highly satisfied or too preoccupied with the Civil War to find fault.

Civil War Days

The war brought an increased workload to the GPO. In 1862, income went up about 10 per cent and in 1863 rose nearly 65 per cent over 1862. The report of the Superintendent of Public Printing for 1865 showed that the cost of public printing and binding for the year ending September 30 was $2,183,010.78—up more than 400 per cent. Inflation in four years of war accounted for some of this increase. Paper is a good barometer of rising costs for the printer. In 1861, map paper sold for 15 cents per pound. In 1865, the contract price was 45 cents per pound. Printers who received $14 per week in 1861 were receiving $24 per week in 1865.

But printing costs were not the only evidence at the GPO that a war was being fought. A unit of federal employees called the Interior Department Regiment was formed. Companies F and G of this doughty outfit were GPO workers, with Company F made up of printers while Company G came from the binding department. Company F was the first organized, early in 1861. It was armed by the government and trained in marching and the use of firearms during specific hours set aside during the day for drilling. At night, its members stood guard duty. In June, 1864, when General Robert E. Lee de-

tached Jubal Early's Corps to menace Washington, Company F
was hastily mustered into federal service. On July 11, 1864,
it marched to a point near Washington's insane asylum and
camped until the following day. Early's troops bombarded the
outskirts of the city, but the Union Sixth Army Corps drove
them back to the Shenandoah Valley. The soldiers from the
GPO's Company F laid down their arms and returned to their
more familiar duties as pressmen and compositors on July 12.
(Because of a delayed muster and the momentary nature of the
threat, Company G, which had never been fully organized as a
military unit, was not dispatched to the field.)

Meanwhile, John Defrees had been busy. In 1863, in a
startling development, workmen in the GPO bindery struck
for higher wages and shorter hours. Although their demand
was hardly unique, the incident is of interest because it was
the first strike in the Government Printing Office. It was settled
quickly and amicably, and the Superintendent described work
as progressing satisfactorily after "a short period." Other matters occupied him more pressingly.

The Superintendent of Public Printing in the nineteenth-
century United States was a prominent political figure with a
preferential place in his Party's "pecking order." Defrees was
quite well acquainted with President Lincoln. In 1863, Lincoln visited the Government Printing Office at Defrees's invitation and addressed the employees. The *Washington Star* of
November 13, 1863, reported that the President asked the
Superintendent to speak to a young lady employed by the
GPO concerning her brother who was a Union prisoner of
war, and Defrees wrote to a friend regarding this incident as
follows:

A poor girl in the employment of the Government Printing
Office had a brother impressed into the rebel service, and was
taken prisoner by our forces. He desired to take the oath of
allegiance, and to be liberated. She sought an interview with the
President who wrote the note asking me to inquire into the facts,

which I did, and the young man was liberated on the President's order.

Defrees also urged Lincoln to "send a message to Congress recommending the passage of a joint resolution proposing an amendment to the Constitution forever prohibiting slavery in the States." His letter to the President on this subject is dated February 7, 1864. (Lincoln replied that, "Our own friends have this under consideration." Just a few days short of a year later the Thirteenth Amendment to the Constitution was adopted by three-fourths of the states.)

Not long after the end of the Civil War and Lincoln's assassination, a familiar figure reappeared on the public printing scene. Cornelius Wendell replaced John Defrees on September 1, 1866. In his first report to Congress, submitted on December 18, 1866, the new Superintendent of Public Printing complained that contracts for paper for public printing had expired on November 30, but that his hands were tied, since control of paper contracts had been turned over to the Joint Committee on Printing by an act of Congress on July 27 of that year. He also noted that the *Army Register of Volunteers* of which 50,000 sale copies had been ordered printed by a joint resolution of Congress was not exactly the success the legislators had hoped, "less than $200 having been realized from the sale of the four parts already issued." (The edition of the remaining four volumes was reduced to 1,000 and was duly documented in the annual report for 1868.)

It is interesting to note that Wendell's attitude on the question of public versus private printing for the government appeared to have undergone a remarkable reversal. As Superintendent of Public Printing, he stated that

A considerable amount of the printing and binding for the government . . . is not executed in this establishment (GPO) or under its control . . . As our facilities are amply sufficient to execute all government printing and binding, and at less cost than by private establishments, I can see no good reason why they should not be executed here.

But Cornelius Wendell had a rather abbreviated tour as Superintendent of Public Printing—six months, to be exact. His place was again taken by John D. Defrees on March 1, 1867.

The Congressional Printer and the Public Printer

On the heels of these changes in the GPO's Superintendency came an unexpected Act of Congress. This legislation provided for the *election* of "some competent person, who shall be a practical printer, to take charge of and manage the GPO" and providing also "that the person so selected shall be deemed an officer of the Senate, and shall be designated *Congressional Printer*." About all that was really affected, however, was the title accorded the head of the GPO—and his salary, which increased from $3,583.33 to a munificent $4,000. All legislation pertaining to the old Superintendent of Public Printing's office was abolished and redesignated as applying to the new Congressional Printer.

On April 15, 1869, a New York Republican, Almon M. Clapp, became the first Congressional Printer. A printer and publisher, Clapp had been a notably unsuccessful candidate for several elective offices, but his record was far better with appointive posts. Prior to his selection as GPO head, he had been postmaster of Buffalo, a position from which he had been removed by President Andrew Johnson in 1866.

The title of Congressional Printer was not to last long. In July, 1876, Congress again repealed all the laws pertaining to the election or appointment of the GPO's head, and specified that from that time he would be called the Public Printer. Under this law, also, the position was to be filled by Presidential appointment, with the advice and consent of the Senate.

Clapp simply exchanged the nameplate on his door for a new one—the one used by all of his successors to date.

More Work and Expansion

In the years following the Civil War, a number of government agencies discovered that the GPO was producing a better product at a lower cost than that of the contractors they had been using. They began to divert their printing to the young office. In 1868, the Patent Office and the Commissioner of Customs took their work from the hands of private printers and sent it to the GPO for execution. In November, 1869, the Commissioner of Customs informed Clapp, "that [GPO work] was very far superior . . . to any of the kind I have ever seen in any customhouse, and incomparably superior to the general average of books."

In 1869, the GPO also took over a U.S. Treasury printing plant and in the process acquired both electrotype and stereotype equipment. This was a valuable addition to the services offered, and in the first year of the new operation, Clapp reported that nearly $10,000 in savings over costs of purchasing duplicate plate work was realized. Two more small printing facilities, each employing one printer, were placed under GPO control in 1870: the plant at the Navy Department and that of the Paymaster General.

However, the need for a larger main plant was growing apace and in his 1870 report, Clapp petitioned Congress, saying: "I desire again to call attention to the imperious necessity of an increase in building accommodation to meet the pressing wants of this office." He enlisted the support of Architect of the Capitol Edward Clark, who reported that his examination of the premises showed "the upper stories of that building (not the GPO proper but a temporary structure used to store overflow volumes awaiting competition) so loaded that I con-

sidered its condition dangerous." The petition was favorably
received and in 1871, a new building, adding about one-third
more space to the Government Printing Office, was completed
at a cost of $45,000. But even this was not enough, so fast did
the workload of the office grow, especially printing for the
executive department. In 1872, Clapp asked for an appropriation to expand along the GPO's west property line. He also
expressed indignation over the regrading of H Street, which
had been raised above the building's first floor level. Presses
and "valuable and delicate machinery" were endangered by
water runoff from the street, he said. This time, Congress
turned a deaf ear to his complaints.

1873: THE *Congressional Record*

In 1873, the GPO commenced printing the proceedings
and debates of Congress, which until that year had appeared
only in privately owned newspapers. The first copy of the *Congressional Record* was printed on March 5 and contained a
full report on a special session of the Senate.

Assuming this responsibility, which remains a principal
GPO function, was an enormous step. The debates of Congress printed in Blair and Rives's (later F & J Rives & Bailey's)
Congressional Globe had grown in cost until in 1871 criticism
of this system of printing legislative debates reached epic proportions, both in the halls of Congress and in the press. The
Globe contract expired in 1871, and after much debate was
rewarded to Rives to continue until March 4, 1873. A tidy
sum of $400,000 was appropriated for this work. Considering
that the cost of printing the *Congressional Record* at the GPO
for the First Session of the Forty-third Congress was $126,000,
the charges of some members of Congress who complained
that the price paid to Rives for printing the *Globe* for two

years was nearly double what it should have been, appear justified.

During the last year of the *Congressional Globe* contract, invitations to bid had been sent to printers across the country requesting proposals for printing the proceedings and debates of Congress. Several were submitted. The Congressional Printer's bid on the work offered to furnish composition of solid brevier (8-point) type at $1.50 per 1000 ems.* Extracts were to be set in nonpareil (6-point). A large majority of the House concurred with the Senate in an amendment that sent the printing of the *Globe* to the GPO. All printing for the executive, judicial, and legislative branches of the government now came under GPO control.

The GPO was producing the proceedings and debates of Congress with efficiency and dispatch, but the private printing community was far from happy about the loss of this lucrative work. The panic of 1873 had heralded a depression that lasted more than three years, and the public was receptive to charges of excessive spending in government. The GPO was not spared, for a committee of the House reported in 1876 on its investigation into the operation of the GPO that the Office was "extravagant to a degree that would bankrupt any private establishment in the country." Two forces were apparently at work, the Democrats who scented victory in the 1876 elections, and the private segment of the printing industry led by Franklin Rives, the *Globe* publisher.

The investigations produced a few illuminating assertions. Theodore L. DeVinne, a respected New York printer, maintained that he could provide the government with printing "far below" GPO prices. His contention was supported by John G. Judd of Judd & Detweiler, a large Washington print-

---

* An em is a type measuring unit equal in length to the height of the character's body. For type that has characters on a body 10 points high, an em is 10 points in length (a point being a seventy-secondth of an inch).

ing house, who declared that GPO composition costs were greater than in his own plant—some 40 per cent greater, to be precise. The minority report recommended returning the contract for printing congressional debates and proceedings to Franklin Rives, claiming that large savings could be made in printing costs. But when the smoke cleared, the minority recommendations lost and the GPO went on printing the *Congressional Record*. (Some changes were made in fiscal and administrative operations as a result of these hearings, but the ultimate loser was the worker at the GPO. The testimony regarding printers' wages resulted in a pay cut in 1877 from a $24 average per week to $19.20 per week. This was 80 cents less per week than was paid to New York printers.)

Clapp at first refused to testify before the House committee. His statement, "inasmuch as I am an officer of the Senate of the United States, your committee has no jurisdiction to investigate my conduct in office as Congressional Printer," emphasized the curious position of the official government printer in the government.

Apparently impressed with the continuing arguments that more space was needed for effective operations, Congress in this period appropriated another $43,800 for the purpose of extending the Government Printing Office building. Two large fireproof extensions were constructed under the direction of Edward Clark. With this addition, the GPO of the 1880's consisted of 160,820 square feet of floor space, or nearly four acres—exclusive of the boiler and coal houses, stables, and other auxiliary buildings. The ground floor of the expanded main building had the press rooms, paper storage, stereotype vault, machine shop, and carpenter shop. In the courtyard were the boiler and coal houses, and the roller house. The second floor contained the offices of the Public Printer, Chief Clerk, Disbursing Clerk, and the Foreman of Printing. Also on this level was the document room, the job room, the stereotype and electrotype departments, and the proofroom. The bindery and the storage areas for binders' materials occupied the third floor. The fourth floor was occupied by the folding room, the *Congressional Record* room, the patent department, and another storage room. The building was equipped with two large elevators for moving materials and work-in-process from floor to floor. A small lift between the first and fourth floors was reserved for rush work and less bulky material.

In the 1880's, about 1,800 people were employed in the Government Printing Office, which by now was tagged "the largest printing office in the world." The nerve center of the establishment was the office of the Foreman of Printing, who exercised general supervision over all production. Records of incoming work received from the U.S. Government's executive departments, courts, and Congress were maintained here. Copy and a "jacket" describing the job prepared by the Chief Clerk was sent to the Foreman of Printing who in turn passed the manuscript to copy preparers. After preparation, the marked copy was given to the Assistant Foreman of Printing for parceling out to individual compositors. Congressional copy came directly from House and Senate printing clerks to the Foreman of Printing.

PUBLIC PRINTER ROUNDS AND HIS REFORMS

Sterling P. Rounds was appointed Public Printer in 1882 by President Arthur to replace the aging John D. Defrees at the end of his third tour. In an effort to ensure compliance with contract weight and quality, Rounds engaged a paper expert to inspect all paper deliveries. He eliminated the use of high-quality paper for disposable and one-use forms. Paper sizes were standardized somewhat with sizes of end products, eliminating much trimming and thereby effecting significant savings. No paper was paid for until it was inspected and approved for use. Rounds also tightened contract performance in the supply of lithographs and engravings. Estimates of costs, in writing, were required before awarding illustration work to suppliers. He assigned regular paydays for employees and established a disbursing office for more convenient payment of workers who formerly had milled around in corridors until paid—or, since withdrawals of money from the Treasury were subject to arbitrary limits, until funds were exhausted.

Taking notice of the new Civil Service Act, Rounds abolished the system of hiring and firing by each foreman and brought some semblance of order into the employment practices of the Office. Patronage, which had to this point played a major part in hiring GPO workers, came under Rounds' fire when he suggested that persons from the District of Columbia and the surrounding states enjoyed an advantage over those from Southern and Western states. He proceeded to appoint greater numbers from the more distant areas in order to equalize the distribution of positions. In time, he also strengthened accounting procedures, abolished the drying room as obsolete, eliminated the annual fiscal deficiency (which had become almost traditional), and cleaned, renovated, and restored the entire plant, greatly improving working conditions for the employees. Sewing-room workers in the bindery were placed on "piecework" instead of salaries of $11 per week, and "care was taken in arranging the scale of wages to give all such employees an opportunity to earn as much by the piece as they were receiving by the week, provided they did the work," according to Rounds's first annual report.

Very little escaped the indefatigable Sterling Rounds. His attention to fire safety is testimony to his energy. He replaced the inadequate water lines in the Government Printing Office with larger mains and supplemented the fire escapes provided in 1878 with canvas chutes for rapid escape from the upper floors. Under his direction, a tramway or fire "trolley" that carried iron water buckets to fight fires on the upper stories was installed completely around the building at the fourth floor. Fire companies were organized, and a hundred feet of fire hose, attached to a standpipe, placed on each floor. A new steam pump supplied pressure for this system. Finally, in a particularly dramatic touch, bows and arrows were provided at strategic locations so that life lines could be shot from windows on the upper floors.

SUCCESSORS TO ROUNDS

Thomas E. Benedict of New York succeeded Rounds on September 13, 1886. After announcing to employees that each of them would be continued in his post "for the time being," he sounded a note that by now could almost be considered standard for an incoming Public Printer. He explained that, while his predecessor had done a commendable job, the Office could stand many improvements, could be operated more efficiently, and needed more space. Benedict ordered that greater use be made of electrotypes rather than printing directly from type, purchased new press equipment, discarded old unproductive machinery, and in general showed a remarkable talent for what today would be called industrial engineering—redesigning workflow and materials-handling throughout the Office. During his first six months, employment dropped from 2,400 to about 2,000, while output went up about 20 per cent. However, Benedict was not insensitive to the needs of his employees. He supported the efforts of craftsmen to obtain wage increases from Congress, which had fixed scales by statute. He also encouraged Congress to grant higher pay for night work and urged that the fifteen days of annual leave obtained for Government Printing Office employees in 1886 be increased to thirty days. (All other government workers had enjoyed thirty days of annual leave since 1883). His views on the employment of apprentices by the government were hardly orthodox and he argued against the use of apprentice labor in the

Government Printing Office. Basically, he questioned the legality of using apprentices and suggested that the number employed and the wages paid them were excessive. He noted that the number of apprentices on the rolls when he took over was seventy-one. A year later this figure had dropped to thirty-five. In his 1887 report to Congress, he summed up his attitude by saying, "My own judgment is that the government should employ only skilled labor, and that it is not beneficial to any class of mechanics to learn their trades in the public service."

Printing demand continued to rise. In 1888, the Government Printing Office produced the largest volume of work in its history. But, despite Benedict's fine record, charges of maladministration and "delays and irregularities" were brought against him that busy year. Among other things, he was scored for improper dismissal of veterans and veterans' widows. However, he was completely cleared of the charges by the Joint Committee on Printing, augmented by the addition of two printers then serving in Congress. In its report, the investigating committee offered the following comment on the discharge of veterans: "The law has been duly observed in making appointments and dismissals . . . the Office is simply a workshop and it should be freed from political influence."

In 1889, Frank W. Palmer of Illinois replaced Benedict as Public Printer. He soon took up his predecessors' cries for a larger, safer building, reporting that: "In my first tour of inspection . . . two kinds of danger to property and human life were apparent within the building. One was from insufficient support and overloaded condition of the second, third, and fourth floors . . . the other . . . liability to fire." Later, he stated that "provision should be made at once for a new fireproof plant on a commodius and accessible site."

In August, 1890, Congress authorized $280,000 for a site for a new GPO building and appointed a commission consisting of Secretary of the Treasury William Windom, Architect of the Capitol Edward Clark, and the Public Printer to select a suitable site for a new plant.

The Commission in December submitted its report to Congress recommending an appropriation for construction of the new building on a site south and east of the old location. Although the Commission was authorized to acquire "either by purchase or by condemnation," and the report was approved by the Joint Committee on Printing, Congress apparently was unwilling to proceed. On February 27, 1891, Congress adopted the appropriation bill with the following amendment: "Provided, That the appropriation . . . approved August 13, 1890, to provide accommodations for the Government Printing Office . . . be hereby suspended."

Not until March, 1892, did Congress again show its interest in the space problem at the Government Printing Office, authorizing the Joint Committee on Printing to locate a site for a new building. No action was taken, however, until the collapse of Ford's Theater on June 9, 1893, occasioned a new plea from Public Printer Palmer on the dangers at the Government Printing Office from overloaded floors. Even then, the only decision was to rent four buildings in the District of Columbia at an annual cost of more than $9,000. In 1894, with the return of the Cleveland Administration, Palmer was relieved of his space and other problems by the reappointment of Thomas E. Benedict as Public Printer. Benedict continued to agitate for a new structure throughout his second term, which lasted three years.

THE ACT OF 1895

On January 12, 1895, Congress codified the laws governing the Government Printing Office and public printing. The Printing Act of 1895, when passed, brought together all the body of law on public printing and added a few new wrinkles. One new section placed all printing offices under the control of the Public Printer—those then in operation and any that might be put in operation later. Statutory exceptions were the plants in the Weather Bureau, the Record and Pension Division of the War Department, and the Census Office. But the Act provided also that the Public Printer, with the approval of the Joint Committee on Printing, could abolish any printing operation, including the excepted plants, wherever "in their judgment the economy of the public service would be thereby advanced." At the time of this Act, Government Printing Office branches were operating in the Treasury, Navy, Interior, and State departments. In addition, despite an earlier law requiring that all government printing be done in the Government Printing Office, a number of separate printing operations were also in existence in the Post Office, the War Department, the Agriculture Department, the Weather Bureau, and the Surgeon General's Office. (In 1910, the Public Printer abolished the printing offices in the Treasury, Interior, and Agriculture departments. His authority to close these plants was questioned, and the Attorney General ruled that the Public Printer's authority extended only to the excepted offices mentioned in the 1895 Act. However, the closed plants never reopened.)

The Act of 1895 also contained an important provision regarding printing appropriations. It required each agency to submit annual printing estimates and declared that the cost for printing in the ensuing year was to be charged against the allotments granted each agency for printing.

But perhaps the most significant provision of the new law was the establishment of the Office of the Superintendent of Documents (see Chapter VI). For years, accumulations of public documents had been growing. The Act provided for the new Superintendent of Documents to receive and store all surplus documents, including those in government offices. It also charged him with the cataloging and indexing of all government publications, both monthly and annually, and with servicing libraries with information on government publications, as well as making sales to the public. The distribution of government documents to the then 420 depository libraries was another duty that fell to the new division. Benedict appointed F. A. Crandall of Buffalo, New York, to the post, and the sixth floor of the Union Building on G Street, N.W., was leased for the Superintendent of Document's use. Crandall went to work with a vengeance on the 150,000 publications that fell into his lap, and the first of many cries of objection from him and succeeding men in the Documents Division over the profligate free distribution of government documents was heard.

New Century, New Building, New Techniques

In 1897, former Public Printer Frank W. Palmer came back again as head of the Government Printing Office (since 1886, Palmer and Benedict had been passing the post of Public Printer back and forth between them). Palmer immediately took up the task he had apparently set for himself during his last tenure—to get not just a new annex, but a new building. In 1898, he was successful. The Fifty-fifth Congress appropriated $225,000 for the purchase of land for an additional building. Later, an amount "not exceeding $2 million" was voted for construction. The Chief of Engineers of the Army designed the structure, with the plans subject to the Public Printer's approval. Construction began on July 10, 1899, and the building was occupied in 1903.

At the turn of the century, the Office was producing about $5 million worth of printing and was considered, at least by the *Washington Times,* the "World's Greatest Printing Office." Supporting this contention was the GPO's acquisition of all Library of Congress printing and binding. At the urging of

Herbert Putnam, Librarian of Congress, the legislature approved the purchase of machinery and materials for the GPO to establish a branch at the Library. This unit was founded to produce the Library's vast catalog card requirements and to perform full binding, repair, and restoration work on Library volumes.

About this time, printers and pressmen were given a raise that brought their wages to $4 a day. Similar wages were also paid to a mixed bag of craftsmen, including saw grinders, leather parers, and blacksmiths. Electricians (a new group, since the Office had only completely converted from steam power in 1897) got the raise as well. Female employees also shared the bounty—although their pay increases were scaled to more modest proportions. "Directresses" received a raise of 26 cents a day, while "gold workers, numberers, press feeders, and sewers" got 8 cents more per day.

With the new century came mechanization. Automatic typesetting machinery was already in use, chiefly in large newspaper plants throughout the country. By the time the Government Printing Office acquired forty-six Linotypes in 1904, 10,000 of Ottmar Mergenthaler's "wonderful machines" had been sold or rented. At the same time, the GPO bought twenty-eight Monotype machines.* The cost for both was nearly $300,000. Other equipment (principally thirty-four new presses) was also purchased to be installed in the new building. All told, Palmer disbursed more than $440,000 for new equipment.

These acquisitions were long overdue, and it was a decidedly practical move to modernize the production elements of the Office when the new structure was occupied. The GPO had lagged far behind other printers in terms of mechaniza-

* The distinction between the two is simple. The Monotype machine casts individual characters while the Linotype machine casts a slug of an entire "line of type."

tion, particularly in type composition. But the Public Printer was still not entirely convinced in 1904 that his new composing machines could efficiently handle "the widely varying kinds of official documents issued by this office." Perhaps Palmer had a premonition, for the year following he was roundly attacked for his extravagances. It was pointed out as a score against him that in his two terms he had served over thirteen years as Public Printer—longer than any previous head of the Office. Also, the provincial and self-protective attitude of craftsmen in the GPO had its effect; most of them violently opposed the use of typesetting machinery as a threat to their job security. President Theodore Roosevelt reacted to the widespread criticism leveled at Palmer and relieved him in September, 1905.

Public Printer Stillings and the Big Delay

In November, Roosevelt appointed Charles A. Stillings of Massachusetts as Public Printer. It was not long before events thrust Stillings into the eye of a congressional hurricane. Lurking deep in the private thoughts of every government appointee must be the nagging horror of a public display of mismanagement, but surely never in his wildest dreams could Stillings have imagined that he would be accused of personally delaying the adjournment of the Congress of the United States and immobilizing the peripatetic Chief Executive of the United States for more than eight hours. But it happened. In characteristic final-day fashion, Congress at the end of June, 1906, flooded the GPO with work. Running at breakneck speed, the Office nonetheless fell behind. Congress—both houses—had to postpone adjournment until the deluge of bills could be properly enrolled. The President and his Cabinet had journeyed to Washington expressly to sign the engrossed bills as they came from the Government Printing Office, and, as the New York Times of July 1, 1906, reported, "The President was obliged to waste the best part of a day sitting around the Capitol with his Cabinet to sign bills. The Senate . . . was obliged to sit and swelter throughout the hottest afternoon and night of the summer." The upshot was a scathing denunciation of the Public Printer and a Senate-ordered investigation by the Joint Committee on Printing.

Apparently, the situation was satisfactorily explained and cooler heads prevailed for not only did the Committee clear Stillings, but it praised his performance as "positively expeditious." However, Stillings' tenure at the Government Printing Office proved to be a stormy two years plus. Early in 1908, he was suspended by President Roosevelt. His downfall was the so-called Rossiter Report, which was ordered by the President following the Public Printer's suspension. The chief objections to Stillings continuing as Public Printer were his rather heavy-handed and expensive attempts to introduce accounting, inventory, and auditing reforms to the GPO. Moreover, nearly $1 million dollars had been spent on new composing machines since 1904. Office production scarcely seemed to justify such a large number of machines—207, to be exact. The report noted that although fifty new Monotype keyboards had been purchased and delivered, only one or two had been placed in operation. The report further recognized a certain amount of employee dissatisfaction but dismissed it as a natural reaction to the discipline prevailing under Stillings.

Henry T. Brian, John S. Leech, and Samuel B. Donnelly followed in rapid succession in the post of Public Printer. Donnelly, former president of the International Typographical Union, had the distinction of being sworn into office at the White House. Under his leadership, the storms of the recent past were largely forgotten and quieter days arrived for the

Government Printing Office. The only ripples in the pond came when the Treasury, Interior, and Agriculture branch printing plants were absorbed by the Office in 1909 and a year later when electric trucks were substituted for horses and wagons.

WORLD WAR I AND THE BUSY 1920's

In 1913, Cornelius Ford of New York replaced Donnelly. Until the declaration of war in 1917, departmental demands were subnormal, but with wartime came urgent and vastly increased orders for printing. Paper supply was short, and the Joint Committee on Printing refused to endorse paper contracts at inflated prices. Only through Ford's personal efforts in appealing to the paper suppliers was sufficient stock obtained to meet the demand. The same conditions prevailed in the ink and other vital materials industries. The Office began manufacturing ink, book-lining paper, and typemetal in an attempt to free itself from the high-priced market for these supplies.

In 1918, GPO production reached its highest point in its history to that time. Printing and binding in the amount of more than $12 million was produced. At the close of the war, the enormous printing requirements of the government visibly slowed and wholesale cancellations of printing orders took place. After the initial dip, however, orders spurred by governmental recovery programs resumed at almost the wartime rate.

With the overwhelming defeat of the Democrats by Warren Gamaliel Harding, and his campaign for a return to "normalcy," Public Printer Ford's days were numbered. On April 5, 1920, he was replaced by George H. Carter of Iowa. Carter at the time of his appointment was Clerk of the Joint Committee on Printing, having served in this capacity for a dozen

years. He was also a printer and thus exceptionally well qualified for his new post. He brought with him from President
Harding a mandate to "stop waste and extravagances," and he
took it seriously. Although he assumed office only three
months before the close of the fiscal year, he returned nearly
$2.5 million to the Treasury in unexpended funds. His 56-
page annual report of 1921 contrasted sharply with the 716
pages submitted by his predecessor.

In another economy step the GPO, in concert with the
newly formed Bureau of the Budget, established an interde-
partmental Permanent Conference on Printing. Carter was
Chairman and carried the intent of the Conference through to
the GPO by organizing a Requisitions Review Board, which
carefully scrutinized all printing and binding orders. The outcome of this full-dress examination was further economies in
government printing.

The vast quantities of paper used by the GPO apparently
had been on the indefatigable Carter's mind for some years.
Fluctuating paper prices were an anathema to the Office,
which by now was using 50 million pounds annually. Earlier,
in his capacity as Clerk of the Joint Committee on Printing,
Carter had drafted a bill to establish a government pulp and
paper mill with pulpwood to be supplied from government–
owned timber stands. Now he recommended a central paper-
purchasing and warehousing authority to prevent departments
and agencies from competing with each other in the paper
market and to bring some order to the government's buying
and use of paper. Under the provisions of the Printing Act of
1895, he established an in-plant unit to test paper and most of
the other supplies and materials used in printing.

Carter's regime is best characterized as one of change. He
reorganized much of the Office, setting up not only the testing
unit but also the photoengraving unit and the Planning Service
Division (see Chapters III and IV). He inaugurated collective
bargaining for the GPO and reinstituted and expanded appren-

tice training.* Through prudent purchases, he modernized much of the production effort. His recommendations regarding fiscal matters pertinent to government printing were adopted by Congress and resulted in simpler and more businesslike methods of executing and accounting for government work. Under his aegis, too, came the substantial and continuing economies traceable to the standardization of government letterhead and form sizes at 8 × 10½ inches. The savings over the years from this deceptively simple change boggle the imagination.

Perhaps the most enduring contribution of Carter's administration was the passage of the Kiess Act in 1924. Basically, this law relieved Congress of the onerous and unfamiliar task of setting wages for the various crafts in the Office and placed the responsibility squarely with the Public Printer. The Act was passed without a dissenting voice. It established a labor-management relationship between the head of the Office and the employees in each craft who were represented by democratically elected committeemen. The initial effect of this law was a wage increase, followed by a sizable increase in printing charges paid by GPO customers. The law also authorized overtime rates and a night differential, which together enabled the Office to attract and keep competent craftsmen and to compete in the day-to-day labor market.

The congressional workload overshadowed that of any other customer department during the 1920's. The *Congressional Record* was late eight times in 1926, and an unbelievable number of bills (nearly 19,000) were dropped into the hopper during the First Session of the Sixty-ninth Congress. Perhaps because of this demonstration of needed service, the legislature responded to the Public Printer's cries for more space, and an

---

* The year 1921 saw a double-barreled drain on Office craftsmen. Strikes in the printing industry attracted journeymen to outside jobs, and the enactment of retirement legislation lured nearly 180 employees into departure. It was partly as a result that in 1922 the GPO re-established apprentice training.

appropriation of $1.25 million was made for an eight-story annex west of the main building. Four years later this structure, which brought GPO floor space to nearly a million square feet, was occupied. The original building on the corner of North Capitol and H streets was still part of the Printing Office complex, although by now chiefly used for storage. It remained an ever-present fire problem, besides being unsightly and in imminent danger of collapse.*

WORLD WAR II

As the lights dimmed in Europe, the Government Printing Office in the late 1930's began feeling a well-defined build-up in printing. Then in 1940, dollar volume rose to a shade over $20 million, while the Office bought nearly $2 million in additional printing and binding, making a total jump of more than 30 per cent over 1939. By 1945, volume had risen nearly 80 per cent over that of 1940. These years, 1940–45, saw unusual demands on GPO employees. Long hours were spent under pressure to fill the enormous requirements of the military—and always on the shortest possible schedules. (If armies travel on their stomachs, their next most urgent need must be for printing.) Of course, quality and accuracy suffered. Supplies, desperately scarce, were controlled by the War Production Board. And hundreds of trained journeymen were lost to the military.

* In 1935, despite—or perhaps because of—the Depression, Congress voted to replace this venerable building. The nation was showing some signs of recovery, undoubtedly spurred by the many federal construction projects, and it was thought the structure planned for the site of the old building would boost area employment. A warehouse was also authorized to be built across North Capitol Street facing the main building, with a tunnel connecting the two to facilitate paper-handling. Construction of the warehouse was completed in 1938, and the new main building, rising on the site of the original Wendell plant, was dedicated in February, 1939, by Public Printer Augustus E. Giegengack of New York, Carter's successor. Occupied in 1940, it remains the home of the GPO.

At the outset, it became clear that, regardless of maximum effort, the GPO working alone could not satisfy the printing demands of the nation at war. In 1929, Congress had authorized the Public Printer to buy printing from commercial plants, the intent being to permit the procurement of various kinds of specialty items. Under the existing War Powers Act, this authority was broadened to include all types of printing. The industry responded promptly. An informal advisory committee was formed among printing industry leaders in thirty-five cities to smooth the way for this expanded program and to supply information and contracts. About 2,000 firms were involved. But despite an early rush to print for the government when paper and supplies for private business were short, the honeymoon of the GPO and the printing industry soon ended, with competition coming from the giant war-industry manufacturers, who had money and priorities for supplies. GPO officials, anxious to maintain the partnership established with commercial printers, developed a system of standard-rate contracts. These agreements enabled the GPO to pick any of the firms that were signatories to a basic contract setting forth rates and types of work. The rates were adjusted to conform with recognized increases in wages and prices. By the close of World War II, printing procured from commercial sources amounted to $50 million annually—more than two and one half times the in-plant volume of the GPO itself just four years earlier.

During wartime, it became necessary to restructure many of the GPO production and planning units. The Planning Division took on much of the organizational form it has today, and in 1943, the Public Printer separated planning from production activities, setting up units called Planning Service, Plant Planning, Commercial Planning, and Typography and Design. A Scheduling Board (now the Scheduling Committee) was created to decide whether work should be done in plant, bought from commercial sources, or waived to departments in order best to serve the particular requirements of each order. Warehouses, perhaps better titled field offices, were organized in various cities. The function of these offices was to provide liaison and control in the areas in which they were situated. Warehouse managers were, in effect, on-the-scene representatives of the Government Printing Office and as such were authorized to buy printing and dole out paper to contractors. These "warehouses" were closed at the war's end.

The war's end brought one new and highly demanding job for the Government Printing Office. When an unprecedented international assembly met in 1945 in San Francisco to establish the United Nations, its unprecedented printing needs became the responsibility of the GPO.

The *Journal* planned for reporting the assembly's debates was similar to the *Congressional Record*. Although *Journal* production was not at first expected to be too difficult, it soon became evident that it would be a large-scale task. Technicians from the GPO were hurried to San Francisco to oversee this work in addition to the other prodigious and urgent requirements that developed.

The U.N. Charter was originally estimated at 150 pages; it finally came to 372. Considering that the Charter was hand set in five languages—English, Spanish, French, Russian, and Chinese—it is almost a miracle that it was printed and delivered at all. To put it mildly, Chinese compositors were difficult to locate. Russian compositors were almost as scarce. Changes and diplomatic alterations made final makeup unbelievably complex. For example, at the last minute, the six signature copies of the Charter were found to lack a single Chinese character. A GPO compositor manually corrected these copies, and the deadline for signing was met.

One of the first orders of normal postwar business at GPO headquarters was a new look for the *Congressional Record*. In nearly seventy-five years, this staid and proper publication had been "beautified" only once—in 1930, when a new type-dress was adopted. A 1948 change in format gave the *Record* a more modern appearance, with a switch from two to three columns improving readability and effecting significant savings in space. Cost avoidance using the new design in actual production amounted to a substantial $150,000 annually and made possible bonus savings to members of Congress wishing to take advantage of reprint privileges (at their own expense) on speeches appearing in the *Record*.

THE 1950's AND 1960's

The GPO barely had time to recover its peacetime breath before the Korean action forced the Office back to something close to wartime operations. Public Printer Augustus E. Giegengack had been replaced by John J. Deviny, wages were being negotiated on a weighted-average formula, and Congress, recognizing the demands upon its members' time, had authorized a ready-reference section for the *Congressional Record*. Called the "Daily Digest," it averaged about five pages and contained a short version of the day's activities, plus a current and an advanced schedule. Commercial procurement, which had been a wartime mainstay and had fallen to a minor role in Office operations, regained its stature. In 1950, $34 million in outside printing was bought. The Chicago and New York "warehouses" were reopened. But the rush was short-lived. The Korean cease-fire heralded a drop in printing expenditures.

In 1953, Public Printer Deviny retired, and a short while later, Raymond Blattenberger assumed the reins of the Government Printing Office. Blattenberger instituted new accounting procedures, realigned work shifts, introduced workflow innovations, created a separate division for offset work, and was the beneficiary of action by Congress establishing a revolving fund for the Government Printing Office. This fund allowed the Office to operate in much the same manner as a capitalized commercial enterprise.

In 1955, the Hoover Commission's report on federal printing came as a shocker. It declared that the total printing bill for government was a tidy $370 million. The GPO produced only $71 million of that amount. The remainder of this enormous volume was provided by 327 departmental printing and duplicating plants, nearly 200 of which were operated by the military. The Commission report also revealed that over and above the GPO's use of paper, the government proper created 25 billion pieces of paper annually. Thus, the role of the Government Printing Office in the growing paper deluge was placed in proper perspective. (In 1969, estimates of the annual federal printing expenditures exceeded a half billion dollars.)

In 1961, following the resignation of Public Printer Blattenberger, John M. Wilson, the Deputy Public Printer, became the Acting Public Printer. Wilson died after serving little more than a month, and on March 9, 1961, President Kennedy nominated James L. Harrison, Staff Director of the Joint Committee on Printing, to be Public Printer. Harrison took office on March 17, 1961, and served until March 31, 1970, when he was succeeded by Adolphus Nichols Spence II. Spence came to the post with excellent credentials, having formerly headed both the Defense Printing Service and the Navy Publications and Printing Service.

Under Harrison, the Government Printing Office entered a period of growth and progress. Dollar volume leaped from less than $100 million in 1961 to more than $200 million in 1969. Documents sales jumped from about $9 million to $20 million over the same period. The far-reaching Harrison policy of sharing the government's printing requirements with industry led to a steady increase in work supplied by contract printers. In 1961, commercial printers provided 42 per cent of the annual volume; in 1970, 57 per cent, or $103 million worth of printing, was done by private industry.

Harrison made strenuous efforts to improve working conditions and environment in the plant, and during his tenure took a keen interest in upgrading the equipment used in supplying the U.S. Government's printing needs. Under his direction, a major part of the Office's outmoded and obsolete equipment was replaced by modern, more efficient machinery. In keeping with nationwide trends in the industry, letterpress was supplanted by offset as the main production method. (See Chapter IV.) Today, offset web presses with high running rates and low plating and press preparation costs keep GPO prices competitive with those of the best commercial firms.

III

The GPO Today:
Obligations and Organization

Modern government is perhaps the most complex activity man has ever attempted. It is infinitely varied and touches on a bewildering assortment of everyday matters. As it is practiced in the American bureaucracy, its indispensable and ubiquitous agent is printing—government printing. Through the printed word, control is exercised, information disseminated, revenue collected and dispensed, security maintained, education fostered, social progress promoted, and the national heritage preserved. Thus, the Government Printing Office has a hand in all the vital functions of the U.S. Government.

The responsibilities of the GPO are set forth in Title 44, United States Code. Section 501 states:

> All printing, binding, and blank-book work for Congress, the Executive Office, the Judiciary, other than the Supreme Court of the United States, and every executive department, independent office, or establishment of the Government shall be done at the GPO, except—(1) classes of work the Joint Committee on Printing considers to be urgent or necessary to have done elsewhere; and (2) printing in field printing plants operated by an executive department, independent office or establishment, and the procurement of printing by an executive department, independent office or establishment from allotments for contract field printing, if approved by the Joint Committee on Printing.

Title 44 was recodified by Public Law 90-620 in 1968. No substantive changes were made, but the language was clarified and a number of obsolete sections eliminated. However, the second exception listed above in Section 501 was effectively changed in 1969.

Government printing policy is developed and interpreted chiefly by the Joint Committee on Printing (JCP) of the U.S. Congress. This policy is disseminated through issuances of the Committee's Printing and Binding Regulations. Issue No. 20, dated March, 1969, transmitted a number of major changes. This document identified all printing as "federal printing"— wording that negates the intent of that part of Section 501 dealing with both "field printing" and "contract field printing." All printing is still to be the responsibility of the GPO, with the same exceptions allowed at the discretion of the JCP as before, but redefining "field" and "departmental" printing as "federal" printing makes it possible for much of the work formerly done in field and departmental plants to be bought from private industry.

In his letter of transmittal for these rules, the Chairman of the Joint Committee on Printing acknowledged the intrusion of the Committee's regulations into the current law but explained that "to avoid unnecessary disruptions of required Federal printing services during this temporary interim period while the new policy direction . . . is being phased into being, departments are advised to proceed as in the past until otherwise directed by the JCP." The new policy direction to which he referred is a long-awaited attempt to streamline government printing operations.

The JCP Chairman added the admonition that work done by all plants owned or operated wholly or in part by the government or at government expense, located on property owned or controlled by the Government "shall not include any items which are determined to be commercially procurable." The new regulations also provided for the establishment of something new: a GPO Field Procurement Office in each of ten national regions corresponding roughly to the regions established by the General Services Administration (GSA). These ten offices, which are being phased into operation, will administer the procurement of government printing for all agencies in the individual regions.

Federal printing requirements are filled by the GPO in a number of ways. Customer agencies can send a duly certified order to the Office stating that "such work be necessary for the public service," and from this point on the problem of delivering a properly executed piece of printing, on schedule, becomes the GPO's problem. The work may be done by the GPO in its own plant. Or its *Printing Procurement Section* (see Chart I) can buy it from the commercial printing industry using one, or more, of its 2,000 qualified suppliers through competitive bidding. Or, if the work fits roughly into one of the GPO-established, open-end contracts, it may be placed directly with a firm that has already submitted the low bid on a certain type of work and been awarded the contract to produce this work at a specified figure for a predetermined length of time.

In the future, departments having a field requirement beyond the capacity of their proprietary plants, will obtain their printing needs through a GPO Field Procurement Office from commercial sources. Exceptions to this method of procurement can still be made, of course, on the authority of the JCP. Also applicable is the waiver provision of Section 504, Title 44, U.S.C., which states:

> The Joint Committee on Printing may permit the Public Printer to authorize an executive department, independent office, or establishment of the Government to purchase direct for its use such printing, binding, and blank-book work, otherwise authorized by law, as the Government Printing Office is not able or suitably equipped to execute or as may be more economically or in the better interest of the Government executed elsewhere.

CHART I

GOVERNMENT PRINTING OFFICE ORGANIZATION CHART

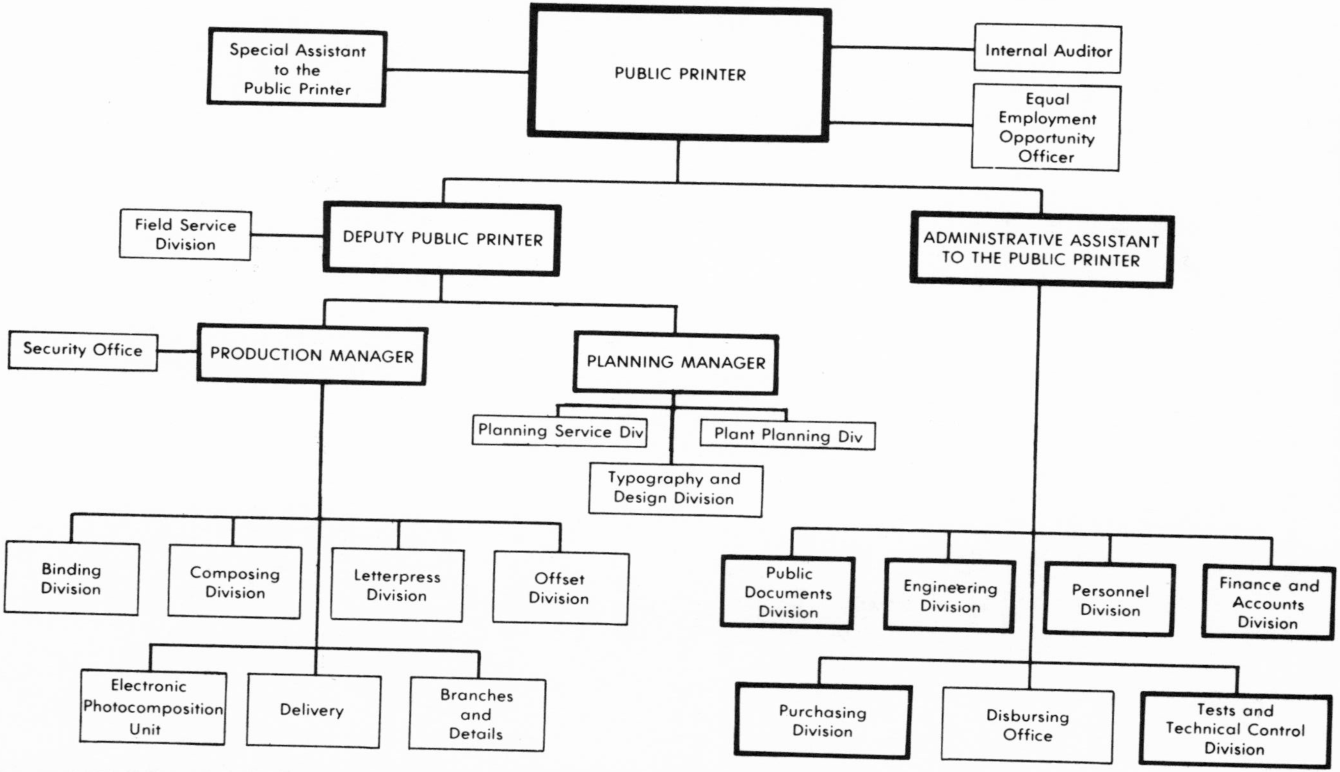

- Special Assistant to the Public Printer
- PUBLIC PRINTER
  - Internal Auditor
  - Equal Employment Opportunity Officer
- ADMINISTRATIVE ASSISTANT TO THE PUBLIC PRINTER
  - Public Documents Division
  - Engineering Division
  - Personnel Division
  - Finance and Accounts Division
  - Purchasing Division
  - Disbursing Office
  - Tests and Technical Control Division
- DEPUTY PUBLIC PRINTER
  - Field Service Division
  - PLANNING MANAGER
    - Planning Service Div
    - Typography and Design Division
    - Plant Planning Div
  - PRODUCTION MANAGER
    - Security Office
    - Binding Division
    - Composing Division
    - Letterpress Division
    - Offset Division
    - Electronic Photocomposition Unit
    - Delivery
    - Branches and Details

The meaning of this waiver is that the Public Printer can return to a customer agency any order that he feels the Office cannot fill and authorize the agency to satisfy its needs by direct purchase from other sources.

The decision as to whether the work is to be done in the GPO or bought rests with the *Planning Service Division,* whose *Requisition Section* in cooperation with the *Scheduling Committee* (see Chart I) makes this determination. Bearing importantly on this decision is the type of printing required by the ordering agency, as well as the GPO's ability to handle the job economically on general-purpose printing equipment. Printing, such as marginally punched, continuous forms for use on computer chainprinters, tabulating cards, and process-color printing, are examples of work that is best produced on special equipment and hence is almost always bought rather than produced in house. General printing is the chief product of the Office proper, and the Government Printing Office is often referred to as the world's largest "job shop." Each day over a thousand orders are received, ranging from simple forms to multivolume sets of hard-cover books.

The Principal Customers

Basic to the production philosophy that has guided the GPO in the years since the end of World War II are the needs of Congress. The large typesetting capability essential for the timely production of the *Congressional Record* (see Chapter V) is available for other tasks only when the million-and-a-half-em nightly production is completed.

Printing for Congress

The *Record* is perhaps the best-known and most important congressional publication. But Congress' other requirements are numerous and varied. Funds for printing the *Record* represent only about one-sixth of the total annual congressional appropriation for printing. The other types of printing needed to carry out congressional business are a very large part of the GPO operation and essential to the legislative processes of the U.S. Government.

The largest single congressional expenditure is devoted to the printing and binding of testimony and supporting facts generated at hearings conducted before the various committees. About 250,000 pages are produced annually. Hearings are normally furnished in "doc-size" pages with a type area of 26½ by approximately 42 picas (the term, short for "document size," derives from the early printing format specified for House and Senate documents).

Envelopes imprinted with the congressional frank, and document franks, also account for a sizable amount of printing. In an average year, 140 million envelopes, and 5.5 million document franks are furnished to members of Congress. Recently, special envelope printing presses were installed in the GPO expressly to meet congressional needs. These presses print from rubber plates that can be rapidly fixed to a steel cylinder with double-faced adhesive tape. They are capable of producing at speeds up to 70,000 envelopes per hour.

House and Senate committee and business calendars total nearly 75,000 pages for an annual session of Congress. These calendars, which list actions on pending and completed legislation, are vital to the orderly conduct of legislative business. Bills, resolutions, and amendments amount to another 130,000 pages. Committee reports on pending legislation make nearly 30,000 pages; and House and Senate documents, consisting of annual reports, engineers' reports, and special reports made by government departments in response to resolutions, supplemental, and deficiency estimates of appropriations, and other congressional requests, amount to still another 25,000 pages.

Each year, Congress prints a document familiar to all who

deal with the federal establishment—the *Congressional Directory*. This volume lists the names of all members of Congress together with brief biographies of each; committee assignments, administrative and operating staffs on the Hill, key officials from the executive and judicial branches, and a wealth of other pertinent information on Congress and the government. Aside from the daily *Congressional Record*, the *Directory* is perhaps the most widely used publication of Congress. This blue-bound volume is grouped with the GPO's "miscellaneous" congressional publications category, which also includes the *Senate Journal* and the *House Journal*, memorial addresses, nominations, the United States Code and supplements, and publications not carrying a document or report number, such as laws, treaties, committee prints, and similar pieces.

The GPO prints all official congressional stationery and stationery items, including letterheads, notices, tags, labels, payrolls, stenographic notebooks, tablets, wall calendars, and blank forms and books—over 60 million separate items each year. Most of the foregoing types of work are given special handling through the Office, a fact that often gives rise to objections from other customers of the GPO who feel that preferential treatment for Congress delays their work. There is some justification for this view, but since the Office is organized and staffed mainly to handle congressional work at night and departmental work on daytime shifts, there is relatively little conflict except in emergency situations.

Executive Department Printing

Under the law, the bulk of all government printing, as we have seen, must be furnished by the GPO. Currently, about a hundred departments, agencies, commissions, bureaus, and offices in the Executive Branch are GPO customers. They range in size from the Army—the GPO's largest single customer, whose printing bill regularly exceeds $25 million—to smaller customers such as the Indian Claims Commission or the American Battle Monuments Commission, whose printing bills rarely amount to more than three figures.

The principle of government that justifies this printing and publishing is one of service—service by the departments to the people of the United States. The Defense agencies, for instance, serve by providing security and protection for the citizenry as a whole, and their mission gives rise to requirements for all types of printing: manuals for fighting men, maintenance and service instructions for armament, research and scientific tracts on advanced weaponry, directories and rosters, strategic and tactical studies and reports, stock catalogs, parts lists, and a host of others. The Agriculture Department, which spends in the neighborhood of $6 million annually, provides printed information on scientific farming methods, conservation, forest land use, farm home industries, rodent and pest control, crop quotas, subsidies, and so on. Nearly every agency produces an annual report, some quite elaborate. Many issue periodicals, many others provide lists and special directories such as the National Library of Medicine's *Index Medicus,* which is published monthly, or the Patent Office's *Official Gazette* issued weekly by the Commerce Department. The list is seemingly endless.

Judicial Printing

The printing furnished to the judicial branch of the U.S. Government by the GPO is small in terms of volume—less than 1 per cent. A special branch of the GPO is housed in the Supreme Court building to meet the special requirements of the highest court. In addition to the Supreme Court, judicial customer agencies include the Court of Claims, the Court of Customs and Patent Appeals, and the Tax Court of the United States.

OFFICE OF THE PUBLIC PRINTER

The duties of the Public Printer have been broadly discussed. The function of the Number Two man in the GPO, the Deputy Public Printer, is somewhat unusual in that he is assigned by law to the "duties formerly required of the Chief Clerk," as well as to the supervision of the buildings occupied by the Government Printing Office. The Deputy also acts in the absence of the Public Printer. In everyday practice, he serves as the officer responsible for production, planning, field service activities, and electronic printing. All other activities are grouped under the Administrative Assistant. (See Chart I.)

The Special Assistant to the Public Printer serves as the public relations officer for the GPO, but the position is a catch-all. In addition to staff writing, speech preparation, and other typical public relations duties, the Special Assistant performs staff research, and is assigned principal staff responsibility for space utilization, and a variety of workflow and industrial engineering functions. Certain types of liaison with Congress and the executive agencies also fall to this office.

GPO ADMINISTRATIVE SERVICES

The Government Printing Office is fundamentally a service agency supplying printing, binding, and allied services to the entire government. But as with most service agencies, it is itself supported by a rather complete set of organic services. Divisional units specializing in financial management, personnel administration, procurement, sales, technical testing, and maintenance and engineering are among these in-plant services.

All of these activities are grouped under the Administrative Assistant to the Public Printer. Through the Comptroller, who heads up the *Finance and Accounts Division,* the Administrative Assistant exercises dominion over all Office fiscal affairs. Through the Director of Purchases, he oversees the *Purchasing Division*'s purchases of supplies, equipment, and commercial printing bought by the Government Printing Office. The Superintendent of Documents heads the *Public Documents Division.* (See Chapter VI.) He also works under the supervision of the Administrative Assistant, who, in addition, is responsible for the work of the *Engineering Division,* the *Tests and Technical Control Division, Personnel Division,* and the *Disbursing Office.* (See Chart I.)

Finance and Accounting

Because the Government Printing Office is capitalized in much the same fashion as a commercial printing enterprise, its financial and accounting practices are of special interest. Until recently, the Government Printing Office was required to appear before the Legislative Appropriations Subcommittee of the Appropriations Committee of each house annually in order to obtain operating capital. From the time the GPO opened its doors in 1861, it struggled with the problems common to such funding until 1953, when Congress established a revolving fund capitalizing it. The original appropriation was $1 million. Congress also agreed to the Government Printing Office retaining collections from its current accounts receivable further to bolster the fund. This action put a value of about $10 million on the original capital available. Periodically, because of the rapid growth of its annual business volume, the GPO has been forced to seek additional funds to augment its capital. In 1963, Congress authorized an increase of $10 million in this fund and in 1967, one of $15 million. If the annual volume in 1953 of some $74 million is contrasted to the volume in 1967, $200 million, the need for extra operating capital is clear.

All of the Government Printing Office's customers budget

for printing in their annual appropriation requests. Most printing estimates are contained in agency administrative requests and are, therefore, difficult to identify. Prior to fiscal year 1923, agency printing appropriation funds were allocated to the GPO when approved by Congress. Charges were made against these funds throughout the year and unexpended surpluses were returned to the Treasury. In 1923, however, agency printing money was appropriated to the agency itself and the GPO began to bill each customer for its own printing and binding.

The Government Printing Office itself prepares an annual budget for submission to the Congress through the Office of Management and Budget (formerly the Bureau of the Budget). Unlike most departmental and agency budgets, the GPO budget was not subject to approval until 1954, and even now no formal hearings are held on its routine items such as personal services, rent, power, and commercial contracts. The Public Printer does, however, as mentioned before, appear annually before the Legislative Subcommittee of the Appropirations committees of both the House and Senate. Two items occupy the attention of these committees: the appropriations for congressional printing and for the Public Documents Division. The first is a paradox, for it requires the Public Printer to justify to Congress *his* estimate of how much printing Congress itself will need for the coming year—a requirement over which the Public Printer exercises no control whatsoever. (However, as a practical matter, the Public Printer's estimates are based on historical analyses, and he is permitted to adjust annual deficiencies in subsequent years —although these adjustments are not always accepted graciously by the committee, especially by minority party members.) The second item, the appropriation for the Superintendent of Documents' operations, which *are* conducted with appropriated funds, is discussed more fully in Chapter VI.

Since 1953, the Government Printing Office has operated on

an accrual accounting system, and it maintains an active capital account with the U.S. Treasury. From this account, the GPO pays its employees, purchases both materials and printing, and meets its financial obligations. Money collected for services rendered, the sale of paper and printing, and such other income as may be derived from disposition of fixed assets, refunds, and the sale of waste paper, is deposited to this account. The revolving fund turns over about five times annually and provides an adequate working capital for normal activities. But more than this, the fund provides a sound financial base for the agency and frees both the Public Printer and Congress from the perennial haggle over appropriations for operating expenses. Each year, in a rather unusual action, the Congress reauthorizes expenditures, in accordance with the law, from the revolving fund. Thus, in effect, the Appropriation committees review the budget of the GPO annually in much the same fashion as the Office of Management and Budget does the budgets of the executive departments.

Watchdogging these annual operating expenses is the General Accounting Office, which maintains an audit team on the GPO premises. This team also examines in great detail the complex transactions that characterize the modified job-cost accounting system used by the Government Printing Office. This audit is required by law, and a report of the GAO's findings is made annually to the Speaker of the House, the President of the Senate, the Director of the Office of Management and Budget, and the Joint Committee on Printing, as well as to the Public Printer. Not until the GPO revolving fund was established did the General Accounting Office become involved in a thoroughgoing examination of GPO accounts, although limited audits of such items as payrolls, travel vouchers, invoices, and bills of lading had been made for many years.

The first complete audit of the Government Printing Office in 1954–55, reported by the Comptroller General, contained many criticisms of accounting procedures then in use. The deficiencies, according to the report, ranged "in significance from bookkeeping errors to major flaws in the application of accounting principles." The GPO was called to task for its operation of the job-order cost system under which it prepared its charges to customers, with the GAO citing the lack of sound standard costs on which technicians could base their computations. Another criticism involved disproportional sharing of production costs by agencies "riding" another agency's requisitions for printing. The Office was also reproached for its methods of setting prices for government publications and its publication inventory systems.

The GAO also suggested several organizational changes bearing on the heavy administrative burdens of the Comptroller and recommended establishing an internal audit program to improve Office management. All of these recommendations were acted upon. Despite the ominous tone of this first evaluation, subsequent reports clearly show that the over-all management of the GPO's varied and complex accounts have met the Comptroller General's criteria and an excellent relationship between the GAO and the GPO has developed. (It should be noted that the GAO's audits are restricted to accounting and administrative functions and are not intended to review the technical aspects of the production of printing.)

Fundamentally, the accounting system in use is designed to recover costs of production, materials, and overhead. At the time a printing and binding requisition is received, whenever feasible the Planning Division prepares a "firm cost" estimate, which is supplied to customers in order that funds may be earmarked to pay the Government Printing Office when final bills are submitted. These estimates depend on the customer's willingness to accept the job as described in his requisition and are expected not to vary more than 10 per cent from the computed cost of a job. The customer pays only the firm estimated cost, although adjustments are permitted to accommodate authors' alterations, transportation costs, job specification changes, and increases in quantities ordered.

Certain types of printing and binding requisitions do not require advance cost estimates. For example, no estimate is supplied on rush work, classified material, or on dated periodical printing. The basis for estimating job costs is the GPO's *Scale of Prices Handbook.* This handbook is constantly being revised to adjust recovery costs in order that neither too much nor too little is being charged for printing. The analysis of current pricing is the principal function of the *Printing Cost Investigation Staff* in the Finance and Accounts Division. This unit also develops and reviews costs for paper and materials used in printing and polices the complex tabulating card reporting system that provides a constant check on individual production costs.

For departmental work, estimates are sent directly to departments. Most congressional work is not estimated except to obligate funds at the end of the fiscal year. For certain private work authorized to be printed for members of Congress at their expense (extracts and speeches from the *Congressional Record*), estimates are sent directly to the Member.

A jacket cost summary is prepared by the *Electronic Data Processing Branch,* and this and the actual jacket become the basis for final billing by the Finance and Accounts Division. Here the cost of each job is examined, reviewed, and developed by the *Computing Section.* The *Billing and Collecting Section* then takes the job costs prepared by the Computing Section and issues billings to customers on a cycle basis.

Each work unit in the Government Printing Office is supplied with an operation and class manual. Listed in this manual are code numbers identifying typical tasks for employees of that unit. At the start of every work day, employees are assigned to their tasks and prepunched tabulating cards are "clocked in" on a printing time recorder. If assignments are changed during the work day, new cards record this change. At the end of the day, cards for every employee are sent to the Finance and Accounts Division for posting and become the basis for payroll and cost preparation. Coded cards for annual and sick leave, nonchargeable hours, and variations from standard rates are also used. Electronic card readers and card punch operators feed this information into the Government Printing Office's computers. A daily report of both employee and machine hours is prepared. Copies of this report are supplied to supervisory personnel as operational control tools. When other than routine work is needed on jobs, exception tab cards are used. These cards carry special rate charges.

The Government Printing Office is one of the earliest agencies of the federal government to mechanize its accounting procedures. In the mid-1930's, the Government Printing Office operated with a tab-card system for accumulating work cost and time and payroll data. Card sorters were used to record and print out payroll and time data as well as inventory information. As the plant expanded and its business grew, the Office adopted the use of electronic accounting machines and reproducers to perform a certain number of basic accounting operations. The reproducers operated at about 150 lines per minute. In 1959, however, the Government Printing Office installed a true automatic data processing system. In that year, it acquired a RAMAC—an IBM-305 electronic computer. In 1961, this was replaced by first one and then another IBM-1401. Later, two IBM-1460's were installed, replacing the IBM-1401 systems. In 1965, the Government Printing Office took a long step forward when it leased an IBM 360-40 system, which replaced one of the 1460's. The remaining 1460 was replaced with an IBM 360-50 in 1967, and a second IBM 360-50 was added in 1969.

The upgrading and sophistication of electronic data processing activities in the Government Printing Office stems from the wholesale accumulation of detailed information on cost production. However, a special additional need for the greater memory capacity of the 360-50's was sparked by the Government Printing Office's advanced work in electronic composition. With the receipt of the first Linotron Electronic Composition System in 1967, and the delivery of the second system in 1968, computer capacity was almost doubled. Today's computer services and support functions are concentrated in the *Data Processing Branch* of the Finance and Accounts Division. Here, in addition to the activities normally associated with processing, retrieving, and reporting information, is the focus of special programming devoted to computer-oriented composition—an operation peculiar in the U.S. bureaucracy to the Government Printing Office. This branch develops programs to enable the GPO to convert raw data received in magnetic tape form to information and coded data that is used for typesetting.

The Government Printing Office's computers are also used to maintain perpetual balances for the constantly changing paper, envelope, and carton inventory. Annual paper use currently hovers around 200 million pounds, and more than 800 separate paper items of various sizes, weights, colors, and finishes are stocked. Nearly 225 million envelopes and 4 million cartons are used each year. Daily reports on stock received and expended are furnished to paper control personnel in the Planning Division, with whom responsibility for reordering rests.

The Comptroller's office not only oversees all operations of the Finance and Accounts Division, but also provides legal services for the Government Printing Office and acts as general counsel for the Public Printer and the agency proper.

Personnel Practices

The Personnel Division is responsible for most of the familiar functions associated with personnel work in the federal government such as recruitment, employment, training, classification, and employee-management and labor-management relations. Excepted are time and leave accounting, safety, and the incentive awards programs, which are assigned to the Finance and Accounts Division, the Engineering Division, and the Office of the Public Printer, respectively.

Since 1895, when by special order of President Grover Cleveland, it was placed in the classified service of the Civil Service, the Government Printing Office has more or less followed the general guidelines issued by the Civil Service Commission for appointment, promotion, transfer, demotion, and separation. However, from time to time the intriguing question as to the legal inclusion of Government Printing Office employees in the classified service has arisen. The original Civil Service Act of 1883 speaks of the "executive civil service." Yet Congress has always considered the Government Printing Office part of the legislative branch, and the Public Printer, answerable directly to the congressional Joint Committee on Printing, must take appropriate cognizance of this fact. Moreover, in 1898, the Attorney General rendered the opinion "that the employees in the office of the Public Printer are not subject to classification and examination under the Civil Service Act." This anomaly will be discussed in Chapter VIII. Suffice it to say here that the personnel policies of the Government Printing Office have been largely influenced by the attitude of the Public Printer toward Civil Service rules and regulations, and the recent heads of the GPO generally have followed the policies and rules of the Civil Service Commission.

The Personnel Division contains eight sections and is headed by a Director, who reports to the Public Printer through the Administrative Assistant. The *Employment Section* is responsible for recruitment, employment, promotion, retirements, and pay plans. It administers the Federal Merit Promotion Program and acts to fill temporary appointment and training program quotas. It also maintains employee personnel folders and operates the group life insurance and health benefits programs for the Government Printing Office.

Classification and position survey services are performed by the *Classification and Organizational Survey Section.* This unit also provides professional assistance in connection with functional structuring within the agency. Studies and staff reports on both organization and wage standards also fall within the purview of this section.

Because of the potential hazards that accompany any manufacturing activity using machinery and chemicals, the Government Printing Office maintains a fairly complete emergency medical unit. The Medical Section employs a staff of professionals to deal with job-connected illnesses and injuries and to provide medical counseling to the Director of Personnel and operating officials in connection with personnel problems of a medical nature.

The *Training Section* plans, develops, and administers the career development program for the Government Printing Office. (See Appendix I.) Aside from the usual supervisory, managerial, and clerical training responsibilities common to most agencies, the section also conducts an in-plant apprentice training program.

Although the statutory authority for training apprentices was contained in the Printing Act of 1895, early attempts to train apprentices met with opposition from the agency head himself (Public Printer Thomas E. Benedict objected to "producing skilled workers at Government expense"), and twenty-seven years lapsed before Public Printer George H. Carter inaugurated a program to teach young men graphic arts skills. Then in 1922, 118 apprentices qualified for appointment in a nationwide Civil Service examination, and, on July 5, the first apprentices began their training. Since that time, except for the years during and immediately following World War II, an in-plant apprentice program has been in operation and has produced hundreds of skilled journeymen. The present curriculum, in addition to regular on-the-job training, includes classroom instruction in grammar, government organization, and technical subjects. Apprentices were formerly indentured for five years. In 1969, the training period was reduced to four years. This period can be further shortened through exceptional performance and extracurricular study.

The Act of 1895 limited the Government Printing Office to twenty-five apprentices. Public Printer George H. Carter recommended that the apprentice authorization be raised to 200, and in February, 1923, Congress agreed. Even under the 1922 union quota system, which permitted not more than one apprentice for each eight journeymen, the Office, then employing more than 1,500 craftsmen, was entitled to such a number.

Normal agency attrition has long required replacement of nearly 300 journeymen annually. An apprentice ceiling set at 200 imposed a real hardship on the Office—and indirectly on the commercial printing industry as well. On a 4-year cycle, an average of only fifty apprentices could be graduated each year. Consequently, upward of 250 journeymen had to be recruited annually from commercial sources. Private firms complained bitterly about the situation, but faced with regular production commitments, the Government Printing Office had no alternative but to continue proselytizing industry printers. Because pay and benefits were somewhat more attractive at the Government Printing Office, the drain on commercially trained personnel continued, becoming especially troublesome in areas near the nation's capital. Efforts to raise the apprentice ceiling, or remove it altogether, met with strong opposition from craft unions. However, in 1969, a bill introduced simultaneously by Senator B. Everett Jordan of North Carolina and Representative Samuel N. Friedel of Maryland was passed that raised the ceiling to 400 and significantly eased the problem.

Since the Government Printing Office operates and maintains its own buildings, it follows that security of the premises and installations rests with the Office. Hence, the GPO employs its own guard force. The unit is under the Personnel Division's **Personnel Relations and Administrative Services Branch**, which also conducts various welfare activities. The Personnel Division's **Employee Relations Section** provides a continuing program aimed at maintaining working relationships and attitudes conducive to efficient production and offers counsel on non-job-related problems as well as advice and assistance to operating officials on employee relations. A separate section is responsible for work in the employee-management field.

Purchasing of Supplies and Printing

The purchasing of materials, equipment, and more than $100 million worth of commercial printing annually is the function of the GPO's Purchasing Division, which is organized into two branches—**General Procurement and Stores** and **Printing Procurement.** The first buys, receives, warehouses, and issues paper, envelopes, machinery, and supplies, and operates the Office communications system. It also maintains established inventories and collects and bales wastepaper and other waste and surplus material for sale or disposal. The second branch is wholly occupied with purchasing printing.

Lists of qualified bidders for all categories of commodities are kept by this Division. Competitive bidding is required for all but a few types of purchases. When a purchase is planned, invitations to bid are circulated to as many qualified suppliers as possible, consistent with the nature of the requirement. Bid forms are mailed to those firms which appear on the appropriate bid lists. If the value of the proposed purchase exceeds $5,000 and time permits, it is advertised in the *Commerce Business Daily*. Printing, binding, and blank-book work, because of scheduling problems, are not advertised in this manner. Any firm interested in having its name placed on the

GPO's list of prospective suppliers can request such action from the Director of Purchases.

Specifications describing Office requirements are sent to prospective bidders. These are prepared by the *Open Market and Contract Section* and either outline the need in precise technical terms or simply describe what is wanted. Specifications must be written so as not to eliminate full and free competition by all qualified and responsible bidders. When a proprietary or patented article is ordered, specifications may call for "brand name or equal." If the items to be purchased demand exceptionally involved technical specifications, or in a case where insufficient time is available to develop full specifications, purchase is also often made calling for "brand name or equal."

Bidders receive an opening date and hour when bids are to be opened. Until that time, they are allowed to withdraw or resubmit bids. Whether a qualified bidder responds to GPO invitations is his decision. However, continued failure to respond is considered sufficient cause for the Government Printing Office to remove firm names from bidders' lists. Periodically, standing lists are purged of inactive bidders.

Of course, contracts are awarded on the basis of the lowest bid, provided the product meets specifications. If the Government Printing Office receives two or more equally low bids, policy dictates that preference be given to bids from labor surplus areas and to small businesses. In evaluating bids by foreign suppliers, 6 per cent is added to the foreign bid price to encourage American manufacturers to produce and sell products to the government. If a small business located in a persistent labor surplus area is competing with a foreign bidder, 12 per cent is added to the foreign-bid price.

As might be expected, except for manufactured printing, the GPO's largest procurement activity centers on paper, envelopes, and containers. Some of these products are furnished to other government agencies and to commercial printers doing contract printing for the government. Because of the obvious advantages, the GPO buys approximately 85 per cent of its blank paper and envelopes on term contracts that vary from three-month contracts for some paper to annual contracts for newsprint. Envelopes and containers are bought for 6-month periods.

The *Printing Procurement Branch* is concerned exclusively with the purchase of printing, binding, and blank-book work. The long-time policy that government printing, except for congressional printing, classified work, or work that must be done in house because of scheduling or other special requirements, be procured from the private economy keeps the already large in-house printing capability in the Government Printing Office from growing larger and more unwieldy. It also gives the government a great deal of flexibility in fulfilling its printing needs by mustering the immense capacity of the private sector of the industry when needs expand beyond normal bounds.

The rules governing the purchase of materials and supplies also apply generally to the purchase of printing. In the main, it is a process of preparing specifications, inviting suppliers to submit bids, evaluating the bids, and awarding contracts. One facet of the GPO's printing procurement operation differs from procurement of general supplies: the GPO's responsibilities include monitoring of the actual manufacturing activities of suppliers.

More than 2,000 firms in nearly every state are listed as qualified suppliers of printing and printing services by the Government Printing Office. In fiscal 1969, nearly 90,000 orders valued at more than $100 million were bought from commercial printers. These orders covered not only routine items but such specialties as marginally punched continuous forms, silk screen work, process color work, gravure, photogelatin work, decals, outdoor advertising posters, and many other types of products in the field of graphic arts.

Composition normally is bought separately on a contract that does not include printing itself. When jobs are small, however, it is often bid in the aggregate, and the successful bidder not only sets the composition but produces the finished product in its entirety. It is also common for the Government Printing Office to furnish "reproducibles" for reprints or sometimes for original printing. Reproducibles may be high-quality press sheets from previous runs, negatives stored for reuse, "repro" (reproduction) proofs, or any of a number of types of material from which a contractor can reproduce the desired product.

By and large, the majority of the GPO's annual volume procured from commercial sources is acquired by contracts established for a yearly term. This type of contract is especially adaptable for items of a repetitive nature such as recurring issues of periodicals, pamphlets, forms, or printing of specialty material—snapout forms, punched continuous forms, and tabulating cards. Annual contracts are awarded on a competitive price basis with the lowest bidder being given an opportunity to accept all work under a typical contract. If, however, the low bidder becomes saturated with work at some point during the year, then the GPO exercises the option of offering this work to the second lowest bidder on the contract. If this contractor in turn has taken as much work as he is capable of producing on schedule, then the third lowest bidder is offered work. In this way, the Government Printing Office can satisfy even the most extraordinary demands for certain types of production.

Cost estimates of work to be procured commercially are furnished to requisitioning agencies, and technicians constantly review samples of products for compliance with specifications and quality standards. The Printing Procurement Branch also maintains progress records of work being done in contractors' plants, makes physical inspections of commercial contractors' facilities, secures and maintains reports on contract compliance matters, and performs regular checks on suppliers' adherence to applicable portions of federal equal employment opportunity regulations.

Testing and Technical Control

The Government Printing Office's annual purchasing activity regularly exceeds $140 million. Of this amount, printing bought from commercial sources accounts for over $100 million. Of the remainder, about two-thirds is spent for paper, envelopes, inks, and other supplies used in the manufacture of printing.

Compliance with specifications is, of course, essential to the competitive bidding system. In order to ensure that raw materials purchased by the Office fully meet product standards, constant testing is necessary. The Tests and Technical Control Division, organized in 1922, and headed by the Technical Director, performs this function and prepares specifications for procurement of materials that are best suited to the requirements of the various processes and techniques used by the GPO. This Division also manufactures limited quantities of inks and adhesives and engages in a modest amount of research. Its research effort, however, lies mainly in solving technical problems as they relate to specific printing jobs.

The Division is comprised of four branches: the *Paper, Bookbinding Materials, Ink and Reproduction,* and *Metals and Chemicals* branches. Paper constitutes by far the largest testing operation. Samplings are taken of each lot and shipment to check compliance with specifications. The Printing Act of 1895, which originated the requirement that the Public Printer compare every lot of paper with a standard of quality fixed by the Joint Committee on Printing, prohibits him from accepting any paper not conforming in every particular.

The *Paper Branch,* composed of a *Research and Specifications Section* and a *Tests and Analysis Section,* is responsible for performing the various types of tests that ultimately determine whether the GPO accepts or rejects paper and paper products received on contract. Three general types of tests are used. The first evaluates physical properties, the second measures chemical properties, and the third gauges the specific printability of samples. All classes of paper are subjected to testing, from newsprint to high quality ledger and index paper.

Physical testing includes bursting strength, folding endurance, tensile strength, and tearing strength. Government printing is oftentimes intended for prolonged usage or historical records. The chemical properties of paper are vital in estimating permanence. Consequently, careful analysis of paper acidity, a principal factor in determining the life of paper, is conducted on all rag-content book, ledger, and index papers. Tests for excess use of rosin in sizing, alpha-cellulose content, and copper number (an index of cellulose impurities) are made. As for printability, paper is examined for smoothness, ink receptivity, surface bonding strength, opacity, thickness, moisture content, color, formation, and general appearance.

The **Bookbinding Materials Branch** consists of a **Laboratory Section** and an **Adhesive Section.** The latter manufactures annually about 150 tons of adhesives, including pastes, flexible glues, gums, and synthetic resins. Synthetic resin adhesives were developed during World War II as substitutes for animal glues and have become very important commercially.* The Laboratory Section exercises technical control over adhesive manufacture and tests both commercial and GPO adhesives for viscosity, adhesive properties, and compliance with established standards.

Nearly one hundred tons of ink are manufactured in the

---

* When the glue on franked congressional envelopes was changed to a colorless, synthetic, plastic-based type, former Speaker John McCormack complained that he could not see the glue and that it was inferior to the old type and would not stick when licked. A meeting was set up with the GPO's top planners and technical people with representatives from the Speaker's office. The GPO added vegetable coloring to the glue to make it look like the old animal glue and the Speaker was delighted—so delighted he called the Public Printer and thanked him.

Government Printing Office yearly for in-house use and use by other agencies. Public Act 222, passed by the Sixty-ninth Congress, authorized this function for the Office. Hence, the Government Printing Office manufactures and sells to government departments not only printing inks, but also mimeograph, multigraph, stamping, numbering machine, addressograph, instrument recording, check signature, laundry marking, postage meter, and drawing and writing inks. The *Ink Section* of the *Ink and Reproduction Branch* has this responsibility. The *Laboratory Section* of this unit conducts chemical and physical tests on the raw materials used for ink manufacture and on the finished products as well.

The *Metals and Chemicals Branch* also has both testing and manufacturing responsibility. The Government Printing Office uses more than 7,000 tons of type metal yearly in its composing and platemaking activities. Type metal, which is an alloy of tin, antimony, and lead, contains somewhat different proportions of these ingredients when used for various machines and processes. (See also Chapter IV.) For example, slug casters use a formula of 4.5 per cent tin, 11.5 per cent antimony, and 84 per cent lead, while Monotype metal is comprised of 7 per cent tin, 16.5 per cent antimony, and only 76.5 per cent lead. The testing and correcting of materials used again and again, which are known as "remelts," is done by professional metallurgists in this branch.

After repeated use, the proportions of the three major ingredients in type metal are altered by oxidation and contamination. Steel trucks called "hell boxes," holding about half a ton, are collected from production units several times each day and are brought to the Metal Room. Here they are dumped onto a conveyor that empties the metal into six gas-fired melting furnaces. After reaching about 650 degrees F, the metal is thoroughly mixed and skimmed of dross. An 8-ounce sample is then taken to the laboratory for an analysis, on the basis of which the type metal is reformulated, skimmed of dross again, and poured into ingots for reuse. These 24-pound "pigs" cool in about three minutes and are delivered to using units in half-ton loads. About forty tons are handled daily.

Over the years, the Tests and Technical Control Division has been responsible for many new developments. Its research accomplishments, which have aided the whole printing industry, are treated more fully in Chapter VIII.

Maintenance and Engineering

In an installation as large as the Government Printing Office, with its varied and complicated functions, maintaining both buildings and machinery constitutes a major activity. The *Engineering Division* is assigned this responsibility. Its head, the Engineering Director, reports to the Public Printer through the Administrative Assistant. Unlike the government generally, which lives and works in buildings as tenants of the General Services Administration, the Government Printing Office owns, operates, and repairs its own structures. Currently, these comprise more than 1.5 million square feet of office, production, and warehouse space. In addition, nearly 400,000 square feet of space is rented for stock and document storage. About half of this rental space is leased from the GSA's huge warehouse complex in Franconia, Virginia, and largely used for paper storage. Commercial rental accounts for the balance, which is required principally to store the 106 million documents in the current inventory of the Public Documents Division. (See Chapter VI.)

The *Office of the Engineering Director* provides professional engineering services relating not only to the maintenance of structures but also to the purchase and installation of new machinery and processes and production layouts.

Maintenance support for the entire office is organized as an on-call service. Where assistance is required, a call is placed to the Engineering Division explaining what is needed. Work is assigned to the section having the specific repair capability, and repairmen are dispatched at once to the site of the trouble. Each call is charged on a labor-materials-and-overhead basis to the requesting section. For other than routine maintenance, job orders are prepared. When minor construction or remodeling is required, a job order estimating the cost of such work is supplied to the section that made the request. After authorization through regular channels, the work is scheduled and performed. Costs again are computed on a labor-materials-and-overhead basis and, in this way, recovered to operate the Engineering Division.

The Division is divided into two branches: the *Mechanical Branch,* which is principally concerned with machinery installations, repair, and maintenance and the *Buildings Branch,* whose chief concern is maintenance and alterations of the structures themselves. The Buildings Branch also contains the *Industrial Cleaning Section,* which performs scheduled and emergency cleaning of work rooms and service areas. In addition, the Engineering Director has responsibility for plant safety, including fire protection, and acts as chief warden for Civil Defense affairs. His staff includes both a safety officer, who represents the Government Printing Office on the Federal Safety Council, and a fire marshal. Safety is a matter of vital concern in an installation engaged in heavy manufacturing and warehousing. Because a great number of printing firms in the country are relatively small, printing plant safety has been rather indifferently treated. The Government Printing Office's active interest in plant safety has contributed to identifying hazards inherent in the printing industry for printers, both small and large.

The Engineering Division also administers a program of preventive maintenance for the Office and maintains complete histories on all the complex and varied items of equipment necessary for typesetting and press work. The large web presses used to print the *Congressional Record,* for example, are taken out of production annually, one by one, during the period Congress is in adjournment and subjected to complete inspection and overhaul. This system has prolonged the efficiency of these presses far beyond their normal life expectancy.

Typesetting and the running of the presses are, of course, the heart of any printing operation. At the Government Printing Office, these functions are especially complex because of the many different kinds of demands made by Congress and the proliferating agencies of the executive branch. In the following chapter, which carries forward the description of the internal structure of the GPO, the way the plant is organized for printing production will be examined.

IV

The GPO Today: Plant and Production

Two basic printing techniques dominate production activities in the Government Printing Office—letterpress and offset. The various functional production units of the Office are organized around these two techniques.

Letterpress is printing from an elevated surface that differs in relief from nonprinting areas. Offset, or lithography, is printing from a planar surface, i.e., one with no significant difference in elevation between the printing and nonprinting areas. Both start with typesetting.

The Government Printing Office possesses one of the largest typesetting installations in the world. Its *Composing Division,* organized as six sections—*Monotype, Linotype, Hand, Job, Proof,* and *Patents*—is equipped with 350 composing machines of various kinds. Annual production of composition now is running in excess of 3.3 billion measurable ems, or about 100 million lines. Both hot metal and cold composition are used, with hot metal predominating. Hot metal composition derives its name from the use of molds or matrices to form three-dimensional relief characters from molten typemetal, while cold composition employs typewriter-like techniques to produce camera copy. The two types of machines used to produce hot metal composition in the GPO are the Monotype and the Linotype, already mentioned in Chapter II. One casts a single character at a time; the other casts a line at a time.

Typesetting Sections

The method used for single-character composing requires a keyboarding machine and a caster and is called the Monotype system. The Monotype keyboard, which is a separate machine, contains 300 keys. It delivers a 4¼-inch punched paper tape resembling an old-fashioned player-piano music roll. This tape is used to activate and control the casting machine that forms a single-character piece of type from molten metal. The caster is air-actuated and contains a die case holding 256 brass dies. As the keyboard-coded paper tape unwinds, it positions a single brass matrix for casting. When the matrix assumes the casting position, hot typemetal is forced into it, the character is formed, chilled, ejected, and the die case moves a new character into place to mold the next letter. The metal line of type is formed letter by letter until the measure width is reached. The caster then moves on to the next line. Generally speaking, this method is slower than other composing processes. Casting speed is about 160 characters per minute. However, despite slowness, and the severe continuing shortage of qualified Monotype keyboard operators, this process, because of its precision, flexibility, and facility with tabular matter, remains a vital part of the Government Printing Office's composition capability.

In addition to processing type by this system, the Monotype Section produces strip leads, slugs, and miscellaneous sorts (type characters) for the entire Composing Division. The Monotype Section also includes a correction unit, where hand compositors insert vertical and horizontal rules to complete tabular makeup, pull proofs for proofreading, hand set difficult composition such as chemical formulas and mathematical equations, and make hand corrections.

The Linotype machine, invented before the turn of the century by a Baltimorean, Ottmar Mergenthaler, is the backbone of typesetting activities in the Government Printing Office and for that matter throughout private industry.* The GPO's Linotype and Patents sections are equipped with more than 165 of these machines. Basically, the machine includes a self-contained keyboard with 90 keys and 180 characters—as opposed to 44 keys and 88 characters on a standard typewriter—as well as a brass matrix magazine, a casting box, and a matrix redistribution system. As the operator strikes a key, a brass matrix containing a female mold of the desired character is released from the magazine and slides into precasting position. Other matrices are key-selected until a line of matrices corresponding to the desired line of type is collected. The line is justified (expanded to exact line length) by mechanical insertion of variable space bands between matrices. The line is moved to casting position, and hot typemetal is forced under pressure against the line of brass molds and chilled. The line of type hardens almost immediately and drops into a galley tray. The brass matrices are then automatically returned to their proper places in the magazine, and the operator is ready for another line-composing cycle. Speed varies according to copy complexity but an average operator can set between one and two lines per minute.

The Hand Section, as the name implies, concerns itself with hand composition. Today, little more than display work and title pages are hand set, as machines have taken over by far the greatest part of typesetting, so this section performs mostly correction and page makeup. Page makeup means assembling the raw galleys and illustrative material into page form—by adding heads and folios and creating finished type pages. On many jobs, customer agencies call for page proofs, chiefly to see how illustrations and type will appear after printing. The

---

* Linotype is a trade name for a linecasting machine produced by the Mergenthaler Linotype Company of Brooklyn, N.Y. Actually, GPO linecasters are only about half Linotypes, the other half being Intertypes manufactured by Harris Intertype of Cleveland, Ohio. In the GPO, both machines and their product are called Linotype.

Hand Section provides these proofs. The production of reproduction proofs also comes under this section. Although there
are several modern-day methods for obtaining camera copy
from type, by far the most common is the "repro" proof. This
is simply a high quality proof, usually pulled on a top-grade
white paper. Special presses in the Hand Section are used for
this work.

The Hand Section also assembles numbers of pages into
forms. Each page is placed in a precise location in order that
the printed sheet has correct margins. In the case of book
printing, these locations must be keyed to the subsequent production plan so that pages are arranged in proper sequence
and relation to other pages after being folded. The arrangement of pages in a form in accordance with a standard plan is
called imposition, and on most letterpress printing is the responsibility of the Hand Section, which also, once a form has
been printed, disassembles it. The type is either stored or
"killed,"* and the furniture† and lock-up devices are saved
for other lock-up work.

The Composing Division's Job Section is responsible for
processing all letterheads, brochures, nonuniform forms work,
and such things as menus for the House and the Senate Dining
rooms. Occasionally, odd difficulties arise for the Job Section.
Some years ago, the Senate restaurant menu was prepared by
a French chef who invariably sent his copy to the GPO's Job
Room in handwriting. He was not an accomplished penman
and frequently had to be called at home to decipher his lun-
cheon plans. One night, after making dozens of phone calls in
an attempt to locate the chef or someone else who could explain an illegible item, an enterprising but disgusted printer
gave up and listed "Navy Bean" as the *soupe du jour* on the
elegant French menu. The reverberations from this commend-

---

* Killed is printing language for breaking up assembled pages into parts.
† Furniture is the term for wood or metal blocks used to fill out space
in the form to be locked up inside a steel frame called a chase.

able but unimaginative substitution were felt in the Public Printer's office, and Public Printer Carter himself paid a visit to the Job Room to admonish the responsible parties.

PROOF SECTION

The Proof Section of the Composing Division has the responsibility for reading proofs on all type that is set in the Linotype, Monotype, and Hand sections. The Proof Section is also responsible for marking all book and pamphlet type composition. Patent composition is proofread and revised in the Patent Proofroom, which is part of the Patent Section proper (described later in this chapter). The Job Section does its own proofreading. Normal proofreading procedure calls for a team consisting of a reader and a copy holder. Unlike many commercial shops, the Government Printing Office employs journeyman printers as both members of this team. Proofreaders read not only for punctuation, spelling, and correctness but are responsible for conformance to style and form standards established by the Public Printer. All copy received from an agency without preparation for printing is set in accordance with the rules published in the *U.S. Government Printing Office Style Manual*.

The GPO *Style Manual*—a 512-page volume setting forth basic printing instructions—is sold by the Superintendent of Documents and is widely used by printers, publishers, editors, authors, and other groups interested in authentic usage in writing and printing.* The *Style Manual* is issued periodically by the Public Printer under authority of Section 51 of the Congressional Printing Act of 1895. The 1967 edition, which superseded the 1959 issue, was approved by the Joint Com-

* When H. L. Mencken was working on his monumental *American Language,* he frequently wrote to the GPO for information about certain word spellings, compounding, capitalization, or some other not completely and universally accepted style.

mittee on Printing on December 12, 1966. The task of revising and reissuing the *Style Manual,* which is known in government circles as the "Stenographer's Friend," falls to the GPO Style Board. The Board is comprised of a chairman and five regular members, all drawn from the proofreading staff. Six ex-officio members also serve on this Board by virtue of their Office positions. They are the Production Manager, the Night Production Manager, the Planning Manager, the Superintendent of Composition, and the foremen of the first and third shifts in the Proof Section.

Fundamentally, the *Style Manual* is a digest of public printing experience. Its rules are based on "principles of good usage and custom in the printing trade," and it contains a veritable treasure trove of information for the individual printer or copy preparer. For example, it tells him that excerpts from the *Congressional Record* are to be set in 6½-pt. type, "Fic & punc" (follow, including capitalization and punctuation), that 12 M. is the proper abbreviation for noon, and that 12 P.M. is midnight. It also explains among many, many other things, that the West Slavic languages as well as Slovene and Croatian have always been written in the Latin alphabet and contains approved transliteration for all forms of the Cyrillic alphabets.

Proofs of galleys set in the Linotype, Monotype, and Hand sections are sent to what is called "Main Proof" either by pneumatic tube or messenger. Here, a deskman parcels out the proofs to be read and keeps track of the material. Proofreading teams, with one man reading the manuscript while the other follows the galley-proof version, check style, spelling, and punctuation. If a statement is inconsistent with the sense of the text, the proofreader is responsible for questioning it by using a circle or query mark. If a statement is obviously erroneous, he can correct it. In the case of quotations, for example, he is required to check the accuracy against an accepted authority and change it to conform. The exception to this is copy marked "fol.lit." (follow literally), on which no changes are made. For questions concerning grammar or construction, the proofreader is expected to indicate the proposed alterations and add a query. All queries must be carried to the author.

After proofs have been marked, they are returned to the section that set the type, where corrections are made, verified, and new proofs pulled. If galley proofs are called for, these are sent to the originating agencies for reading.

PRINTING PATENTS

The Patents Section, which is a complete printing plant within the Government Printing Office, is equipped with sixty-four Linotypes, lock-up stations, and a number of flatbed letterpresses. The basic function of this section is to compose, proof-read, and print patent specifications, trade marks and designs, and to set all composition for the *Official Gazette* of the U.S. Patent Office and its indexes. The *Gazette* prints about 430,000 copies each year, and nearly 12 million copies of patents, trademarks, and designs are produced annually.

Manuscripts and drawings are sent weekly to this unit from the Patent Office, which is part of the Department of Commerce. GPO employees detailed to the Patent Office prepare patents and trademarks for printing. At the present time, fourteen preparers are assigned to the Patent Office. When preparation work is exceptionally heavy, this force is supplemented by details from the Patent Proofroom.

The Patents Section averages about 1,300 patents each week. The drawings, which accompany all patents, are sent from the Patent Office directly to a contractor who prepares multiple copies. The Office sets type from the manuscript. When the type is set, proofs are pulled, and are given a proof-reading in the Patents Section. Once the patent has been revised, the type is locked in a form and copies are printed directly from the type.

The average patent is printed in 125 copies. A few, known as "hard copies," are for file-and-search purposes and are printed on heavy 100 per cent rag ledger sheets. The balance of the 125 copies are produced on 32-pound writing paper. Once the printed copies are finished and collated, they are sent to the contractor who has reproduced the drawings. The text, or the description, is bound together with the drawings associated with each patent and the completed patents delivered to the Patent Office. One hard copy goes to the inventor. It is bound with a ribbon, and its cover is embellished with elaborate scrollwork—very much like a stock certificate.

In addition to patents, the Patents Section produces 400 trademarks and forty designs each week.

The Government Printing Office operates three weeks in advance of the patent publication date. Patents go on sale by the Patent Office, according to law, at noon each Tuesday. (The Patent Section in the Government Printing Office uses a strange calendar, which has only Tuesdays listed on it to keep track of patent schedules.)

It is not unusual for patents to be issued that were filed twenty to twenty-five years ago. Some of these, because of their sensitive nature, have only recently been declassified in order that the patent could be issued. A patent can consist of only one page, including text and drawing, or it can contain up to 300 drawings and several hundred pages of descriptive text. The filing fee is $65 for each, and includes all claims up to ten. For each claim over ten, an additional fee of $2 is charged.

Once the original patent has been printed, the type is returned to the makeup bank for preparation of the *Official Gazette*. The number, the title and the description of each patent is removed from the text of the patent claim proper, and made up into pages employing a two-column format. As for the patent drawings, one view of the patent is specified for reproduction along with the description in the *Official Gazette*. These illustrations are produced in black and white print form by the GPO in the Offset Negative Section of its Offset Divi-

The Government Printing Office is pictured as it has appeared in successive stages of development. The Wendell plant (top), acquired in 1861, can be contrasted with the massive structures now occupied by the world's largest general-purpose printing plant (bottom). Also shown is the plant as it looked on a wintry day near the turn of the century (next to top) and as it appeared in the early 1920's (next to bottom).

CONGRESSIONAL RECORD.

DEBATES AND PROCEEDINGS OF THE FORTY-THIRD CONGRESS.

SPECIAL SESSION OF THE SENATE.

IN THE SENATE.

TUESDAY, *March* 4, 1873.

Hon. HENRY WILSON, Vice-President of the United States, having taken the oath of office at the close of the last regular session of the Forty-second Congress, took the chair and directed the Secretary to read the proclamation convening a special session of the Senate.

The Secretary (Hon. GEORGE C. GORHAM) read the proclamation, as follows:

A PROCLAMATION

Whereas objects of interest to the United States require that the Senate should be convened at twelve o'clock on the fourth of March next, to receive and act upon such communications as may be made to it on the part of the Executive:

Now, therefore, I, ULYSSES S. GRANT, President of the United States, have considered it to be my duty to issue this, my proclamation, declaring that an extraordinary occasion requires the Senate of the United States to convene for the transaction of business at the Capitol, in the city of Washington, on the fourth day of March next, at twelve o'clock at noon on that day, of which all who shall at that time be entitled to act as members of that body are hereby required to take notice.

Given under my hand and the seal of the United States, at Washington, the twenty-first day of February, in the year of our Lord one thousand eight hundred and seventy-three, and of the Independence of the United States of America the ninety-seventh.

[L. S.]

U. S. GRANT.

By the President:

HAMILTON FISH,
Secretary of State.

The VICE-PRESIDENT. The Secretary will read the names of the newly-elected Senators.

The list was read as follows:

Hon. Bainbridge Wadleigh, of New Hampshire.
Hon. Justin S. Morrill, of Vermont.
Hon. Orris S. Ferry, of Connecticut.
Hon. Roscoe Conkling, of New York.
Hon. Simon Cameron, of Pennsylvania.
Hon. George R. Dennis, of Maryland.
Hon. Augustus S. Merrimon, of North Carolina.
Hon. John J. Patterson, of South Carolina.
Hon. Simon B. Conover, of Florida.
Hon. George E. Spencer, of Alabama.
Hon. Stephen W. Dorsey, of Arkansas.
Hon. John B. Gordon, of Georgia.
Hon. Lewis V. Bogy, of Missouri.
Hon. Thomas C. McCreery, of Kentucky.
Hon. John Sherman, of Ohio.
Hon. Oliver P. Morton, of Indiana.
Hon. Richard J. Oglesby, of Illinois.
Hon. Timothy O. Howe, of Wisconsin.
Hon. William B. Allison, of Iowa.
Hon. John J. Ingalls, of Kansas.
Hon. Aaron A. Sargent, of California.
Hon. John H. Mitchell, of Oregon.
Hon. John P. Jones, of Nevada.

When the name of Mr. Conkling was called,

Mr. HAMLIN said: Mr. President, owing to some inadvertence the credentials of the Senator-elect from New York have not been presented in this body. It is a matter of public notoriety that he has been elected; and, in accordance with the usage of the body, I move that the oath of office be administered to him.

The VICE-PRESIDENT. The question is on the motion of the Senator from Maine.

The motion was agreed to.

As their names were called the respective Senators-elect came forward, and the oaths prescribed by law were administered to them, with the exception of Mr. Wadleigh, Mr. Ferry, Mr. Gordon, Mr. Spencer, and Mr. Jones, who were not present.

The Senators-elect having been sworn and taken their seats in the Senate, the following Senators were present:

From the State of—

Maine—Hon. Hannibal Hamlin and Hon. Lot M. Morrill.
New Hampshire—Hon. Aaron H. Cragin.
Vermont—Hon. George F. Edmunds and Hon. Justin S. Morrill.
Massachusetts—Hon. Charles Sumner.
Rhode Island—Hon. Henry B. Anthony and Hon. William Sprague.
Connecticut—Hon. William A. Buckingham.
New York—Hon. Roscoe Conkling and Hon. Reuben E. Fenton.
New Jersey—Hon. Frederick T. Frelinghuysen.
Pennsylvania—Hon. Simon Cameron and Hon. John Scott.
Delaware—Hon. Thomas F. Bayard and Hon. Eli Saulsbury.
Maryland—Hon. George R. Dennis and Hon. William T. Hamilton.
Virginia—Hon. John F. Lewis.
North Carolina—Hon. Augustus S. Merrimon and Hon. Matthew W. Ransom.
South Carolina—Hon. John J. Patterson and Hon. Thomas J. Robertson.
Georgia—Hon. Thomas M. Norwood.
Florida—Hon. Simon B. Conover and Hon. Abijah Gilbert.
Alabama—Hon. George Goldthwaite.
Mississippi—Hon. James L. Alcorn and Hon. Adelbert Ames.
Louisiana—Hon. J. Rodman West.
Texas—Hon. J. W. Flanagan and Hon. Morgan C. Hamilton.
Arkansas—Hon. Powell Clayton and Hon. Stephen W. Dorsey.
Missouri—Hon. Lewis V. Bogy and Hon. Carl Schurz.
Tennessee—Hon. Henry Cooper.
Kentucky—Hon. Thomas C. McCreery and Hon. John W. Stevenson.
West Virginia—Hon. Arthur I. Boreman and Hon. Henry G. Davis.
Ohio—Hon. John Sherman and Hon. Allen G. Thurman.
Indiana—Hon. Oliver P. Morton and Hon. Daniel D. Pratt.
Illinois—Hon. John A. Logan and Hon. Richard J. Oglesby.
Michigan—Hon. Zachariah Chandler and Hon. Thomas W. Ferry.
Wisconsin—Hon. Matthew H. Carpenter and Hon. Timothy O. Howe.
Iowa—Hon. Willam B. Allison and Hon. George G. Wright.
Minnesota—Hon. Alexander Ramsey and Hon. William Windom.
Kansas—Hon. Alexander Caldwell and Hon. John J. Ingalls.
California—Hon. Eugene Casserly and Hon. Aaron A. Sargent.
Nebraska—Hon. Phineas W. Hitchcock and Hon. Thomas W. Tipton.
Oregon—Hon. James K. Kelly and Hon. John H. Mitchell.
Nevada—Hon. William M. Stewart.

INAUGURATION CEREMONIES.

The persons entitled to admission on the floor of the Senate Chamber having been admitted to the places reserved for them, the President, Hon. ULYSSES S. GRANT, entered the Senate Chamber, accompanied by Mr. CRAGIN, Mr. LOGAN, and Mr. BAYARD, members of the Committee of Arrangements, and was conducted to a seat in front of the Secretary's desk, and the members of the committee were seated on his right and left.

Nearly a hundred years separates these two cover pages of the *Congressional Record*. The upper page was the first produced by the GPO, and it carries the proceedings of an extraordinary special session of the Senate, convened by President Ulysses S. Grant to debate irregularities in the elections of 1872.

Congressional Record

United States of America

PROCEEDINGS AND DEBATES OF THE 91st CONGRESS, SECOND SESSION

Vol. 116 WASHINGTON, TUESDAY, MARCH 17, 1970 *No. 41*

Senate

The Senate, as in legislative session, met at 11 o'clock a.m. and was called to order by Hon. GEORGE MCGOVERN, a Senator from the State of South Dakota.

The Chaplain, the Reverend Edward L. R. Elson, D.D., offered the following prayer:

Almighty God, our Father who bids us come before Thee with clean hands and pure hearts, qualify us now to serve Thee. Cleanse us and make us new. Grant us the pure hearts of those who see God. Preserve us from the hypocrisy which magnifies evil so as to appear worse than we are; or the artificiality which pretends to be better than we are. Help us to ring true to what we really are—human beings saved by Thy redemptive love, forgiven when repentant—a people who walk and work conscious of Thy judgment, kept by Thy grace, aware of Thy guidance, ever striving for the establishment of that city whose builder and maker is God.

In the Redeemer's name. Amen.

DESIGNATION OF ACTING PRESIDENT PRO TEMPORE

The PRESIDING OFFICER. The clerk will read a communication to the Senate.

The assistant legislative clerk read the following letter:

U.S. SENATE,
PRESIDENT PRO TEMPORE,
Washington, D.C., March 17, 1970.

To the Senate:

Being temporarily absent from the Senate, I appoint Hon. GEORGE MCGOVERN, a Senator from the State of South Dakota, to perform the duties of the Chair during my absence.

RICHARD B. RUSSELL,
President pro tempore.

Mr. McGOVERN thereupon took the chair as Acting President pro tempore.

THE JOURNAL

Mr. BYRD of West Virginia. Mr. President, I ask unanimous consent that the reading of the Journal of the proceedings of Monday, March 16, 1970, be dispensed with.

The ACTING PRESIDENT pro tempore. Without objection, it is so ordered.

MESSAGES FROM THE PRESIDENT

Messages in writing from the President of the United States submitting nominations were communicated to the Senate by Mr. Leonard, one of his secretaries.

EXECUTIVE MESSAGES REFERRED

As in executive session, the Acting President pro tempore (Mr. MCGOVERN) laid before the Senate messages from the President of the United States submitting sundry nominations, which were referred to the appropriate committees.

(For nominations received today, see the end of Senate proceedings.)

MESSAGE FROM THE HOUSE

A message from the House of Representatives, by Mr. Hackney, one of its reading clerks, informed the Senate that pursuant to the provisions of section 2(a), Public Law 91-213, the Speaker had appointed Mr. BLATNIK and Mr. ERLENBORN as members of the Commission on Population Growth and the American Future, on the part of the House.

The message also announced that the House had passed, without amendment, the bill (S. 3427) to increase the authorization for appropriation for continuing work in the Missouri River Basin by the Secretary of the Interior.

The message further announced that the House had passed the following bills of the Senate, severally with amendments, in which it requested the concurrence of the Senate:

S. 227. An act to provide for loans to Indian tribes and tribal corporations, and for other purposes,

S. 743. An act to authorize the Secretary of the Interior to construct, operate, and maintain the Touchet division, Walla Walla project, Oregon-Washington, and for other purposes; and

S. 2062. An act to provide for the differentiation between private and public ownership of lands in the administration of the acreage limitation provisions of Federal reclamation law, and for other purposes.

The message also announced that the House had passed the following bills, in which it requested the concurrence of the Senate:

H.R. 1187. An act to amend the act of August 7, 1961, providing for the establishment of Cape Cod National Seashore;

H.R. 4145. An act to provide for disposition of estates of intestate members of the Cherokee, Chickasaw, Choctaw, and Seminole Nations of Oklahoma dying without heirs;

H.R. 12858. An act to provide for the disposition of certain funds awarded to the Tlingit and Haida Indians of Alaska by a judment entered by the Court of Claims against the United States;

H.R. 12878. An act to amend the act of August 9, 1955, to authorize longer term leases of Indian lands at the Yavapai-Prescott Community Reservation in Arizona;

H.R. 14855. An act to amend the act of August 31, 1954 (68 Stat. 1026), providing for the construction, maintenance, and operation of the Michaud Flats irrigation project;

H.R. 14896. An act to amend the act of October 15, 1966 (80 Stat. 915), establishing a program for the preservation of additional historic properties throughout the Nation, and for other purposes;

H.R. 15143. An act to amend title 10, United States Code, to provide the grade of lieutenant general for an officer serving as the Chief of the National Guard Bureau, and for other purposes; and

H.R. 15700. An act to authorize appropriations for the saline water conversion program for fiscal year 1971, and for other purposes.

HOUSE BILLS REFERRED OR PLACED ON THE CALENDAR

The following bills were severally read twice by their titles and referred or placed on the calendar, as indicated:

H.R. 1187. An act to amend the act of August 7, 1961, providing for the establishment of Cape Cod National Seashore;

H.R. 4145. An act to provide for disposition of estates of interstate members of the Cherokee, Chickasaw, Choctaw, and Seminole Nations of Oklahoma dying without heirs;

H.R. 12858. An act to provide for the disposition of certain funds awarded to the Tlingit and Haida Indians of Alaska by a judgment entered by the Court of Claims against the United States;

H.R. 12878. An act to amend the act of August 9, 1955, to authorize longer term leases of Indian lands at the Yavapai-Prescott Community Reservation in Arizona;

S 3813

WIRLING, SHRIEKING SPECULATORS ON THE MAIN FLOOR. THE LINES IN HIS FACE DEEPENED.

"'I HAVE BEEN HERE BEFORE,' HE MUTTERED. 'I CAME AS GOV-ERNOR OF SOUTH CAROLINA TO SELL THE BONDS OF MY STATE. I KNOW WHAT A HORDE OF WOLVES THEY ARE. THESE ARE THE MEN WHO HAVE THE NATION BY THE THROAT.'

"SO FOR TWO DAYS SENATOR TILLMAN WENT ABOUT IN THE STRONGHOLDS OF THE MONEY KINGS OF AMERICA SEARCHING FOR FACTS.

"'THERE ISN'T A DROP OF PATRIOTIC BLOOD IN THIS CROWD,' HE SAID. 'AND YET IT WRITES THE LAWS AND CONTROLS THE POLICY OF THE COUNTRY. NOTHING BUT A REVOLUTION CAN OVERTHROW

SENATOR TILLMAN'S ALLEGORICAL COW.

This cartoon, designed by Senator Tillman, shows his idea of the present American situation. The cow, symbolical of national resources, is feeding on the produce of the farmers of the West and South, while her golden milk is all drawn by the "sharpers," gamblers, and speculators in Wall Street.

SENATOR TILLMAN'S ALLEGORICAL COW No. 2.

In this cartoon Senator Tillman shows the result of the attempt of the farmers to turn the big cow around, to let her feed on income tax in the East while they should milk her in the West and South. But the cow, as Senator Tillman draws her, was not a reversible cow. As soon as she tried to feed on income tax the Supreme Court seized her by the throat as a reminder that she must do her eating exclusively in the agricultural regions. The farmers in the West are disappointed and get no income-tax milk.

The cutting edge of this cartoon struck deep into some of the tenderest parts of the congressional body, and reaction was swift and lasting. This illustration is the only one to appear in the *Record*—ever!

The storage of paper is a major problem for a printing operation using a million or more pounds each day. Until construction of the GPO's own modern warehouse in 1938, paper was held and handled in a shedlike structure (shown above). Building No. 4 (shown below), located across from the main GPO buildings, contains five levels—two below grade—and is connected to the plant by a tunnel under North Capitol Street.

he heartbeat of any printing plant is its press equipment. Above is a web-fed otary press purchased in 1908 for $8,250 to print money orders for the Post ffice Department. This press was capable of printing at a speed of 2,000 npressions per hour (iph). The GPO's modern web equipment prints at speeds f 22,000 iph and costs many times more than this early machine.

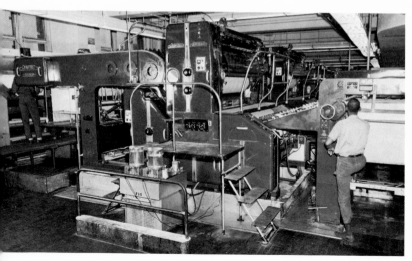

his is one of the GPO's newest sheet-fed offset perfecting presses. Nearly fifty fset presses of various kinds and sizes give the Office an enormous cylinder pacity.

Computing costs and preparing work jackets were wholly manual operation at the turn of the century. This is a view of the Computing and Jacket Section of about 1900. Note the banks of file drawers from floor to ceiling.

Most of the GPO's accounting operations are now computerized including billing, inventory control, time records, and payroll. Several ultrasophisticated electronic systems currently handle this work and prepare magnetic tapes for the GPO's pioneering electronic photocomposition devices as well.

his is a photograph taken around 1920 in the Job Composing Section, where
ie then prevailing systems for setting type were virtually unchanged from
utenberg's time.

own here is the control console of the GPO's ultra-high-speed photocom-
sing system. Operating from magnetic tapes, this apparatus can set type at
e incredible rate of 1,000 characters per second, providing a fully made-up
ge, even of complex tabular material, in about fifteen seconds.

The sale and distribution of government publications grew rapidly after the creation of the Public Documents Division under the Printing Act of 1895. The retail bookstore (shown here) opened on the first floor of the "Documents" building in 1921.

Annual sales of government publications now amount to nearly $70 million and each year GPO retail bookstores serve more than a quarter of a million customers. Shown below is the main bookstore as it appeared in 1969.

sion. (See pages 89–90.) As the drawing is photographed, its size is logged and sent to the Patents Section in order that sufficient space can be left in the makeup to permit insertion of illustrations at the head of each patent description. The completed composition, with space left for illustrations, is converted into a reproduction proof. This reproduction proof is then sent to the Offset Division, where the drawings are inserted to appear with the description, and the entire patent is photographed to page size for the *Gazette*.

The *Official Gazette* is printed by the offset process in slightly less than 10,000 copies each week. Patent attorneys, inventors, and businesses concerned with new developments can subscribe to it for $50 per annum. Those interested only in trademarks can subscribe to the trademark section, which is bound separately, for $12 per annum. Single copies of the *Gazette* can be purchased for $1.25 each, and of the trademark section for 25 cents each.

Press Work

As we have seen earlier, Government Printing Office production is divided about equally between the letterpress and offset printing processes.* Prepress and press activities differ widely for the two processes and are therefore discussed separately.

Letterpress Prepress Work

Printing from relief images can be accomplished using a variety of image carriers—the most common being type itself. In the Government Printing Office, as elsewhere, such printing

---

* According to the Commerce Department's Business and Defense Services Administration, the American printing industry is also about equally divided between offset and letterpress, although *Outlook 1969,* BDSA's annual review of industry, says that the offset process now has more than 50 per cent of the market.

is confined to short-run work using flatbed presses and sheet stock. Type characters (Monotype or foundry type) or multiple-character slugs (Linotype or Ludlow) together with illustrative material, if any, are assembled in a steel frame, called a chase, and locked in position with expanding steel wedges called quoins. This steel frame with its locked-in burden is sent directly to the pressroom from the Hand Section, for printing.

For longer runs—over 5,000 copies approximately—a more durable image carrier is needed. In the Government Printing Office, relief image carriers, or plates, of various kinds are available from the *Platemaking Division.* Two sections, the *Stereotype Section* and the *Electrotype Section*, are engaged in making plates of typecast material.

Because it is relatively cheap and quick to produce, the stereotype plate is most common. It is made from a thick, fibrous paper mat containing a controlled amount of moisture on which a female image is impressed from a locked-up type form. The mat is "roasted" to drive out the residual moisture, leaving the image-bearing paper hard and dry. The mat is then placed in a water-chilled casting box where molten stereotype metal is poured against it. The metal hardens almost immediately, and the paper mat is stripped off, leaving a positive cast of the original type. The mat is stored for further use. The plate is shaved to the proper thickness and beveled at the head and foot, and unwanted areas are machined away with high-speed routers; after inspection, it is ready for the press. Stereotype plates are provided in either flat or curved form.

The Government Printing Office also provides a mat service, whereby stereotype mats are furnished at low cost and in large numbers for multiple-point shipping. Since stereotype casting equipment can be found in almost every newspaper plant, agencies can in this way avoid the high costs of shipping heavy plates to multiple users. In the past, the Veterans Administration and the Social Security Administration both used this method for getting spot messages to the public in local newspapers. Altogether, the Stereotype Section produces almost 100,000 plates each year. Mat production can vary from about 5 million to more than 20 million per year.

For higher quality reproductions and longer press runs, electrotype plates are used. The matrix or mold in this process is made from sheet vinyl and is produced under heat and pressure. This mold reproduces the finest detail from a master image, which may be type or another plate. After molding, the vinyl is made electrically conductive by spraying it with silver nitrate solution. Once prepared in this way, the mold is immersed in a copper sulfate bath where copper is plated from large copper anodes onto the face of the mold until the deposit is thick enough to retain the image—usually about .002 inch. When greater wearing properties are required, the deposit is allowed to grow thicker by longer immersion in the bath. Once the copper shell has formed, it is separated from the mold, and lead is poured on the back of the shell to make a rigid plate. After trimming and leveling, the plate is ready for press. Where rotary press equipment is to be used, electrotypes are curved to fit the plate-carrying press cylinders. Copper electrotypes can also be given an especially durable surface by electroplating with nickel or chromium.

The Electrotype Section produces about one million square inches of printing plates annually. This Section also can produce both flexographic (rubber) printing plates and vinyl plastic plates. The latter are cheap to reproduce in large numbers. They are light in weight and can be shipped at small cost to be used as a printing medium by even poorly equipped shops. This plate is often used by the State Department and the U.S. Information Agency for shipment abroad.

Drawings and photographs for letterpress printing are produced by a third section within the Platemaking Division, the *Photoengraving Section.* Copy is photographed by process cameras, and the resulting negatives are used to transfer the image to a metal plate. The process resembles that used to make photographic prints on paper, except that metal is used as the light-sensitive emulsion carrier. In the Government Printing Office, magnesium and copper are the most common plate metals.

The metal is prepared by scrubbing to remove all grease and foreign matter. Then it is coated with a light-sensitive emulsion that becomes insoluble in water when exposed to light. The image transfer is made by printing through the clear portions of the negative using high-intensity lamps. After exposure, the unaffected emulsion is washed away with water, leaving the light-hardened portions intact. Following this step, the image is "fixed" and dyed to make it visible and the plate is baked to harden the image and make it acid resistant. After cooling, the plate is etched with a high-acid-content emulsion. By virtue of its special chemical properties and the physical means of applying it to the face of the plate, the etchant erodes the bare metal vertically but not horizontally. The result is a relief duplicate of the copy, except that it has been laterally reversed in the photographic steps. These plates are "blocked" (glued to wooden bases to make them the same height as the type they will accompany) and are then ready for press—or electrotyping or stereotyping.

Plates made from photographs, called halftones, can also be produced on copper or magnesium in much the same manner as regular photoengravings.

Two other plates produced by the Government Printing Office Photoengraving Section are also worthy of mention since they are relative newcomers to the graphic arts. They are "wraparound" plates and Dycril plates. Wraparound plates are thin metal image carriers that must be used on special wraparound presses. They are etched rather shallowly—about .010 inch as opposed to about .030 inch for regular plates—and hence must be wrapped skintight around press plate cylinders to prevent printing the plate bottoms during reproduction. The entire press cylinder is covered by the plate in wraparound printing, and the plate is very similar to an offset plate except that the image is in shallow relief. Dycril is a patented photopolymer material that has the property of being hardened by exposure to a high-intensity, ultraviolet-rich light source. It is hardened through its entire thickness, and after exposure the nonhardened areas can be washed away by a weak alkali solution. Relief plates prepared from this material exhibit exceptionally durable running properties and excellent ink-transfer qualities. However, at this writing, the relatively high cost of Dycril is inhibiting its greater use in the GPO.

The Photoengraving Section also produces overflow offset negative work (see below) as well as stamping dies for the bindery.

Offset Prepress Work

The offset process in the Government Printing Office today accounts for slightly over half of in-plant production. Because of the process's closely knit procedures, all offset activities were brought together in a single division in 1954. Prepress work of the **Offset Division** is done in three sections: **Offset Preparation, Offset Negative,** and **Offset Platemaking.**

Copy for all printing by the offset method is received by the Offset Preparation Section. Here, the raw manuscript and illustration material are subjected to such preliminaries as may be required subsequent to production. Camera copy received directly from a customer agency, is sized for photographing, and data sheets with detailed production instructions are prepared. If reproduction proofs are called for, composition and proofs are ordered. Copy then goes directly to Offset Negative where it is photographed.

In the Offset Negative Section, which is equipped with three semiautomatic 40×48-inch process cameras, plus several smaller ones, negatives are prepared and delivered to strippers who inspect and assemble them into pages. Newer compositing techniques are used to combine illustrations and text, wherever possible.*

The Offset Negative Section produces both line and halftone negatives, the latter in screen rulings up to 300 lines per inch for exceptionally fine detail work. During World War II and the Korean conflict, Air Force target mosaics were produced with these ultrafine screens.

Offset Platemaking receives negatives from the Offset Negative Section for processing. Negatives are assembled into large "flats"—the determining size being the plate size that the press itself will accept. Negatives of pages are taped to a semiopaque paper—each page in its proper sequence and location. The paper is then cut away from each image area so as to permit light to pass through each negative during the "burning."

A metal plate, usually aluminum, is roller-coated with a light-sensitive emulsion and after drying is used to "burn," or print, the image areas of the prepared flat. This is done by exposing the plate—through the negative—to high-intensity light, which hardens the image of the printing areas and makes it insoluble in water. Next, a special lacquer is applied to the entire plate, the exposed portions of which accept the lacquer and form an ink-receptive image. The plate is then sprayed with water and the nonprinting areas are cleared of both unexposed coating and the lacquer by sponging, after which a weak acid etch and a gumming solution are applied to the plate to ready it for the press.

Deep-etch plates, which are used for high-quality and long-run printing, are prepared in much the same fashion, but with completely different chemistry. Positives are used rather than negatives, and the image areas are deliberately lacquer-

---

* Compositing is precombining several negatives by contact printing methods, so that a single negative is furnished for platemaking, rather than groups of negatives, which must be hand assembled.

hardened and chemically reinforced, using the stencil-type image formed by the positive.

For runs of half a million or more, the Offset Platemaking Section is also equipped to supply bimetal type plates that feature a copper image.

The Pressrooms

The **Letterpress Division** consists of the **Job Press, Main Press, Web Press,** and **Postal Card** sections. The GPO is equipped with most types of letterpresses, including flat bed, rotary, and web. Flat bed presses predominate since much of GPO's work is short run, print-from-type jobs. The running speed of flat bed presses is not high, but simplicity and ruggedness make them invaluable for bills and hearings. Of the sixty-one flat beds in the Main Press, eighteen are referred to as "bill" presses and constitute "the racetrack." (The second nickname stems from the unrelieved urgency of the congressional work that occupies this equipment full time. In the first months of a session of Congress, it is not unusual for the number of bills to be printed to average 200 a day. During that period, a single press may change forms ten times per shift.)

Rotary presses print exclusively from plates curved to fit intimately on plate cylinders. On a rotary press, an impression is created with each revolution of the cylinder. (Flat beds produce only one impression for every two revolutions.)

When rolls of paper are used to feed rotary equipment, the paper is threaded completely through the press and printing is continuous. Such presses are called web presses from the "web" of paper strung through the rollers. A web press is by far the fastest type of printing press. The Government Printing Office's letterpress web equipment is capable of folding, pasting, perforating, and stitching following the actual printing operation. The *Congressional Record* is produced on web equipment. (See Chapter V.)

The Letterpress Division is also equipped with a number of specialty presses. The newest equipment is of the wraparound variety and uses thin metal or metal-backed photopolyneer plates that completely cover the plate cylinder. The plates are shallow-etched. Wraparound presses operate at high speeds, employ a special inking system designed to deposit a coating of ink on the relief image without fouling the etched areas, are capable of excellent ink transfer, and need almost no form makeready.* Several embossing presses for the production of fine engraved stationery and certificates print from intaglio plates furnished mainly by the U.S. Treasury's Bureau of Engraving and Printing. This equipment was installed to fill requirements for the President, Vice President, and Cabinet officers, all of whom are authorized engraved stationery. This type of stationery is also authorized for diplomatic correspondence by the State Department.

The bulk of the government's printed envelope needs are provided by the Government Printing Office. Congress alone orders nearly 150 million franked envelopes yearly. Special high-speed presses, printing from rubber plates, are used for this work.

The Government Printing Office also produces over a billion postal cards yearly—a sizable task, although the demand for postal cards is diminishing as postal costs increase. The Letterpress Division's **Postal Card Section** is located in the GPO's warehouse across North Capitol Street and represents perhaps the most highly automated activity in the Office. Because of the strict security required (postal cards are quite negotiable), the Section was isolated from main plant operations when the GPO's new warehouse was occupied in 1938. This Section is equipped with four specialty presses capable of

---

* Makeready is the building up or relieving of pressure to produce an even transfer of ink.

producing a million postal cards per shift. Each press carries twenty curved steel plates. These plates are produced by the Bureau of Engraving and Printing and are virtually indestructible. Before postal rates began to escalate, necessitating increasingly frequent changes, some of these plates had been running continuously for more than fifteen years. These web presses are fed from rolls of white card stock, thirty-three inches wide and weighing more than half a ton. At the same time the stock is printed with the familiar royal purple postal card ink, knives slit it into ribbons. Choppers, working perpendicular to the axis of the paper flow, chop out individual cards, delivering them into single-card piles. The press counts the cards and bands them into individual packages of fifty. Conveyors then carry the banded packages of fifty to a station that wraps five of these packages. The wrapped packages, containing 250 cards, are automatically loaded into cartons holding either 5,000 or 10,000 cards, which are sealed and delivered to skid-loading stations. Recently, the GPO began direct shipment of postal cards to fifty-four points throughout the United States. When the cards arrive at these points, they are placed in the regular mail stream and dispatched to individual post offices as far down the postal ladder as third and fourth class installations.

This new service has brought about some interesting encounters between the Government Printing Office and postmasters of small post offices. Connor, Montana, with a population of five persons, found itself with 2 million postcards for sale. The local postmaster had ordered 2,000 cartons instead of 2,000 cards. In 1969, an Iowa postmaster wrote that his need for cards had increased because "an abnormal amount of local girls" were getting married and "a large amount of showers" were being held. He went on to say that they had only one wedding in June but in July "at least ten girls got the notion." The GPO filled his emergency order. In another crisis visited upon a South Carolina postmaster by a local Jaycees

"Girl Watcher" contest, the Government Printing Office hurried a shipment of postcards to the beleaguered official.

In recent years, the Post Office Department has shown an inclination toward multicolor cards of a commemorative type. The GPO's equipment is not designed to produce such material with the same efficiency as it has the single-color card. Since the Bureau of Engraving and Printing is better equipped for this special type of color work, it will probably take over this color card production.

The Postal Card Section also manufactures overseas aerogrammes, distant cousin to the World War II V-Mail. Printed in two colors on light weight paper and gummed on press, the aerogramme is die cut to form a sheet of writing paper that can be folded and sealed to make a private envelope. Aerogrammes can be mailed anywhere in the world at a standard rate. Annual production ranges over 30 million pieces.

The *Offset Pressroom* is part of the larger Offset Division. Generally speaking, the offset printing method is faster, requires less makeready and uses a far less costly plate. Offset presses fall into two large families, sheet-fed and roll-fed. The Government Printing Office's sheet-fed offset presses are equipped with plate cylinder pin register systems, which permit rapid plate installation to hairline tolerances. The offset method draws its name from the fact that the inked image is transferred from the plate to a rubber blanket, which in turn transfers the image to the paper. Although the chemistry of the offset process has become quite sophisticated in recent years, it is still basically a grease-attracting, water-repelling, physical phenomenon that underlies the method.

The GPO operates more than forty rotary offset presses ranging in size from 17×22 inches to 43×60 inches. Each press is intended to match the required sizes of certain standard products. Although the majority of government work is printed in one color, the GPO maintains a modest two-color capability in its offset pressrooms. Also available are several perfector presses, which complete a product—printing front and back of each sheet—in one pass through the press.

Roll-fed offset presses employ the same principles as offset sheet-fed presses but, because of the continuous web of paper being moved through the press and the folding and cutting equipment at the delivery end, are many times more efficient. The GPO's web equipment consists of two 25×38-inch roll-fed presses capable of delivering 20,000 32-page signatures in the 6×9-inch family per hour, and a single 35×50-inch press, which will print at approximately the same speed and deliver two 32-page signatures in the 8½×11-inch family. Each of these presses, by virtue of its flying paster component, can continue to print while changing from one roll of paper to another. All of the offset roll-fed presses are also equipped with hydraulic packers that expel trapped air from printed signatures to facilitate those operations which follow press-work. These presses print both sides of the paper simultaneously. After receiving the image, the web of paper is passed through an open-flame gas oven, which sets the ink, and then over chilling rollers cooled by a refrigerated-water system. Following this, the web of paper is slit, folded, and chopped to form individual signatures. These signatures are sent directly to the bindery for trimming or other finishing operations.

The GPO Bindery

The *Binding Division*, consisting of the *Pamphlet Section*, *Book Section*, and the *Blank Section*, is one of the GPO's largest. It is charged with the job of "packaging" most of the printing. When press sheets or signatures are delivered to the Bindery, the desired product may be case-bound books, pamphlets, single sheets, or pads. For bookwork or pamphlets, printed press sheets are machine-folded to form page-sequenced packages, or signatures. The maximum signature size in the GPO is thirty-two pages, although many private firms use forty-eight pages or even sixty-four pages in a signature when stock weight will permit proper folding. Once folded, the signatures are loaded into stations on gathering equipment that assembles the desired number in the proper order to make an entire book or pamphlet.

The signatures are held together by wire stitches or are sewn together. Sewing is preferred for quality products since sewn books will lie flat when opened. For small pamphlets, saddle wire stitches are used. Signatures are inserted one into the other and a wire staple is driven into the back fold. For larger products, such as the *Congressional Record*, a side stitch is used. Binding machinery used for the *Congressional Record* will side-stitch through as much as a 1-inch thick product. Most of these operations, exclusive of sewing, are performed by the Pamphlet Section, which also does covering, trimming, tipping, inserting, signature pressing, and storage.

When a case-bound book is wanted, signatures go to the Book Section where they are assembled by large gathering machines. Here the collected signatures are sewn together, and a combination machine then "rounds" them, giving the book its characteristic concave back, and prepares them to receive the "hard" cover. Covers are made separately and placed on the book by a special machine. Once covered, each book is inspected and placed in a hydraulic press until it is properly formed and dry. The Book Section also stamps covers and back strips in gold, imitation gold, and colors, and performs hand binding. The GPO produces nearly 4 million case bound books annually.

Forms work, which customarily consists of single-sheet products, does not require folding and hence is sent directly from presses to cutting machines. These huge guillotines cut and trim individual forms from the larger sheets delivered by presses. Some presses are capable of printing up to twenty-eight standard 8×10½-inch forms on a single pass. Once trimmed, the forms may be drilled, stapled, or padded. Perforating is normally done on press. The familiar multiple-copy type of form that abounds in government is often assembled from varicolored press products together with carbon interleaves by the Bindery. But normally, because of the special nature of this work, and the fact that many outside printing firms specialize in manufacturing these forms, most customer requirements are filled by commercial printers.

An entire unit in the Bindery is maintained to rebind, restore, and repair old books and other library material. The chief users of this service are the Library of Congress and the special libraries of the legislative branch. Bookbinders assigned to this unit are real craftsmen in the finest tradition of the art. New bindings for old documents are made by hand. Rare books and special editions are painstakingly restored, employing the ancient crafts of marbling (applying the spidery colorful patterns to end sheets and book edges), gilding, and leather hand tooling. Presentation volumes, such as those of the Presidents' Papers prepared for the Chief Executives' personal libraries, are bound in special morocco bindings and are showpieces of the binder's art.

The reader who has stayed with this necessarily technical account of the GPO's structure as regards plant and production is by now well aware that, more than any other single government agency, the GPO is above all a "shop." As such, it produces a very wide variety of printed material.

The next chapter describes in detail the production of the *Congressional Record*—a daily, or rather a nightly, job that is historically the GPO's most important function. Here, printing and politics merge.

V

The *Congressional Record*

Just before dawn on almost every day that the U.S. Congress is in session, a flurry of activity stirs the neighborhood several blocks from the Capitol building as half a dozen gray-green panel trucks, with yellow stripes around their middles and yellow emblems on their doors, begin to snort and cough in the warrens around the Government Printing Office. These are GPO route trucks, warming up. They are loaded with the first-off copies of the proceedings and debates of the U.S. Congress, better known as the *Congressional Record*. In another hour, the route trucks will have delivered the *Record* to the metropolitan residences of more than a hundred senators and congressmen who wish to ingest the preceding day's legislative activities with their toast and coffee less than twenty-four hours—sometimes less than twelve hours—after these activities have been concluded.

The highly organized, semi-automated routine that makes possible such rapid progress from the spoken word to the printed page actually starts in the Capitol, where reporters record the proceedings of Congress in shorthand. Congressional debate reporters are a breed apart and are totally devoted to their task. There are six reporters in the Senate and six in the House of Representatives. Each reporter has one transcriber and two clerks.

These reporters use two folio systems—both quite uncomplicated—to number the records of debate in order to keep them in proper sequence. (Folio in this case refers only to the reporter's copy.) Keeping the records of debate in proper order is very important when it comes to assembling the *Record* copy, especially for the House, where the copy has to be checked and revised by four or five hundred congressmen before it can be dispatched to the GPO for printing.

The Senate reporters use an hour folio system, in which the hour is divided into six segments, one for each reporter. The first reporter records ten minutes of floor debate and is then supplanted by another reporter. Each hour has 100 folio numbers allocated to it, and each reporter is assigned a block of numbers The second hour the Senate is in session begins with folio 100 and runs through 199. Another 100 folio numbers are allotted to each succeeding one-hour increment, whether the preceding 100 numbers have been used up or not. The folio system permits the foreman of the *Record* at GPO to tell how much copy is yet to come. If, for example, he knows that the Senate met at noon and was in session until 6 P.M. when he receives folio 500 indicating the beginning of the fifth hour of proceedings (5 P.M.), he knows that he is handling copy for the final hour of proceedings. The House of Representatives finds a half-hour folio system more suitable, since it allows representatives to receive copy for revision more quickly. In the half-hour system, each of the six reporters spends five minutes every half-hour recording debate. In both houses, a reporter who has taken down his allotted minutes of debate and been replaced by another reporter then returns to his office, where he reads his notes into a recording device. His transcriber types the remarks, and after a final check by the reporter, the sheets are given to a clerk who turns the copy over to the appropriate members for revision—but not until the clerk has recorded each folio and the names of the members holding it. This information constitutes an "out" list; as copy is returned after revision by congressmen, it is checked off the list.

At the close of the daily session, the approved copy, to-gether with the out list, is delivered to the Government Print-ing Office by messenger. A duplicate copy of the out list is retained by the messenger, who is notified when the copy is ready for printing and can be picked up. Almost a hundred years ago, Congress considered constructing a pneumatic tube between the Government Printing Office and the Capitol to speed up transmission of congressional documents for print-ing. Work was begun in 1873, the year the GPO printed the first issue of the *Record,* but the shell surrounding the tube was not strong enough to support the weight of the earth, and the project was abandoned before completion. In the early 1900's, messengers used bicycles to transmit the copy for the *Record.* Today, they use small panel trucks to shuttle back and forth from the Capitol to the Printing Office.

The copy is delivered to the foreman of the *Record* at the Government Printing Office. If Congress is still in session, the foreman receives as much of the *Record* as is ready for print-ing. He is also given a record of assigned folios so that he can identify the reporter responsible for any part of the transcript in question. If it is necessary to check a phrase or to locate a missing page, it can best be done by telephoning the reporter who took the notes. Reporters carry their notes with them at all times, and rarely fail to provide the GPO promptly with the information needed.

What Goes into the *Record*

Each daily *Congressional Record* consists of four parts when both houses are in session: The House proceedings and debates, the Senate proceedings and debates, the "Extensions of Remarks," and the "Daily Digest." One day the Senate proceedings occupy first place, the next day the House pro-ceedings.

By definition, the *Congressional Record* is a "substantially verbatim" account of the proceedings and debates of the Congress.* "Substantially" as here used means that members of Congress have leeway to extend their remarks and to insert extraneous matter—speeches, letters, text of bills, pertinent magazine articles, newspaper editorials, and the like—in the Extensions of Remarks. Each member is limited to one or two such insertions each day. The Joint Committee on Printing polices this arrangement for both houses through its rules and regulations, but Congress frequently grants permission for several extensions or revisions at a time, and members often obtain permission for further extension if an item exceeds two printed pages. Other standard exceptions to the rule are: excerpts from letters, telegrams, or articles concerning a speech delivered during congressional debate; communications from state legislatures; addresses or articles by the President, by members of his Cabinet, by the Vice-President, or by members of Congress themselves.

Usually, the *Record* is printed daily every day that one or both houses are in session. However, the Joint Committee on Printing can direct that a very small issue be held and combined with the following day's issue. The Joint Committee also permits material to be submitted for printing in the *Record* for a specified number of days after Congress adjourns.

The "Daily Digest," which appears in the final pages of each issue, presents a condensation of chamber action, brief notes on matters under committee consideration, a list of bills signed

---

* It is *not* the official minutes of congressional proceedings. These are issued at the end of each session of Congress in a very limited number as the *Journal* of each house. House and Senate journal clerks at the Capitol assemble copy for the manuscript each day. This copy is set into type and page proofs are returned to the journal clerks who hold the proofs until the end of each session. The entire manuscript is then sent to the GPO for printing and binding into a single volume for each session. The House *Journal* makes about 1,200 pages and the Senate *Journal* about 800 pages per session. The journals of the House and Senate, which are not offered for sale, constitute the true proceedings of each house and contain no speeches or extraneous material.

by the President, and the program immediately ahead for the Congress. Digest editors for each body, attached to the offices of the Secretary of the Senate and the Clerk of the House, keep track of chamber action from the floor. Information on committee activities is sent daily to the editor's office.

When the Digest copy is completed for each day's session, it is sent to the GPO where copy preparers in the Proof Section ready it for composing. Reference page numbers for each chamber action item appearing in the *Record* proper are also added, making it necessary that this part of the *Record* be completed last.

PRODUCING THE *Record* AT THE GPO

The GPO "night people," like the congressional debate reporters, are a breed apart. Most like to work under fluorescent light rather than sunlight. They get premium pay—15 per cent over and above day rates for the same work—but few would trade places with day employees even were the pay scales not more attractive. Producing the *Congressional Record* and other urgent overnight jobs inspires much the same spirit and excitement that can be found on a newspaper—especially a morning paper. Prior to the convening of each Congress, a certain number of printers, pressmen, and bookbinders must be selected to round out the regular night force. Many of those drafted for a limited "hardship" tour find the highly charged "this job's gotta go tonight" atmosphere to their liking and stay on after the tour's end.

The night moves quickly.

As fast as the foreman of the *Record* receives copy, it is subject to what is called hasty preparation. This entails indicating type sizes, ensuring a sequential connection in folios, and checking the matter destined for the Extensions. Whenever proceedings refer to bills, reports, and other government documents, GPO copy preparers are responsible for supplying accurate excerpts or frequently the entire texts for insertion in the *Record*.

The deadline for copy is 9 P.M.—with the exception of copy containing tables, which must be submitted not later than 7 P.M. since all tabular matter must be set on Monotype machines and rules must be inserted by hand—both relatively time-consuming tasks. It is seldom possible to obtain all copy by deadline time, especially when the session has been lengthy. When the preparer comes across an "out" in his copy, he indicates the approximate number of "galley slugs" (type-high metal bars) that are to be inserted in the galley (a metal tray of type set in lines) by the compositor to allow space for the material to come. It is not uncommon for the number of outs in House copy to reach forty or fifty. As each out comes in, it gets priority handling so as not to cause a delay in making up pages.

If a member of Congress holds his speech material beyond the deadline, a notation is inserted in the *Record* such as: "Mr. Jones of Maryland addressed the House. His remarks will appear hereafter in the Extensions of the *Record*." When Mr. Jones' speech is received, it is printed in the Extensions of a later issue.

The prepared copy is turned over to a deskman, who passes it to the men who actually set the type—the Linotype operators. Each operator handles what is known as a "take"— enough copy to make approximately one galley of type. When the take is complete, the operator returns the copy and type to the deskman and picks up another take from the desk. A proof is then pulled of the material set in type, and both proof and copy are sent by pneumatic tube to the proofroom above. After typographical errors have been corrected, a revised proof is inspected, and any remaining errors are corrected.

Because of the severe *Record* schedule, revisers (normally Proof Section positions), are assigned to the Linotype Section, as are imposing specialists, the men who place the material for plating so that the margins, folding sequence, and page sequences are correct. A page referee and a page reviser are also on hand in the Linotype Section to expedite *Record* composition and makeup.

The *Record* begins to take shape as galleys of type are assembled into pages, and the compositor who is making up the pages inserts the appropriate date and page number at the top of the assembled page. Proofs of the made-up pages are then inspected to make certain that heads and page numbers are correct and that pages run in the proper sequence. A second reviser makes still another check for errors.

After one more, final check by the copy preparer, the two-page forms are locked in metal frames and cast into stereotypes. As described in greater detail in Chapter IV, the stereotype mats are treated with heat in a curved roaster to remove moisture and set the image, then placed in casting boxes, where molten lead is poured against the face of the mats, forming curved plates. These plates are trimmed, shaved to the proper thickness, and, after checking by the stereotype reviser, sent to the pressroom. Schedules call for the last plate to be ready for press at 2:15 A.M.

The presses on which the *Congressional Record* is printed are double-deck rotary presses, each capable of printing from four to sixty-four pages at a speed of 20,000 impressions an hour. The presses are equipped with automatic roll splicers, and the paper is fed continuously from rolls. At present, the average daily *Record* requires about thirty 46-inch rolls of 64-pound newsprint, or about fifteen tons for the average issue. Since approximately 49,000 copies of each daily *Record* are printed, the total on-press time is about two-and-a-half hours.

The presses produce folded signatures, which are gathered, stitched, and trimmed on automated machines in the Bindery. Copies to be mailed are fed directly into mailing machines that wrap, roll, and seal individual copies, using previously stenciled address wrappers.

The first copies off the press are given to the routemen, who have been standing by to deliver yesterday's *Congressional Record* to those senators and congressmen who have requested such service.* Hard on the heels of the route trucks come the vans that deliver copies to the House and Senate office buildings, the Supreme Court, and the White House. These are closely followed by copies for distribution at the Capitol. Other copies have been accumulating on the delivery platform for delivery by daytime-shift personnel to the profusion of departments, agencies, offices, bureaus, and commissions throughout the city.

In the meantime, other copies of the *Congressional Record* that have been wrapped and machine-addressed are placed in conveyor belt into as many as 400 mailbags, tagged with state and city destinations and arranged in the proper sequence to meet train departures to various sections of the country. The mailbags are dropped by spiral chute to a continuous conveyor, which twists its way under North Capitol Street and deposits the bags inside the Post Office over 1,000 feet south of the GPO complex. About 3,000 of these copies represent paid subscriptions. The Public Printer is required by law to furnish the daily *Record* to subscribers at the rate of $1.50 per month. By and large, however, the bulk of the *Record* subscribers receive their copies free. Each senator is authorized to receive one hundred copies of the daily *Record* and each member of the House sixty-eight copies for free distribution to constituents and such other persons as he may designate. Executive departments of the federal government, state governors, and embassies also receive free copies, as do foreign countries that extend a reciprocal service.

Schedules call for home-delivered copies of the *Record* to leave the Government Printing Office by 6 A.M., Capitol Hill copies by 7 A.M., and mailing copies by 8 A.M., although large volume, late copy, or complex material may occasionally make it impossible to adhere rigidly to these hours. In all prob-

---

* President Nixon's staffers now get very early delivery of the *Record* to prepare for 7:00 A.M. briefings at the White House.

ability, however, within a few hours of the time the last copies have left the GPO, both the Senate and the House will once more be in session and the whole process will be repeated nightly until Congress adjourns.

Approximately 2,500 copies of the daily *Congressional Record* are set aside each night for a biweekly accumulation, which is indexed and bound for the use of congressional and other federal agencies and personnel. The binding is green, which distinguishes these two-week sets of the *Record* from the regular "bound" *Record,* traditionally red, produced in approximately 2,500 sets at the end of every session of Congress. The makeup, presswork, and binding of the red bound *Record* is used as filler work during the period Congress is in adjournment. Type set for the daily *Record* is reused after an additional proofreading. The Extensions and Digest are removed, except for the material that was received too late to be included in the proceedings, which is inserted intact in the body of the *Record* from which it was perforce omitted. Because of the relatively small number of copies required, this work is printed on flat bed presses. The bound *Record* for the Eighty-ninth Congress, Second Session (1966) runs to twenty-three volumes, including one volume entitled the *Congressional Record—Its Past and Its Future.* *

THE *Record* FORMAT

The appearance of the *Congressional Record* today does not differ markedly from the first issue, which consisted of two and one quarter pages and was devoted almost entirely

* No official publication of the proceedings of the U.S. Congress was undertaken until 1824, when the firm of Gales and Seaton began publication of the *Annals of Congress* in forty-two volumes. The *Annals* covered the proceedings and debates of both houses of Congress from 1789 to 1824 and included congressional correspondence, state papers, public documents, and laws, making these volumes a singularly important source of the nation's early legislative history.

to President Ulysses S. Grant's brief inaugural address. Only one major change in format has been made in nearly 100 years. In 1941, the *Record* changed from a two-column to a three-column makeup. Oddly enough, this was a return to the *Congressional Globe* format of 1837–73 (see Chapter I). There have been a number of minor alterations, however; the text typeface was changed in 1905, when Linotype machines outmoded hand composition, and again in 1930. Type for headings and speech captions have undergone a series of changes, and the eagle and the seal in the masthead have been simplified for better reproduction. Recently a more readable, Gothic typeface has been introduced for tabular matter.

The ultraconservative appearance of the *Congressional Record* occasionally draws critical fire from contemporary typographic circles, but the classic format is retained by choice. Congress is acutely aware of the functional mission of its daily publication and has consistently resisted any attempts to "jazz up" the design. Illustrations are strictly forbidden. The only drawing ever to appear in the *Record* created such a furore that it has remained unique in almost a century of publication.

The Senate unwittingly gave its unanimous consent to the publication of this drawing on October 3, 1913, when Senator B. R. Tillman of South Carolina, firebrand, nonconformist, former governor of his state, and a senator for eighteen years, requested the Senate's permission to reprint in the *Congressional Record* an article he had prepared many years before for the Sunday March 1, 1896, issue of the *New York World*. The matter under debate was the income tax, which had been declared un-Constitutional by the Supreme Court but had been recently enacted into law via a Constitutional amendment. The original Tillman story had included a cartoon that pictured what the *World* called Senator Tillman's allegorical cow. In the first half of the cartoon, the cow, a rather elongated animal, was feeding on the produce of Western and Southern farmers and being milked by Wall Street "sharpers, gamblers, and speculators." In the second part of the cartoon, the cow had been turned around to demonstrate the animal's "irreversability," ascribed to the income tax. Hands labeled "U.S. Supreme Court" were interfering with the cow's milk production by choking it, while two additional Wall Street figures stood by, thumbing their noses at the frustrated Western and Southern milkers and their empty pail. (See reproduction in photo section.)

When the cartoon appeared in the *Record,* Congressional reaction was violent—so much so that no relaxation of the policy outlawing illustrations in the *Congressional Record* is to be expected in the foreseeable future—even though this incident took place over fifty years ago.

But if the format of the *Record* has changed surprisingly little, its size has not remained constant over the years. The *Record* for the Forty-Third Congress (1873–74), the first issued by the Government Printing Office, ran to 9,018 pages. The Eighty-Ninth Congress (1965–66) accounted for 70,229 pages. The average number of pages is steadily growing, boosted no doubt by longer sessions and the sheer volume of floor colloquy. In 1964, the average was 154 pages per issue, and in 1967, 210 pages. Several 320-page dailies have been issued. The largest *Record* for a single day, incidentally, was issued for October 10, 1965. It was printed in three parts, due to limitations imposed by bindery stitching equipment, and contained 704 pages.

With paper costs inching upward and with craft wages subject to yearly increases under the Kiess Act (see Chapter II), the cost per page is also rising. If the number of pages in the daily *Congressional Record* for the fiscal year is divided into the total cost of the daily, biweekly, and bound copies and the indexes, the cost per page for the fiscal year 1964–65 was $96. The cost three fiscal years later was $115 per page.

Page volume is relative to the number of days the legislature is in session. The complexity of contemporary problems, the burgeoning population, and the ever-increasing involvement of the legislative branch in governmental affairs all presage longer sessions and lengthier proceedings. Projections point to an average daily *Record* in excess of 400 pages by the year 2000.

VI

The Public Documents Division

Librarians are generally pictured as quiet reservoirs of reserve and dignity. And so they generally are, unless confronted with inefficiency and lack of order in their special field. Before the Printing Act of 1895, the methods in vogue for distributing public documents left much to be desired and frequently drew fire from professional librarians. As a case in point, listen to the words of the secretary of the Lyceum Library in Houston —oldest library in Texas, founded while the state was still a republic. He was quoted in 1895 as complaining:

> There is no doubt in our minds that the distribution of public documents heretofore has been too promiscuous among persons who did not appreciate their true value. For instance, we find some valuable public documents in secondhand book stores for sale, thus abusing the generosity of the Government. It has been said that some Members of Congress have in the past disposed of their quota of public documents otherwise than in the manner intended by the Government. Abuses have existed, without a doubt. In order to remedy this defect in distribution, we would respectfully suggest that in the future no one but public depositories receive public documents. Others desiring the same should be permitted to purchase the desired publication from the United States Government at actual cost.

Before this new printing law, distribution and storage of government documents was a hopelessly haphazard operation. Copies of documents were ordered with little regard for public or official interest. Of the 420 official depositories, some were overwhelmed by mountains of government publications, while others received no regular distribution at all. Copies ordered for congressional use accumulated in members' offices until no storage space remained, at which time senators and representatives dispatched them to home libraries to crowd shelves often already jammed with other documents that had been obtained by direct distribution. Not wishing to offend members of Congress, successive public printers stored leftover publications until natural deterioration solved the warehousing problem. In addition, no standard system for titling government documents existed. Consequently, practical cataloging was virtually impossible.

Distribution of government documents to libraries in the United States was first specifically authorized by the Act of 1813. This law called for one copy of the journals and documents of the Senate and House to be sent to each university and college, and to each incorporated historical society in each state. At first, the Secretary of State assumed the duty of distributing these publications, although no specific assignment of the function to him can be found. Later, other officials of the government were given this duty including at one time, the Clerk of the House, and, at another, the Librarian of Congress.

In 1857, the responsibility for documents distribution was transferred to the Secretary of the Interior, who was also authorized to designate libraries to receive these publications. In 1858, a joint resolution permitted each representative to designate a depository from his district, and in 1859 senators were provided with authority to assign one depository each. Today, each representative is permitted to designate two depository libraries within his own district and each senator two at large in his state.

The Act of 1869 actually established the post of Superintendent of Public Documents in the Department of the Interior. All of the aforementioned acts applied only to the documents of Congress. But when these acts were passed, most of the executive department publications were issued in the congressional series as well. The Act of 1869 stated that "all publications of the executive departments not intended for their special use, but made for distribution" would be sent to depository libraries. It also added to the total number of depositories by including the state and territorial libraries, the libraries of the eight executive departments, and the libraries of the Naval and Military Academies.

On January 12, 1895, however, Congress codified the various laws pertaining to printing in one comprehensive package. Much of this Act of 1895 concerned itself with establishing a new post within the Government Printing Office proper—the Office of the Superintendent of Documents. This individual was to be subordinate to the Public Printer but was to exercise full authority over the tangled government documents situation. The problems concerning the receipt, care, and distribution of government documents were perplexing, but F. A. Crandall, the first Superintendent of Documents, gave some indication of his grasp of conditions in his opening comment to the Public Printer. Addressing himself to the cataloging chaos in his report of 1896, he said:

> There is probably not a man living who could tell off hand what is the subject matter of part 2 of part 2 of volume 4 of part 5 of No. 1 of part 2, volume 14, of the House Executive Documents of the Fifty-first Congress, second session. One might as well try to commit to memory lettering on a Chinese tea chest as charge one's mind with such a rigmarole.

The Government Printing Office was fortunate that its first Superintendent of Documents was both knowledgeable and systematic. He devised a method for orderly storage and arrangement of the flood of publications that under the law now came into his custody. He undertook indexing the documents under his care and organized what he hoped would become a complete documents library. He restructured the system of depository library distribution and suggested ways in which exchanges could be made between depository libraries. He re-interpreted laws that had penalized small libraries for failing to meet arbitrary regulatory standards.

He was also responsible for a more effective arrangement for printing and binding depository copies, eliminating much of the "back-to-press" cost associated with printing "reserve" volumes. He recommended substituting order blanks for gratui-tous congressional distribution of volumes, thus saving thou-sands of dollars in unwanted documents. Many other innovations can be attributed to this excellent public servant, all of which resulted in the elimination of duplication and waste in the document activities of the federal government.

The Act of 1895 called for the Government Printing Office:

1. To sell at cost any public document in its charge, the dis-tribution of which is not specifically directed by law.
2. To receive from any government office any document pub-lished for sale.
3. To have general supervision of the distribution of all public documents.
4. To prepare and print at the close of each Congress a com-prehensive index (Document Catalog) of public documents.
5. To prepare and print at the close of each regular session of Congress a consolidated index (Document Index) of con-gressional documents.
6. To index such single volumes of documents as the Joint Committee on Printing shall direct.
7. To receive all accumulations of documents from the several executive departments, bureaus, and offices of the govern-ment, and annually to take over their surplus for distribu-tion or sale.
8. To prepare and publish a Monthly Catalog of Government publications, which shall show the publications printed

during a month, where obtainable, and the price thereof.

9. To thoroughly investigate the condition of the designated [library] depositories.

10. To distribute the documents as issued to the designated depositories.

In general, this law still determines the responsibilities of the Public Documents Division.

Although the new division began its work in leased quarters on the sixth floor of the Union Building near 7th and G streets, N.W., it now operates from the oldest of the Government Printing Office's four buildings on North Capitol Street. At this writing, in addition to 131,000 square feet of office and storage space in these structures, more than 200,000 square feet of warehouse space is rented in the metropolitan area for document stockpiles. This stockpile now numbers over 110 million copies and comprises more than 27,000 different titles.

Generally, the Public Document Division's functions fall into four broad categories; sales, distribution, the depository library system, and the Documents Division library, all of which are concerned with the handling and orderly placement of material printed by the government in the hands of users in both the public and private sectors of our society. There is considerable overlap in these functions, naturally, but for convenience, they are treated separately in the following pages. First, let us look at sales.

The GPO as Bookseller

Since 1895, U.S. Government book and pamphlet sales operations have come a long way. In that year, the work of fifty employees resulted in sales of $889. Today, with more than 500 employees, the Superintendent of Documents' book sales constitute a major business operation. In fiscal 1968, they amounted to nearly $17 million. Perhaps this substantial growth in the sale of government-printed material is representative of a newer, brighter curiosity on the part of the American people about their government. Certainly the quality, content, and topical range of government documents is expanding. Today, the Superintendent of Documents publishes about fifty separate subject price lists intended to show what is available. Such groupings as Occupations (33A), Finance (28), American History (50), Mining (58), Education (31), Space (79A), National Parks (35), and Government Periodicals and Subscription Services (36) are typical. Many government sales publications have reached bestseller proportions. First on the list of government bestsellers is a Children's Bureau publication—a 108-page booklet on infant care that sells for 20 cents and since its issuance in 1913 has sold 15 million copies. Four of the top five booklets on the government's bestseller list concern children. In addition to *Infant Care;* the titles are *Prenatal Care, Your Child from One to Six,* and *Your Child from Six to Twelve.* Altogether, they have sold over 32 million copies. (Interestingly, the commercial record bestsellers in nonfiction are in the same subject field—Dr. Benjamin Spock's books, with total sales of 18 million.)

The Superintendent of Documents obtains sales copies of publications chiefly from the Government Printing Office proper, "riding" departmental printing orders for the number of copies he estimates he will need to meet the public demand. Originally, in 1895, sales copies were acquired from stock returned by libraries or from "extra" departmental copies. Reprint authority was granted in 1904, but did not include congressional material, although such material was obtained from various sources and sold to the public. By Joint Resolution, May, 1922, reprint authority for congressional documents was given. Only since that date has it been possible for the Superintendent of Documents to function as the sales source for all government printing.

Despite reprint authority, it does not follow that a supply of every government document is available through the Superintendent of Documents. Unless estimates for riding the original departmental printing reasonably anticipate the public's interest, it is oftentimes impractical to go back to press in order to accommodate a relatively small market. Consequently, buyers occasionally find a certain publication is "out of print." If, however, enough interest is shown in a specific publication, the Superintendent of Documents will go back to press especially to satisfy an unpredicted demand.

Long experience with government documents enables the Superintendent of Documents to project public interest with exceptional accuracy. Since he must absorb the cost of printing and, if necessary, the reprinting costs, as well as the costs of unsold publications, he exercises great care in preparing his estimates. More often than not, he must judge public appetite, knowing little more than the title and subject matter of an upcoming document. The ordering agency recommends the number of copies to be ordered based on expected interest. But the Superintendent of Documents must temper this estimate with his own knowledge of the hard realities of bookselling, and various considerations diluting an agency's natural enthusiasm for its own publications affect his judgment when ordering sales copies. These are: (1) the extent of free distribution; (2) agency and media promotional campaigns, and finally and most important (3) the effect of inclusion on the Public Documents Division's "Selected List of Government Publications." Some 900,000 potential customers receive this biweekly list, which can explode demand for a particular title from a few copies to bestseller proportions overnight.

The Warren Commission Report on the assassination of President John F. Kennedy is a prime example of the Public Documents Division's extraordinary sensitivity to a potential book market. Commission members suggested that sales of the summary report would approximate a million copies. The Superintendent of Documents rode the original printing order for 150,000 copies. In the five years following the issuance of this volume, roughly 149,000 copies have been sold. Twenty-six hundred sets of the full 26-volume series were ordered, and to date something in excess of 2,400 have been sold.

It is interesting to see what national publicity does to government book offerings. When the Bayer Aspirin Company ran a nationwide ad extolling the virtues of aspirin in treating rheumatism and quoting a 5-cent Public Health Service folder on rheumatism, the sales impact of this modest document was stupefying. Also, it apparently makes little difference whether the publicity is derogatory or not. General Dwight D. Eisenhower in his Presidential campaign disdainfully referred to a Department of Agriculture pamphlet entitled "The Use of Tools in Dishwashing" as an example of a waste-ridden bureaucracy. The Superintendent of Documents was forced to reprint this pamphlet to fill a flood of orders. A similar rush of orders followed the late Senator Styles Bridges' lampoon on the floor of Congress of another Agriculture publication entitled "Planning the Bathroom."

Sales by the Superintendent of Documents are handled through mail orders and through authorized retail Government Printing Office bookstores located in several cities throughout the United States. There are now ten bookstores operated by the Superintendent of Documents, and more are planned. Five of these are located in the Washington, D.C., area. The main bookstore occupies part of the first floor of Building No. 1 at 710 North Capitol Street. Retail outlets are also operated in the United States Information Agency, 1776 Pennsylvania Avenue; the Department of Commerce, 14th Street between Constitution Avenue and E Street; the Department of State, 2201 C Street, and the Pentagon. The State Department outlet is open only to a limited number of persons—those permitted to enter the restricted State Department building proper.

Bookstores are also operating in Chicago, Illinois; Kansas City, Missouri; San Francisco and Los Angeles, California; and Boston, Massachusetts. All of these stores are self supporting, meaning that receipts exceed the operating costs of the facility. This is a relatively new program of the Government Printing Office; the first bookstore outside of Washington itself was authorized and opened in 1967. But the instant public acceptance of these outlets promises well for the bookstores soon to be opened in other metropolitan areas throughout the country.

Congressional authorization must be obtained for the opening of government bookstore facilities, since an initial outlay of federal funds is required. In addition, space must be available in federal buildings. The Kansas City bookstore is unique in that it is a part of the three-in-one information center operated by the U.S. Government, with the Civil Service Commission, the General Services Administration, and the Government Printing Office participating in the enterprise. Originally conceived as part of the President's program to improve services to the public, this center can provide a wide range of information on jobs and federal employment, procurement of materials and equipment for the federal government and, of course, government documents from the bookstore facility, which caters to both the particular and general curiosity of the public concerning the U.S. Government.

The San Francisco facility has already become the largest seller of government publications among all government bookstores, with the exception of the main bookstore located in the Government Printing Office itself. Opened in January, 1969, the San Francisco store served 5,820 customers in the first full month of operation with total sales for that period amounting to $17,649.29.

Although these retail activities have been very successful and tend to relieve pressures on the mail-order operations at the main office, they still represent only a fraction of government book sales. In 1968, nearly 70 million publications were sold by the Public Documents Division. Of the $17 million-plus total, bookstores accounted for slightly over $1 million.

Prices for government documents, as one might suspect, are considerably lower than similar documents produced by commercial publishers. The Revised Statutes approved in 1874 called for the Congressional Printer to provide extra copies of any document printed at the Government Printing Office at cost of production, plus 10 per cent. Subsequent changes to the laws pertaining to the sale of government documents raised the added percentage to 50 per cent over costs of production. Title 44, Sec. 71, U.S.C. reads, ". . . said cost (of publication) to be estimated by the Public Printer and based upon printing from stereotype plates . . ." (Stereotype production costs were about midway between "printing from type" and printing from high quality electrotypes.) Subscriptions to periodic publications were computed on the same formula. As production and distribution costs continued to rise throughout the ensuing years, regular adjustments to selling prices of documents were made. In 1968, however, a major overhaul of the selling formula resulted from a study of the entire publications pricing structure.

For many years, hearings before the Legislative Appropriation subcommittees of the Senate and House Appropriations committees produced a certain empathy between the Superintendent of Documents and committee members. The cause of this warmth was the profit shown through the sale of public documents, which consistently exceeded the amount of the annual appropriation for operating the Public Documents Division. However, as the costs of printing and distributing publications rose steadily from 1953 to 1968, the gap between funds returned to the Treasury from the sale of publications and the appropriation narrowed dangerously. In 1968, the Superintendent of Documents said that "unless publication prices are adjusted, the deficit between earnings and appropriation will exceed three or more millions of dollars in the near future."

In response to this warning, the GPO reluctantly reworked the entire pricing system. The formula finally developed kept the 50 per cent markup in printing costs and added a 25 per cent surcharge for administrative expenses, a 25 per cent surcharge for postage (documents mailed to customers are sent under the U.S. Government frank, but postage based on the number and weight of each item is billed to the Superintendent of Documents monthly by the Post Office Department), and a 25 per cent contingency factor for absorbing back-to-press costs. This last item enables the Superintendent of Documents to reprint publications in accordance with the law and the public demand and to retain the original selling price if reprinting is necessary. The contingency factor also cushions the costs of disposing of out-of-date documents and unmarketable material.

The *Document Division's Sales Planning Section,* as its name implies, is responsible for promoting the sale of government documents. (See Chart II.) Sales promotion takes the form of general lists of material offered to the public, including the biweekly Selected List, news releases, and flyers. It operates the retail bookstores, both local and in other cities, as well as directing the preparation of government publication exhibits and special direct sales at such affairs. Displays of this sort are in constant demand from conventions and conferences of all sorts. Currently, the Public Documents Division is averaging about one such meeting each month. In 1968, for example, exhibits were prepared for the American Society of Agronomy in New Orleans, the Beautiful American Festival in St. Louis, National Library Week in the Pentagon, and the Conference of International Chiefs of Police in San Francisco.

Document sales are also the concern of several other government departments and agencies. At present, 171 offices of the departments of the Interior, Commerce, and Labor, the

CHART II

ORGANIZATION CHART OF PUBLIC DOCUMENTS DIVISION

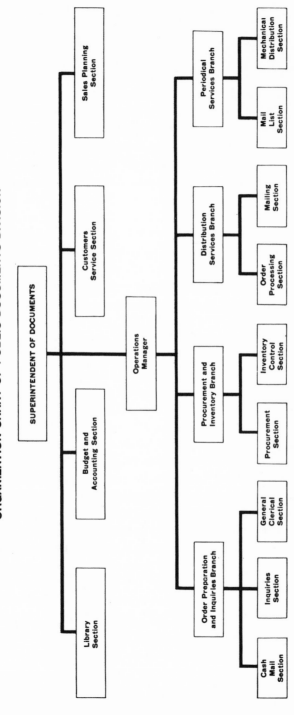

Internal Revenue Service, and the Small Business Administration act as consigned agents for the Public Documents Division. This arrangement began in 1922 when the Department of Commerce contacted the Superintendent of Documents about acquiring a stock of selected publications to be made available in its field offices. The Superintendent of Documents quickly agreed. Title 44, Section 72a, United States Code empowered the Superintendent of Documents to designate "any Government office his agent for the sale of Government publications under such regulations as shall be agreed upon by the Superintendent of Documents and the head of the respective department or establishment of the Government." Consigned agent annual sales are now averaging almost 1 million dollars. Most departments concentrate on stocking their own publications, but more and more are maintaining supplies of "tie-in" material published by departments and offices whose areas of interest parallel or overlap.

MAIL-ORDER AND OTHER DISTRIBUTION

The Public Documents Division mail-order business begins with the receipt of thousands of orders, letter orders, and inquiries daily.* In 1968, more than 1.7 million inquiries were received. This flood is accepted in the *Order Preparation and Inquiries Branch* of the Public Documents Division from the *Office of the Operations Manager.* (See Chart II.) Here, clerks sort the letters by envelope size and slit each piece by machine. Bundles of letters are then made up into "units of mail," by weighing; each contains approximately fifty letters.

* The Superintendent of Documents is now receiving 20,000 to 60,000 letters each day. Not all this mail is meant for him, however. For example, just before April 15 each year, he receives several hundred income tax returns from confused taxpayers who believe that since his title appears in small print on their tax forms, he is the government official to whom all things must be rendered.

These units are taken by mail openers and are burst so that coins which may be caught in envelope corners are released. The return name and address is checked, and the letter is dated. Payment is removed, verified against the amount stated in the letter, and placed in one of several pouches designated for coins, money orders, stamps, or prepurchased Documents coupons. Checks are kept with orders.

At this point, orders are divided into three categories: (1) those without remittances such as inquiries, (2) those with remittances other than cash, and (3) those containing checks. The mail is then passed to machine operators who insert orders into an accounting machine that imprints the letter or order with a certification, an identifying number, the amount received, the type of payment, and the date. The tape from this machine is then sent with the payment pouches to auditors who reconcile the tapes with receipts. Receipts are dispatched several times each day to the U.S. Treasury, where they are credited against the Superintendent of Documents' account. Finally, the order-filling process begins.

Inquiries received without remittances are sent to the *Inquiries Section* of the *Order Preparation and Inquiries Branch.* Here, in the interest of speed and simplicity, preprinted order forms and appropriate subject-price lists are marked in answer to requests for information, attached to each inquiry and dispatched to the *General Clerical Section* for envelope typing and mailing. Each reply carries an appropriate order form to facilitate ordering by the inquiring customer.

Inquiries that cannot be handled with preprinted forms are sorted into two groups, those carrying specific item titles and those containing questions about certain subjects or identifiable publication series. These are sent to a reference unit where clerks use catalogs and reference files to prepare replies. Again for speed, replies are noted directly on the customer's letter, an order form is attached, and this material is sent to the *General Clerical Section* for addressing and mailing.

The Superintendent of Documents receives a wild variety of letters from all over the country. For example, a Texas man wrote to inquire about "a book about pregnancy," explaining that he needed it immediately as his wife was in "that condition." He added, "You will be doing a big favor for us newlyweds, as we just got married yesterday." A "college psyche grad" wanted information on "asparodictics." He helpfully explained that the "FBI, the Narcotics Bureau, and the U.S. Public Health Service" had all "flatly refused to tell me a thing." A young man from Modesto, California, wrote: "Gents, I'm a kid and I like fishing, but worms cost one penny each, and they ain't no good. I found some and now I will raise my own worms and sell them too. Do you guys have any books on worm raising?" A general letter of complaint from a New York correspondent stated that

Some time ago I remitted a check in advance payment for a subscription to the magazine *Approach* which, as you know, is the Naval Aviation monthly for pilots. I received a notice thereafter advising me that my subscription would begin with the August issue of said magazine. This morning's mail brought not *Approach* but *Agricultural Research* with two cows grinning at me from the cover. The only interest I have in farming is the farmer's daughter, and the only chickens I'm interested in come frozen at the super-market. I hope the farmer who's getting my *Approach* doesn't get reckless with his tractor and try a snap roll over church on Sunday morning. Can you look into it for me, please?

In order to assist in answering such questions, Documents Division reference files are maintained in such fashion that entry can be made by subject, title, or author. For example, a question concerning a publication such as "Growing Potatoes in Virginia" can be identified using the major locator "growing," or under files on "potatoes," or by isolating subject titles on "Virginia."

By far, the highest percentage of orders for government

publications comes as a result of the Public Documents Division's own promotional mailings, including the Selected List of Government Publications and special inserts concerning new or unusually interesting offerings. The Selected List, as already noted, is unbelievably productive, showing a return-order rate of more than 52 per cent. Names and addresses, formerly held on address plates, have recently been placed on magnetic tape for better servicing. A high-speed label printer operating from this tape prepares 5-line address labels at a rate of 135,000 per hour. Other new equipment inserts and seals envelopes, and fixes labels. Each month, 25,000 changes are made to this list.

Through an ingenious color-rotation scheme, order forms from the selected list are coded for quick sorting. Mail generated from this source is sorted by color and by list, and forwarded to the *Order Blank and Selective Item Unit* of the *Order Processing Section.* This mail presently is handled on a 10-working-day cycle. Stacks of publications are stored in bins in exact order form order. Clerks draw items by number, insert publications in either envelopes, cartons, or "jiffy bags" and place them on conveyors. These conveyors carry packages to a mail sack area where items are placed in mail bags and dropped by spiral chute to the basement of the Government Printing Office, where a multiple conveyor system forwards sacked mail under North Capitol Street to the Washington Post Office.

Letter orders—that is, requests for publications in letter form—are subjected to a series of sortings. First, single publication requests are isolated, and then subsorted according to predesignated documents storage locations, most of which are keyed to specific agencies, i.e., Agriculture, Interior, Commerce, etc. Clerks fill orders from shelf or bin stock and package and mail in much the same fashion described above. Letter orders for more than one publication are forwarded to the *Cash Mail Section* where clerks locate preprinted cards representing each document requested. This card identifies the storage location of a particular publication. Cards, one for each document, are sent together with the letter orders, to a scheduling desk where both letters and cards are identified as a multiple order. Letters are sent by pneumatic tube to the Order Processing Section and cards to the proper storage units where publications are drawn. Orders are reassembled with the original letter orders and then wrapped and mailed in the regular manner. Cycle time is approximately twenty minutes for this system. One exception to this routine exists. On orders amounting to $20 or more, individual orders are registered and, for obvious reasons, tracing records maintained.

The actual wrapping and mailing of orders is done by the *Mailing Section* of the Distribution Services Branch.

Distribution involves not only response to individual mail-order requests for publications but much more. Under existing law, departments of the government can engage the Documents Division's distribution capability to place individual or selected items in the hands of the public. This is done on a reimbursable basis, with the Documents Division recovering all costs. These publications may be printed by the Government Printing Office, a contractor, or by the departments themselves. The Superintendent of Documents, however, has the option of accepting or refusing such work based upon an evaluation of his current workload.

Departments and agencies of the government are leaning more and more toward periodical publishing, and the list of dated periodicals grows steadily. About 400 publications are presently handled by the Documents Division on a regular publication routine, and servicing their subscription lists is a sizable task. In excess of 1,200 separate mailing lists are maintained in the Division's *Periodicals Services Branch.* This unit processes all subscriptions for periodicals and is responsible for addressing, label preparation, and list maintenance. It is equipped with inserting, sealing, collating, folding, and mailing machines, as well as duplicating machinery for reproduction of forms and letters used in servicing periodical accounts.

The Distribution Services Branch is also charged with distribution to the depository library system. At the present time, there are nearly 1,000 such authorized depositories for government documents.

THE DEPOSITORY LIBRARY SYSTEM

The Depository Library Act of 1962 set the theoretical total of designated depositories at 1,340, but due to redistricting after each decennial census, some congressional districts now have three official depositories. Once a library becomes an official depository, it cannot be removed from the list and another designated in its place when a new member of Congress is elected. The Superintendent of Documents, however, can purge it from the list if the library fails to comply with the laws governing the operation of a depository.

The 1962 Act introduced a new dimension to the government documents depository system. It authorized the designation of not more than two libraries in each state and commonwealth as regional depositories. Designation of such libraries was vested in the senators, and in the case of Puerto Rico, the resident commissioner. Regional depositories must already be official depositories and must be approved by the top library authority in the state. The major difference between regional and regular depositories is the requirement that regional depositories accept and retain at least one copy of all government publications made available to depositories. This includes not only printed but microfacsimile material as well. Other responsibilities include interlibrary loan, reference service, and assistance for regular depositories in the disposal of unwanted government publications.

Regular depositories receive one copy of all publications of the U.S. Government, but on a preselected basis. Lists of groups and series of government publications are supplied to depositories for use in determining the types of documents they wish to receive.

The mechanics of depository library distribution are simple to explain, but with the numbers of depositories growing almost daily and the flood of new publications, plus the changes in selections by depositories, distribution is complex in actual operation. The *Planning Service Division* (see Chart I) has the responsibility for seeing that work jackets for printing carry the numbers of copies needed for depository use. This information is forwarded by the Documents Division's *Library Section*, which, receives amendments to depository choices. Since depositories are permitted to select any item printed by the government that is not classified or intended strictly for the internal administrative use of the ordering agency, the number of documents distributed to depositories is quite large —nearly 10 million items in 1968. This total includes material printed by the Government Printing Office, work contracted for by the Government Printing Office, and a substantial amount of printing produced in departmental plants or ordered by departments directly from private contractors.

THE DOCUMENTS DIVISION'S LIBRARY SECTION

One of the most vital assignments relegated to the Documents Division by the Act of 1895 was the preparation and publication of monthly, annual, and biennial indexes. This task is performed by the Library Section. The monthly list, known not too surprisingly as the *Monthly Catalog of U.S. Government Publications,* is compiled by title and serial number. The price, if a sale item, is also listed. An annual index is issued for each volume and is of inestimable value to librarians and others having a need for keeping in touch with government publishing. This unit also compiles the *Numerical Lists and Schedule of Volumes of Congressional Documents and Reports,* which is specifically called for in the law.

The Library Section also prepares the list of publications from which depositories make their selections—*The Annotated Class List of U.S. Government Publications.* This list is revised and issued annually, and depositories may choose to receive certain items, stop others, or rework their lists of selections at any time. For convenience's sake, available documents are divided into classes. At the present time, there are some 2,200 subject areas. Many of these classes are numbered and refer to specific issuances. For example, a depository may elect to receive all of the Geological Survey's Water Supply papers, or all of the Department of Agriculture's Farmers Bulletins. As one might suspect, assembling this data is a continuing process, subject to constant amendment, consolidation, or reclassification.

The Library Section employs about a dozen professional librarians, and a complement of technicians, library assistants, and clerk-typists. Much of this staff's available time is spent cataloging documents for inclusion in the Documents library.

Of special interest is the unique system of classification for government publications known as the Superintendent of Documents' Classification System. It was first explained by William Leander Post, who was then in charge of the library, in the preface to the *List of Publications of the Agriculture Department, 1862–1902, Department List No. 1,* issued by the Superintendent of Documents in 1904. Post assigned credit for originating the system to Adelaide R. Hasse, who first employed it in cataloging Agriculture Department publications for 1841 to 1895 while she was assistant librarian in the Los Angeles Public Library. (The Agriculture Department published this listing as its *Library Bulletin No. 9* in 1896.) The system has been expanded as government cataloging has grown, but in essence it still reflects the original work of Miss Hasse.

The system groups together publications of any government author—the "author" being federal bureaus, departments, and agencies. The organizational structure of the U.S. Government is followed, with each executive department and agency, the judiciary, Congress, and other major independent establishments assigned a place in the scheme determined by alphabetical designations—as "A" for Agriculture, "JU" for Judiciary, and "NS" for National Science Foundation.

To identify subordinate bureaus and offices, numbers are added to the symbols. The figure "1," for example, designates the parent organization and the secretary's or administrator's office. Subordinate bureaus are assigned other numerical identifiers and a period follows the combination of letters and numbers. The second breakdown identifies series of publications common in government, and this number is followed by a colon. For example: 1:annual reports; 4:circulars; 8:handbooks and manuals. Tie-in publications pertaining to large groupings are indicated by a shilling mark: 4: circulars; 4/a: separates from circulars (numbered); 4/b: separates from circulars (unnumbered). The class stem is thus created for various series of publications: A1.10: Agriculture Yearbook; A77.22: Agricultural Research Service, *USDA Consumer Expenditure Survey Report*. Individual book numbers follow the class stem. For example, Department of Agriculture Leaflet 381 would be A1.35:381. Its second revision would be A1.35:381/2.

Generally, these are the rudiments of the system although it should be noted that congressional documents and documents of certain other author-departments receive special treatment too detailed for this volume.

A basic weakness of this system of classification is that, because it is dependent upon the organizational structure of the government for its rational order, changes in the fundamental position of subordinate bureaus and offices under departments or the creation of new departments and subsequent transfers of bureaus upset the classification scheme. However, it must be said that the system has withstood the test of time and with a few basic alterations still satisfies the needs of librarians for a government document classification discipline. (The Library of Congress does not use this system but relies on the standard Dewey Decimal System for government documents.)

We have seen that the first Superintendent of Documents decided very early that an urgent need existed for a complete library of government publications and set out to correct this deficiency. He was exceptionally successful. Although there are a number of publications issued prior to 1895 of which no copy can be found, the Documents Division library today contains the most nearly complete set of government publications in existence—some 1.9 million books, pamphlets, and maps. In 1968, its acquisitions amounted to 28,455 items. Of course, compared to the Library of Congress collection of nearly 60 million items and 1.5 million annual rate of acquisitions, the GPO collection is small. But this library is all the more remarkable in that when the Office of the Superintendent of Documents was created, its stock was obtained from overages returned by libraries or extra material given irregularly by Government Printing Office customers.

Readers wishing additional information regarding the items in this library or those on sale through the excellent educational resources service of the Public Documents Division are advised to write to:

The Superintendent of Documents, Government Printing Office, Washington, D.C. 20402

VII

GPO Relationships with Congress and Other Agencies

The Government Printing Office is among that small but select group of agencies in the legislative branch—a group that also includes the General Accounting Office and the Library of Congress. Not unnaturally, the GPO traditionally has been oriented toward congressional service and inclined to respond more smartly to legislative requirements than to those of the executive and judicial branches—even though its mandate covers *all* government printing.

Early Congresses provided the drive that resulted in the establishment of a captive printing service within the Government, and from the very start, Congress, through its committee system, exercised authority over the majority of Government Printing Office activities. In 1875, Chief Justice Morrison R. Waite of the Supreme Court stated that "the Government Printing Office superintendent seems to have a department of his own, in which he is in a sense supreme. Certainly he is not under control of any of the executive departments. Apparently he is more responsible to Congress than to any other authority." This view held true for many years. In a House Appropriation Committee hearing in 1928, George H. Carter, the Public Printer at that time, declared:

Senator Root once said in a debate in the Senate that the Printing Office is an anomaly in our system of administration; it is

132

neither under Congress nor any executive department. The Public Printer is appointed by the President and confirmed by the Senate, but other than that the President does not exercise any active control of its management. The Joint Committee on Printing acts as board of directors for the GPO and to that body the Public Printer has to look for advice and counsel, and for the approval of many of his purchases, such as paper and machinery. Otherwise, the GPO is an absolutely independent establishment and the Public Printer has to assume entire and sole responsibility for its management. However, the Joint Committee exercises, and has always exercised, in my experience of twenty years, a very close and keen observation over the operation of the Office. Our purchases of machinery have to be submitted to that committee.

But despite all this and a Comptroller General's decision in 1932 that the Government Printing Office was a part of the legislative branch, in 1943, an Act of Congress relating to the military deferment of persons employed by the government stated: "For the purposes of this section . . . the GPO . . . shall . . . be deemed an agency in the executive branch of the Government."

THE GPO's CONGRESSIONAL INFORMATION SECTION

Although there may be confusion as to the Government Printing Office's position in the organizational scheme, its first loyalty is clear cut. Relations with the Congress and congressional staffs are very close. The GPO's Planning Division maintains a special Congressional Information Section that is the focus of attention for members of Congress and committee personnel. If the city desk on a newspaper has a government counterpart, it would have to be the desk of the Chief of the Congressional Information Section. At the outset of a new session of Congress, inquiries to this unit reach a fever pitch. On the first day of the Ninety-First Congress, for example, on top of an already scarcely normal workload, nearly 3,000 public bills were ordered printed. Although a public bill is printed in only about 2,800 copies (private bills call for 900 copies), each one is given special handling to assure on-time delivery. The Congressional Information Section is the printing control and contact point not only for the 535 members of Congress, but also for the several thousand staff people serving those members and the legislative infrastructure. As presently organized, there are thirty-seven standing committees of the House and Senate. To the casual student of the legislative process, printing may appear to be of relatively minor importance to committee action. But measured by the urgency as expressed to the Congressional Information Section, it would seem to be indispensable to the orderly actions of the nation's highest deliberative body.

Bills and stationery vie with each other for first place in printing orders. Even after the flood introduced in the early days of a session, bill printing averages about 200 per day throughout a session. Stationery serves as an advertising medium for the Congress, inasmuch as a new Congress, after reorganization, is alive with fresh committee assignments, which all committee letterheads carry. Many members also list their committee positions on their official letterheads. Naturally, new stationery becomes one of the first items required from the Government Printing Office.

Following hard on the heels of the flurry of activity on stationery come questions and complaints to the Congressional Information Section on the *Congressional Directory*. This 1,000-page volume is printed for each session and contains everything from names and addresses of members of Congress and most major government officials in all three branches, to names of those authorized admission to the press galleries. The alphabetical list of members of Congress also carries notations as to which are married, which have unmarried daughters, and "those having other ladies with them."

The majority of inquiries concern the personal biographies, which are a vital part of the Directory. Most requests for additions, changes, and deletions are referred to the Joint Committee on Printing, whose staff assembles this material and is, in effect, the preparer and publisher of this document. But habitually, most staff assistants and clerks contact the Chief of the Congressional Information Section for assistance and guidance.

After the initial flush of opening business, as Congress settles into its busy routine, inquiries accelerate concerning the bread and butter of the legislative processes—hearings and committee prints. Hearings are fairly straightforward matters, although their production occasions questions concerning schedules and numbers of copies. Committee prints are quite another kind of animal. For the uninitiated, these prints contain majority opinions, minority views, and occasionally "individual views" or "separate views." What is carried in these working papers is consistently vital to the passage or failure of legislation. Committee prints are therefore always "hot" and always attract the most urgent sort of attention. They carry a very short-time deadline. Most committees meet at 10:00 A.M., and rarely is committee print copy available far enough in advance to allow routine handling. When assessing the liaison work of the Congressional Information Section it helps to remember that this small unit—four people—handles more than $20 million in congressional printing and binding annually. Nor can we forget the enormous interest of our legislators and their staffs in what appears daily in the Number One publication of the Government Printing Office, the *Congressional Record*. The error rate of the *Record* is the envy of every printer, but errors do creep in, and when they do, the telephone traffic to the Congressional Information Section rises sharply. Several years ago, to the embarrassment of the Government Printing Office, Mr. Blatnick, the distinguished and very senior congressman from Minnesota, was listed in the *Record* as Mr. Beatnik. In another document, an article on a trip of President Lyndon B. Johnson's to California was headed, "President Johnson on a Fun Raising Trip to California." Calls on this item, in which some employee helpfully forgot the "d," were definitely unfunny.

Another recurring inquiry concerns the prayer that opens each congressional day and is printed in the *Record*. At regular intervals, this prayer is offered by a rabbi. When the word God appears in a Jewish prayer in the *Record,* it is set as "G-d," since Hebraic use of the word "God" itself is thought to deify the actual document on which it is printed and GPO style therefore dictates the use of a dash between the "G" and the "d." Rarely does this appear without drawing a number of questions from the "Hill" and from the subscribers and readers of the *Record*.

The Joint Committee on Printing

Although the GPO has day-to-day contact with the Joint Committee on Printing, its "board of directors," most of its relationships with the Committee are more or less routine. But since this body is charged with using "any measure it considers necessary to remedy neglect, delay, duplication, or waste in the public printing and binding and the distribution of Government publications," it becomes a vital and constant force in many activities of the Office. The Joint Committee on Printing not only has statutory authority over the classes of work done outside of the Government Printing Office, as well as full authority over the establishment of printing capabilities elsewhere in government, but contracts between the Government Printing Office and commercial contractors also must be approved by the Joint Committee on Printing.

Perhaps the closest cooperation between the Joint Committee on Printing and the Government Printing Office surfaces in the procurement of printing papers and supplies and equipment. Although the funds for such purchases come from the Government Printing Office's account with the Treasury, the Joint Committee on Printing, through its broad powers of oversight, exercises careful control of major purchases by the Office. This care is especially evident in its monitoring of paper purchases, which amount to about 40 million pounds every three months.

When paper stocks fall below certain levels, the Paper and Materials Control Section of the GPO's Plant Planning Division prepares a purchase request for the amount and type of paper needed to restore the inventory. If the required type of paper is available through an existing contract, the Purchases Division simply calls in delivery on the contract. This contract, of course, must have had prior approval of the Joint Committee on Printing. If the paper is not available on an established contract, the Purchasing Division must resort to procurement on the open market through regular competitive bidding. In this instance, of course, the approval of the Joint Committee on Printing must be obtained before the award to the low bidder. For standard papers, a quarterly contract is let, while the newsprint contract is awarded for an entire year. Cartons and envelope contracts operate over a six-month period.

The members of the Joint Committee on Printing are not, of course, personally involved in the details and complexities of such contracts. The pick-and-shovel work is done by the Committee on Paper Specifications, which is appointed by the Joint Committee on Printing. It consists of thirteen members, including two members of the Joint Committee staff, plus the Staff Director, and the Assistant Staff Director. The Government Printing Office is represented by its Director of Purchases, the Deputy Technical Director, the Planning Manager, the Deputy Comptroller, and the Supervisor of the Paper

Testing Branch. The balance of the membership is made up of departmental representatives and one representative from the National Bureau of Standards. The Staff Director of the Joint Committee on Printing is the chairman. The most recent report of the Committee on Paper Specifications contained 125 pages, and the accompanying schedule recommended purchase of 205 lots of paper totaling 40,218,000 lbs.

A technical subcommittee of the Paper Specifications Committee exercises another rather important function. It is responsible for a document entitled *Government Paper Specification Standards* issued by the Joint Committee on Printing, which contains physical and technical criteria for hundreds of kinds of papers used by the entire federal establishment, and, of course, by the Government Printing Office. Such details as tensile strength, opacity, thickness, curl, grain, color, finish, formation, and cleanliness are all carefully specified for each type of paper.

This manual is in looseleaf form to facilitate changes, and it mandatorily governs types, grades, weights, and colors of government papers. The preface in the current issue explains to prospective suppliers that

> . . . each specification and its standard sample represent the lowest quality of paper that will be accepted. Paper suppliers shall adjust material and processes, and make such tests as may be required, in order to insure the delivery of finished paper complying with the applicable specification and standard sample.

Thus, the Joint Committee on Printing and the Government Printing Office through its prominent representation on this working committee wield considerable influence over the enormous amount of paper used in government.

By the same token, the Joint Committee on Printing makes its authority felt in reviewing all purchases made by the Government Printing Office. Each week, a list of items bought is sent to the committee. Approval for major purchases naturally must be obtained prior to committing funds. Those classes of items requiring previous approval before acquisition are listed in the Joint Committee on Printing's "Government Printing and Binding Regulations." Some examples are cameras, casting machines, cutters, photocomposers, and printing presses. These rules apply to the purchase of printing, binding, and related equipment by any government agency including the GPO.

The Appropriations Committees

Relations with other congressional committees and Congress itself are on an as-needed basis and are concerned chiefly with printing and binding. An exception to this generality is the annual series of hearings on Office appropriations. Since the Government Printing Office proper operates on a revolving fund, it does not face the annual traumatic haggle over operating funds. Except for infrequent requests for additional money to increase this fund, the Office is relieved of this burden. But although the Government Printing Office does not receive an annual appropriation, the Public Printer is not wholly spared the problems of justifying the use of public funds. The Public Documents Division *does* request an annual appropriation, and the Public Printer, as the head of the agency in which this Division reposes, is charged with explaining the Documents Division budget. Since the Government Printing Office is part of the legislative branch, its budget is reviewed and approved by the subcommittees on Legislative Appropriations of both the Senate and the House. Moreover, it is the Public Printer who must review and justify the annual estimates for congressional printing and binding. Each year, this is a major presentation and calls for full-dress treatment. Estimates are prepared for each principal product supplied the Congress. These are twelve in number and in 1969 ranged from the largest category, "Hearings," ($5,050,000), to the smallest, "Publications for International Exchange," ($200,000). The total appropriation was $24.6 million, of which $2.5 million was for the estimated deficiencies in previous appropriations. Herein lies a traditional bone of contention—the deficiency appropriation. It offers a tempting target for probing by committee members who fail to appreciate why the annual estimate for congressional printing cannot be more accurate. The explanation is not simple, and it habitually prompts much lively colloquy between members and the Public Printer.

Estimates for congressional printing and binding for fiscal year 1970 were submitted to the then Bureau of the Budget (now the Office of Management and Budget) nearly two years —September, 1968—in advance of the hearings. These estimates were projections of all orders to be submitted by Congress between July, 1969, and June 30, 1970. Keep in mind that some of the work sent to the Government Printing Office during this period might itself require several years to complete and much time before bills could be submitted for payment. The Public Printer is, in fact, required to forecast price rates as much as five years or more in the future. Pay increases and fluctuating paper prices are but two of the factors that make such a task virtually impossible. The clincher, however, is attempting to predict the volume of work that will be ordered by Congress. The *Congressional Record* offers an excellent example of the dilemma faced by the Public Printer in his estimates.* Despite the fact that many increases are built into his cost projections, they are largely guesswork based on historical data and experience. In 1963, the estimate for *Congressional Record* pages was 22,000. Even though Congress adjourned early—September 26—page volume reached

* Fortunately, not all the work of estimating congressional printing needs must be done entirely by the Public Printer. Projections for congressional printing of the *Federal Register*, including the *U.S. Government Organization Manual*, the *Public Papers of the Presidents of the United States*, the *Weekly Compilation of Presidential Documents*, and the *Supplements to the Code of Federal Regulations* are supplied by the General Services Administration's National Archives and Records Service, Federal Register Division, and become the basis for GPO estimates.

30,089. In 1964, the Public Printer estimated that Congress would order 30,000 *Record* pages. That Congress was extraordinarily lengthy—the full calendar year—and page volume soared to 36,638. The deficit resulting from the estimated volumes for these two years alone totaled about $1.5 million.

Committee hearings are even more difficult to forecast and represent the largest item in appropriation requests. Oftentimes, while the work is done in one fiscal year, the requisition is dated the previous year, and all charges are applied according to that date. This is common in hearing documents, which accumulate throughout the duration of the hearing. Many hearings drag on for months and months awaiting witnesses, and since the printed hearing is almost entirely testimony, the printing schedule proceeds only at the rate at which the hearing proceeds.

Tom Steed of Texas, the able Chairman of the House Subcommittee on Legislative Appropriations, in 1965 attempted to explain to his colleagues the system of deficiency appropriations and why the subcommittee had adopted this method rather than some other method for authorizing funds to the Government Printing Office for congressional printing and binding. In part, he said:

> The difficulty they [the GPO] have always had in knowing how much money they are going to need just more or less forced this system. If we appropriated a lump sum that had $2 or $3 million more than they actually used, you do not know whether to hold that in reserve for those recurring reorders and have surplus money hanging around, or whether to get a supplemental. This just seemed to be the easiest way to do it because you are only putting up money here for what actually happens.

THE CUSTOMER AGENCIES

The distinction of being the GPO's largest customer commonly belongs to the Department of the Army. In 1968,

Army's annual expenditures topped those of Congress by more than $8 million. By contrast, the GPO's smallest customer was the National Capital Transportation Agency, which spent $31.51 with GPO in 1968. Among the more than one hundred clients ordering printing, binding, or service, the Army and Congress are followed in annual expenditures by the Navy, Air Force, General Services Administration (GSA), and Health, Education, and Welfare (HEW).

All major customer agencies and many smaller ones are organized to include publications offices. Most are staffed with highly qualified technicians, many of whom are expatriates from the Government Printing Office. A high percentage have strong publication-planning backgrounds. This is both a source of pride and exasperation for the Office. Pride stems from the knowledge that those trained in the methods and procedures at the Government Printing Office now wield great power and influence in the exciting world of government printing. Their experience and technical and administrative know-how makes the enormous publishing effort of the federal establishment move. Exasperation often results from the very same qualities that inspire pride—the inclination of exceptionally effective publications managers to introduce detailed technical directions into administrative requisitioning channels. The final effect of this is to literally peek over the shoulder of the Government Printing Office's production team and make unnecessary suggestions. Such attempts on the part of departmental publications people invariably create shallow conflicts. Happily, this is an inconvenience, not a deterrent, to effective production. The accepted response by the Government Printing Office is a polite "thank you, but you just tell us what you want and we will supply it."

Perhaps the most abrasive matter with which the Government Printing Office must contend is a first cousin to that discussed above. This is the subject of pricing and billing. Because most customer agencies operate on fixed publications budgets, their interest in prices is understandably great. This fact was instrumental in bringing about the "firm estimate" policy some years ago. Many agencies must commit funds for printing by quarterly periods, and, since their estimates are sometimes delayed for numbers of reasons, timeliness becomes vital and is especially important as quarterly deadlines approach. This means that the Government Printing Office is constantly faced with the specter of insufficient recovery for services performed. Unless its prices reflect its costs of production, this specter can materialize and become all too real. Only constant fiscal alertness to all cost elements brings a measure of order and keeps the Office on the black side of the ledger. But, unfortunately, this does not mean that agency publications officials are always sympathetic with the GPO's fiscal problems. Although rate increases are no more palatable to the Government Printing Office than to its clients, and are only reluctantly applied when other alternatives are impractical, rising costs of labor and material in recent years have forced the issue. Such occasions frequently bring inquiries on the relative cost of printing in the Government Printing Office as compared with outside firms, and periodically the Government Printing Office is called upon to defend its prices against complaints that it charges too much. In every case, it has been shown that GPO prices are competitive with those in the industry.

For a number of very good reasons, the GPO restricts information that actually pinpoints charges. Printing is in most respects a custom operation, with one job seldom exactly like another. Publishing the scale of prices, which is composed almost entirely of exceptions to standard charges, would, it is believed, surely lead to great confusion among customers attempting to judge what would apply to a specific job. To give a few examples, some foreign language composition might be charged at double price. But composing the more familiar tongues such as French or Spanish might only call for one-

and-a-half times the regular price. If a halftone engraving is made in magnesium metal, it might cost only two-thirds of the cost of a copper engraving, but there are instances—not necessarily apparent to customers—in which magnesium is unsuitable. The imponderables in presswork that alter the standard scale of prices number in the dozens. Among these are printing on gummed stock or cloth-lined stock; overprinting, perforating, scoring, or slitting on press; and extra press washups. The same applies to operations at every stage of production. Many decisions must be made immediately before or even during the production cycle that can drastically influence the final price to a customer. It should also be remembered that the GPO keeps a running check on cost recovery in order to keep its activities in the black. This necessitates periodic revision to the scale of prices which would be further complicated if these scales were widely distributed to agencies.

Other factors color both pricing and productivity in the GPO, and in opposite ways. For instance, the Office labor costs are a cut above those in industry generally, and its fringe benefits, including federally supported hospitalization, insurance, and annual and sick leave, are especially good—and costly. Volume buying on a competitive-bid basis, however, offers a solid advantage to the government. Additional savings are attributable to the fact that the GPO pays neither rent nor taxes. Thus, GPO operating costs are lower than private industry's conveniently offsetting its somewhat higher labor costs. As for productivity, GPO output-per-craftsman averages compare favorably with commercial output, although such comparisons are difficult to make accurately. When man workloads for machine composition are contrasted with commercial figures available, the GPO averages are several hundred ems-per-hour greater than job plant averages and considerably more than that as compared to newspaper averages. Some claim that this disparity is due to inconsistencies in comparing workloads and classes of work. Probably the continuous flow of work in the GPO, with few gaps in the stream, has more to do with the high productivity than any superiority on the part of GPO journeymen. Still, from time to time, craftsmen who apparently have been adequate performers elsewhere cannot hold a GPO job because of an inability to maintain what the Office considers satisfactory machine production.

From time to time, when commercial plant workloads are light, printing firms submit bids at, or even below, manufacturing costs in order to maintain production tempo. When this occurs, the commercial price for a specific job can drop below GPO costs. But regular cost reviews of work procured through commercial contracts continue to bear out the contention that the cost of obtaining printing from private printers shows no appreciable benefit over the costs of obtaining it from the Government Printing Office. Since the Office is the largest buyer of printing in the nation, these reviews can hardly be overlooked or ignored. Despite these facts, agencies occasionally seek authority to buy directly from commercial sources, either because they desire special effects or results or are convinced that under a unique set of circumstances they will be able to realize savings. Machinery exists for enabling an agency to do this, but only within rather narrow limitations. Section 504, title 44, U.S. Code states that

> The Joint Committee on Printing may permit the Public Printer to authorize an executive department, independent office, or establishment of the Government to purchase direct for its use such printing, binding, and blank book work, otherwise authorized by law, as the Government Printing Office is not able or suitably equipped to execute or as may be more economically or in the better interest of the government executed elsewhere.

Relatively few waivers are granted annually—something on the order of a few hundred out of a total job input numbering about 350,000. Long experience has demonstrated the wisdom and economy of such a policy. Routine and special audits of bills for work done on waivers seldom show either lower costs or any identifiable advantage to the government or to the ordering department. In the majority of instances, GPO "know-how" and a wide familiarity with the printing capabilities of most of the nation's largest and best-qualified printing houses suggest that the interests of the government are best served by permitting the Government Printing Office to produce the printing in house or itself place such contracts with the industry.

An excellent example of agency/GPO cooperative effort is shown annually in the production of the enormous and complicated requirements of the Internal Revenue Service (IRS). Many different types of products are turned out each year, and—as every taxpayer knows—they become the principal revenue-collecting instrument for the U.S. Government. Most taxpayers fail to realize the care with which these forms are designed and manufactured, or the painstaking study and planning that take place to make the forms readable and simple to execute. (But does the recipient of a sting notice the bright body colors and diaphanous wings of the bee?) Long-standing intimacy between the Internal Revenue Service and its printer, the Government Printing Office, has produced an innovative series of changes, both in format and manufacturing methods. One worthy of mention is the technical wrinkle that permitted use of both writing paper and newsprint in the No. 1 tax package. Ink-receptive stock for that part of the tax form which is completed by the taxpayer, and newsprint for the instructional material, is interleaved, printed, folded, slit, and pasted on press. The effect of this production gimmick is a whopping savings in stock costs.

A number of years ago, the IRS indicated an interest in using a preprinted, piggyback label on its largest tax package. This label, designed to offset taxpayer errors in personal identification such as social security numbers, street addresses, and names, was intended to serve as an address for sending the forms to the prospective taxpayer and as an accurate identification of the taxpayer returning his completed tax form. The key to its use was a die-cut window in the cover of the package. GPO officials were told by experts in web-press production that die-cutting high speed webs of paper was a technological impossibility. But since the requirement for this package exceeded 30 million copies, both schedule and cost favored web-press printing. At this point, the GPO's own experts got busy with IRS technicians. Between them, they designed and satisfactorily printed with rotary dies on the web cylinders. The result made practical the use of the piggyback label and reduced incorrect entries by taxpayers to an acceptable level.*

A more recent and somewhat more visual departure from the familiar appearance of income tax forms came in January, 1969. In that month, over 30 million taxpayers were treated to a multicolor invitation from the Internal Revenue Service. Dark blue ink was used for the body of the form, and bright red spot lines highlighted the key parts. Some taxpayers in the East were even more startled to find a blue tint printed over the entire form with only entry spaces left completely white.

Color in tax forms is hardly new. In 1954, instructions were printed in blue and in the Philadelphia region, a reddish-brown color was employed in 1960. But the use of two-color forms in 1969 ('68 tax year) was an abrupt departure from tradition. It was introduced not without some pain. Initially, discussions were held with the Joint Committee on Printing staff, since the use of color must, according to the Committee's printing and binding regulations, make a "demonstrably valuable contribution" to the product. The Government Print-

---

* One negative effect of this innovation was the inability of commercial contractors to supply such forms on GPO contracts. Consequently, this package was produced in plant until 1967. In that tax year, a large business-forms firm using much of the die-cutting know-how developed in the Government Printing Office obtained the contract to produce this package. Today, several firms possess this capability. But even so, the broad bidding base that the GPO enjoys on most work was, and still is, somewhat restricted by this special requirement.

ing Office felt at the outset that the enormous requirement would severely limit the bidding competition as few firms were able to produce and deliver such quantities on schedule. The Internal Revenue Service's position centered on two considerations—improved readability and the promise of reducing taxpayer errors still further. IRS figures showed that out of 76 million tax returns, about 7 million contained mistakes of some sort. Nearly 2 million social security numbers alone were either omitted completely or were in error. Officials estimated the cost for correction approached nearly $2 per error. Supposedly, color highlighting could significantly lower the taxpayer error rate and, therefore, the costs associated with tax collection. After a round of meetings, general agreement was reached, and the Joint Committee on Printing approved the two-color form. The Government Printing Office had some reservations concerning its ability to procure the forms within projected costs and on schedule. But since it did not possess an in-house two-color capability of sufficient magnitude to guarantee delivery and was faced with a heavy congressional workload planned for its high-speed web equipment, there appeared to be no other feasible course of action but to acquiesce and buy the forms commercially.

The 1968 tax form program began in mid-October of that year. The GPO's own presses required nine weeks of around-the-clock production to complete the in-plant portion of the work and used about 4 million pounds of paper and 25,000 pounds of ink in printing nearly 11 million 48-page booklets. These booklets were packed in 100,000 cartons and shipped directly to Internal Revenue Service distribution centers across the nation. Commercial contractors used an additional 13 million pounds of paper in preparing the 32 million two-color packages.

The results of this program were very successful, and somewhat of a surprise to everyone, with final costs for the forms below expectations. Unfortunately, an analysis of the accuracies traceable to the use of two-color forms were rather inconclusive, principally because of the relatively small sampling—200,000 forms—but IRS officials were satisfied that in two particularly troublesome spots the two-color forms showed a definite improvement over the one-color form. These were the social-security-number entry and the signature block spaces. The Internal Revenue Service claimed a more than 50 per cent drop in errors and omissions. At $2 per correction projected over the 2 million errors recorded in the previous year, $2 million in correction costs alone were probably avoided.

The services offered by the Government Printing Office to other government agencies generally parallel those which may be found in any well-staffed printing house. Although requisitioning procedures are pretty much standardized, a sizable cadre of specialists and technicians is available for consultation with agency representatives having unusual graphic arts problems. Technical conferences with departmental printing people are encouraged in the interest of both efficiency and economy. The Typography and Design Division, for example, is organized to provide advice on copy preparation to agencies very early in the planning stages. Oftentimes, prior to the development of either text or illustrations, departmental technicians confer with layout and format specialists to determine how best to present material for printing. Suggestions as to methods of printing, paper and cover stock, typefaces for body and display, and money-saving shortcuts are some of the subjects thoroughly aired in these meetings.

The use of color often pits the departmental publications people against officials of the Typography and Design Division representing the GPO. Under current regulations of the Joint Committee on Printing, any use of color in government documents must be justified in accordance with very specific guidelines. In such matters, compliance with these regulations is a function delegated to the GPO. The fundamental basis for controversy stems from the departments' never-ending competition for readership attention, in which agency representatives feel that color gives their publications a definite advantage. Consequently, they strive to include multicolor material in many of their printed pieces. Because of the additional cost and time required to produce this type of work, control is necessary, and the Government Printing Office is given authority to arbitrate these matters. If the work meets the criteria established by the Joint Committee on Printing, no problems are presented. However, if the ordered printing fails to meet Committee guidelines for color printing, or is marginal, the Government Printing Office must indicate approval or disapproval. Usually, when the Government Printing Office refuses to recommend the use of additional colors, the matter is closed, but in instances when agency representatives feel strongly about a certain job and cannot convince officials of the Typography and Design Division that multicolor printing is justified, the agency can appeal directly to the Joint Committee on Printing.

Color is not the only matter adjudicated by the Government Printing Office. The excessive use of illustrative matter, illustrations not entirely related to the transaction of public business or tending to aggrandize individuals, or illustrations that are not in good taste or are offensive to "proper sensibilities," are also subject to scrutiny by GPO officials acting as watchdogs for compliance with Joint Committee on Printing regulations. This quasi-regulatory function of the Government Printing Office occasionally tends to create friction in the Office's relationships with customer agencies.

COMMISSION RELATIONSHIPS

One of the most difficult situations bearing on GPO customer relationships develops when for any number of reasons temporary committees or Presidential commissions are created to study, report findings, and recommend actions. Overnight, a staff is assembled, frequently with membership both from within and without the federal establishment—some experienced and others total newcomers to publication management. In most instances, these temporary commissions are satellited on a regular agency for administrative support. It is not surprising, therefore, that the clear, familiar lines of authority sometimes become badly tangled, with resulting disruptive effect on service agencies such as the Government Printing Office.

The Warren Commission, or the President's Commission on the Assassination of President Kennedy, is an example. It was formed on November 29, 1963, seven days after John F. Kennedy was killed in Dallas. Almost a year to the day after the Commission was formed, the Warren Commission Report, consisting of twenty-six volumes, was released to the public. In the interim, this enormous study—nearly 18,000 pages— not only was printed and bound, but was manufactured under the strictest sort of security. The job of pagination and the use of footnotes and exhibit material created almost insurmountably difficult problems for the printer. Added to this was a gigantic correction undertaking complicated by the use of nearly twenty consulting attorneys, most of whom worked in their home offices scattered across the country.

The manuscript for the report began coming to the Government Printing Office in sizable increments in early May, 1964. The Composing Division, which nicknamed the Warren Report "The Monster," had the responsibility for putting the manuscript into type. As report folios were set into galleys of type, proofs were pulled and sent to the Commission for revision. Usually, proofs went to consultants for reading in distant cities. On the return of the proofread material, which had already received two readings by the Government Printing Office, corrections were made. The next step was page makeup and proofing. Page proofs, after again being double-read by the Government Printing Office, were dispatched to the Commission, which repeated the distribution to consultants for further review and correction.

At the Commission proper, it was not unusual for five to ten proofs to be given to staff and secretarial assistants for reading. An Office technician was assigned to the commission to help transcribe the multiple corrections sometimes made by a half dozen people to a single "R," or revise proof. This proof then became the basis for revision by the GPO. By far the greatest number of changes consisted of editorial changes or departures from the original manuscript. This, of course, constitutes the most expensive type of correction, known in the trade as "author's alterations." Such alterations, frequently calling for a complete reset of one or more pages, are an anathema to printers. Often they require repagination of a complete volume and frequently reindexing.

Ostensibly in the interest of speed, the Commission, when the first copy was sent to the Government Printing Office, appended a rather lengthy list of key words to be spotted and checked for spelling. "Neeley" Street was to be changed to "Neely" Street, and "DeMar," which was spelled five different ways in the manuscript—De Mar, Demar, Demarr, DeMarr, and DeMar—were among those to be corrected. In point of fact, this type of correction could have better been accomplished in the manuscript and would have been much less expensive—and time-consuming.

Because of the size of this single job and its explosive contents, special security measures were necessary. Monitors were assigned to watch production activities throughout the entire production period from May until October. Both staff and equipment were physically isolated. Despite these unusual precautions, when the late Dorothy Kilgallen, in an exclusive *New York Journal American* story, quoted word-for-word testimony by Jack Ruby, the GPO security system came under suspicion. A painstaking investigation satisfied GPO officials and Commission members alike that the leak did not emanate from the Office. However, it was never satisfactorily explained where Miss Kilgallen did obtain her information. Chances are, as *Newsweek* stated in its issue of August 31, 1964: "Although the Commission has tried to maintain a screen of secrecy, it has been as effective as a sieve. While the leakage has been kept to a minimum in Washington, newsmen in Dallas and other cities have easily breached Commission security." The GPO came out with completely clean hands despite literally hundreds of employees being exposed daily to information that media representatives eagerly sought. An Associated Press story summed up the security situation: "The Printing Office has an impeccable reputation of preventing leaks on secret government documents and advance leaks on publications with future release dates."

It should be noted that no criticism of the value of temporary and special commissions is intended here. Despite the administrative and communications problems, the end-products of such bodies are almost without exception factual, well-organized, quality publications that testify to the flexibility and mutual adaptability of both the Government Printing Office staff and the staffs assembled by these commissions. Certainly, the Warren Commission Report was an outstanding demonstration of what can be achieved under the most awkward and adverse conditions imaginable.

THE GPO AND THE WHITE HOUSE

There still remains one special relationship to discuss. That is the association between the Government Printing Office and the White House. The consanguinity between the President (usually as represented by his staff) and the Government Printing Office is as close or as remote as the President desires. Some chief executives take a great interest in what happens at the GPO, possibly remembering the often extraordinary accomplishments of the Office in printing their speeches in the *Congressional Record* when they were members of Congress. Others rarely acknowledge the existence of the agency once they have nominated a new Public Printer or decided to continue an incumbent in the position. They concern themselves with the larger problems which they inherit, and the Public Printer is left largely alone to fulfill his less spectacular commitments.

Occasionally, Presidential authority over GPO operations is tested—not always with success. For example, in 1906, President Theodore Roosevelt directed that the Public Printer adopt a revolutionary spelling reform for all government printing. His action was inspired by his evident enthusiasm for the work of the Spelling Reform Committee, a group headed by Professor Brander Matthews and financed by philanthropist Andrew Carnegie. This committee was composed of a number of distinguished educators and scholars. The outcome of their continuing study was a list of 300 words that they recommended be spelled according to a simplified and logical pattern. The Public Printer received a letter from the President instructing him: "Please hereafter direct that in all Government publications of the Executive Departments the 300 words enumerated in circular shall be spelled as therein set forth. If anyone asks the reason for the action, refer him to Circulars 3, 4, and 6 as issued by the Simplified Spelling Board." The effect of this directive came as a thunderclap in the English-speaking community. Battle lines formed and the news media took up the cudgel and mace. Opponents greatly outnumbered the advocates, but the storm raged hotly. Newspapers throughout the country printed news stories, editorials, the list of offending 300 words, and Letters to the Editor departments were swamped.

Most of the words were merely standardized and simplified. "Plough" was made "plow," "programme" was made "program," and "honour" was made "honor," for example. But when "though" was made "tho" and "through" was made "thru," and fifty-two past participles were phoneticized, such as "fixt" for "fixed" and "exprest" for "expressed," it was too much for the traditionalists. The *New York Times* of August 25, 1906, prematurely reported that the President's directive would rapidly advance the cause of spelling reform. Tongue in cheek, the *New York World* of the same date suggested that under the reformed spelling system, a Thanksgiving proclamation might appear; "When nearly three centuries ago, the first settlers kam to the kuntry which has bekom this grat republick, tha confronted not only hardship and privashun, but terible risk of their lives. . . . The kustum has bekum nashnul and hallowed by immemorial usaj."

The order of the President caused a predictable furor in the halls of Congress, chiefly bearing on whether these instructions applied to legislative documents. But since Congress adjourned June 30, no reaction was immediately forthcoming. Not so elsewhere. The New York State Commissioner of Education declared that his department would not follow President Roosevelt. A London paper suggested that "the President overrates his powers." Public Printer Charles A. Stillings was trapped in the middle but on December 3, Congress returned and its mood was decidedly hostile to the idea. The issue was settled summarily when Congress attached as a rider to the printing money bill stating:

> No part of the compensation provided by this act shall be paid to the Public Printer unless he shall, in printing documents authorized by law or ordered by Congress or either branch thereof, conform in the spelling thereof to the rules or orthography recognized and used by accepted dictionaries of the English language.

The vote in the House was 142 to 25, an indication of just how strongly the legislators felt about this matter. Thus, the Congress prevailed over a powerful President. Public Printer Stillings had little choice but to follow the clear-cut directive from Congress, and, because of the absurdity of adopting two systems of spelling—one for executive department printing and one for legislative printing—he could not comply with the previous order from the White House.

In recent years, relations with 1600 Pennsylvania Avenue, or more accurately with the Executive Office of the President next door, have been considerably less controversial. During the Kennedy years, printing was not only routine but included items of special interest. Mrs. Kennedy's luncheons and dinners, both formal and informal, always called for special menus, the copy for which was calligraphed by a White House artist. This copy inspired a personal response on the part of GPO craftsmen to see that the printed results were in high quality and delivered on time. State dinners and special affairs, such as Pablo Casal's appearance, also meant printed programs upon which exceptional care was lavished to supply something out of the ordinary in design and execution. Much the same sort of requirement and reaction to Presidential needs prevailed throughout the Johnson Administration.

As far as the Government Printing Office was concerned, the Johnsons generated every bit as much excitement as their predecessors did. Ladybird's involvement in beautification, as well as the First Family's social schedule, developed a more-than-average amount of printing. The Office's relationships with President Johnson's aides were consistently good. But it was apparent right from the start that Lyndon Johnson knew what he wanted, in printing as in other matters. Thus, when a brochure intended for a remembrance to a select number of figures at or near the power center of the Johnson Administration was delivered to the White House late one snowy Friday, a Presidential aide almost beat the messenger back to the GPO with the word that it wasn't what the President wanted. Despite the proofs and the stock having been previously approved, the GPO set out to correct it. But just enough special paper and cover stock had been purchased to complete the job. After frantic calls to a local paper supply house, a vehicle was sent to the firm's warehouse late at night. The booklet contained a process color halftone of the President, and the white margin of this page carried the President's signature. One complaint was that the color of the signature did not match the ink in the President's pen. The other objection was to the typeface used for the monogram "LBJ" stamped on the cover. It was a Cheltenham face in which the "J" projected below the line of the "L" and "B." Suffice it to say that the GPO corrected both problems and next morning delivered the finished work to the White House lawn where an aide took off by helicopter, followed the Presidential "chopper" to Andrews Air Force Base, and saved the day.

White House printing expenditures are relatively small and devoted to work directly connected to the affairs and activities of the President. The preparation, administration, and funding of other documents in which the White House has a special interest, often are assigned to an executive agency. For example, the series, *The Public Papers of the Presidents*, which was started in 1957, is of continuing importance to the incumbent President, but the National Archives and Records Service of the General Services Administration has the legal responsibility for their execution.

These papers, recommended for compilation by the National Historical Publications Commission, answered the need for an orderly documentation of Presidential messages and official commentary. Except for the period between 1896 and 1899, when Congress authorized the publication of James D. Richardson's extensive work covering Presidential papers from 1789 to 1897, no systematic means for preserving this material existed. In the interim, private compilations were issued, but they did not enjoy the stamp of officialdom. *The Public Papers of the Presidents* is done in hardbound volumes— ordinarily one for each year, although President Johnson's papers had to be divided into two annual volumes because of the large amount of material generated in the White House during his administration. These volumes contain a variety of subject matter, including full textual presentation of Presidential news conferences. Proclamations, executive orders, and similar documents required by law to appear in the *Federal Register* or the *Code of Federal Regulations* are not included but are carried by number and subject in an appendix. Presidential messages and reports required by statute also appear in appendixes.

Each President indicates his personal choice of colors for binding his papers. Truman chose gray and blue; Eisenhower red and black; Kennedy blue and maroon; and Johnson green. Special skins are purchased by the GPO, and a presentation copy is handbound in full leather for the President's personal library. These copies are unique except for sample copies prepared as models and are superb examples of the bookbinder's art. In 1968, Public Printer James L. Harrison and Administrator of the General Services Administration Lawson Knott journeyed to Independence, Missouri, to convey the final volume of the ex-President's papers to Harry Truman for inclusion in the Truman Library.

In all of its relationships with its customer agencies, the Government Printing Office remains a service agency—one staffed and equipped to fulfill a functional mission. Whatever regulatory or control duties which may accrue to it are, as we have seen, drawn from statutory authority delegated or assigned by the Joint Committee on Printing. Relations with the agencies it serves are not without occasional friction, but by and large this friction is confined to familiar problems of schedule and prices and rarely reaches proportions to attract public notice. In the next chapter, we shall examine a few instances when it has—and discuss more everyday relations between the Government Printing Office and the public.

VIII

The GPO and the Public

The GPO's work is performed wholly in the public interest, as is the work of all government agencies. Unlike agencies of lesser visibility, however, it is never far removed from the public's concern and scrutiny. Printing houses, publishers, suppliers, unions, libraries, schools, and research firms make up the GPO's public dominion. Together with the individual citizen, this clientele has a special and often keen interest in what the Government Printing Office is doing.

THE PRINTING INDUSTRY

Contact with many of the nation's printing houses is understandably close. As a buyer of printing and printing services spending in excess of $100 million annually, the GPO usually is a coveted customer for most firms. But not all. Because of the needle-sharp competition and a certain amount of unavoidable red tape connected with selling printing to or through the Office, some private printers steer clear of government printing. Still others consider the Government Printing Office an active rival for printing work, holding the view that the government should not provide services that are available from commercial houses. This latter position varies inversely in intensity as the economic health of the printing industry rises and falls. When the industry is enjoying boom

159

conditions, criticism of government printing is irregular and desultory. The chief, and more or less traditional, antagonist is a loose federation of state and regional employing printers, banded together to promote printing interests and to lobby for these interests. This group opposes the principles of government printing. When times are slow for the industry, opposition ranks swell greatly and complaints about Uncle Sam's printing polarize around this organization.

In attempting to assess the validity of the theory that the government should not compete with the private sector of the economy in printing, a brief overview may be helpful. Quite aside from the convenience and service offered by a proprietary printing activity, the relative share of the nation's printing business represented by the Government Printing Office's volume furnishes a revealing perspective. In recent years, the printing and publishing industry has reflected the steady rise in the nation's gross national product. A rule of thumb pegs printing and publishing volume as contributing about 3 per cent of the national annual output of goods and services. In 1968, printing and publishing volume amounted to about $25 billion. The Government Printing Office's volume in this year was roughly $200 million—or less than 1 per cent of the national total. About half of the GPO work was actually done by commercial printing houses, so that the in-plant volume accounted for less than .5 per cent of the United States's printing and publishing volume.

It should be pointed out, however, that industry groups do not target in exclusively on the Government Printing Office proper. Much of the critical fire is reserved for "field" or "departmental" printing plants, about 330 of which are presently operating. "Field printing" was inaugurated to accommodate exclusively the need for government printed matter outside of the District of Columbia. In 1919, Congress exempted such printing from the mandatory requirement that all work be done in the Government Printing Office, and today a substantial portion of government printing is produced in field plants. In 1961, about fifty of these plants were labeled "departmental printing plants." Of this number, fifteen are now located outside of the District of Columbia.* Some are engaged in producing only maps and charts, but the government also operates plants in Germany, the Panama Canal Zone, Japan, France, Newfoundland, the Marianas, Guantánamo Bay, England, Italy, Puerto Rico, and the Philippines. To give some idea of the magnitude of this type of effort, the plant in Kawasaki, Japan, was a million-dollar operation in 1964.

At the end of World War II, vigorous complaints were heard concerning the absence of control over the proliferation of federally operated printing plants throughout the United States. A survey was conducted jointly by the Government Printing Office and the Bureau of the Budget to provide the Joint Committee on Printing with up-to-date information on the validity of these complaints. The result was the closing of many of the small field plants and the legalization of others where the Joint Committee on Printing recognized "the need for timely in-house and secure printing services." Industry groups have maintained an unrelenting pressure against these smaller plants and this type of federal printing. Undoubtedly, as time goes on and both the government and private industry learn how to operate in concert to meet federal printing needs, more small plants will be closed.

The trend for government to remove itself from printing activities where it is clearly in competition with the private economy has grown, in part because in many instances the government can contract for services heretofore believed its exclusive province. As with the defense agencies' employment of private management firms to study strategic and even tac-

* Although the terms "field" and "departmental" were eliminated in 1969 by the Joint Committee on Printing, the plants and their work are still largely unaffected.

tical problems and military logistics, so is it with printing. The only phase likely to remain sacrosanct is congressional work or top-rated security work in which the national interest must be protected by controlled exposure.

As greater amounts of printing are procured from commercial sources, adequate liaison with all these sources becomes more necessary. Printing being a largely custom operation calls for the closest sort of cooperation between buyer and seller. Faulty or ambiguous specifications must be clarified before production begins. During production, quality control must be maintained and after completion, delivery on schedule guaranteed. At any point in the procurement stream, technicians must be available to ensure that the printing supplier receives whatever assistance he needs to fulfill his contract obligations. These functions are the responsibility of planners in the GPO's Printing Procurement Section, who are constantly in contact with firms printing for the government. Contract compliance officials are also assigned to this Section and are available for trouble-shooting assignments.

THE PUBLISHING INDUSTRY

The publishing industry, as opposed to the printing industry proper, represents quite another relationship for the Government Printing Office. The GPO does not have a publishing function. Everything, except for internal publications, is written and prepared by its clients. This fact is not clearly understood by the public or even by the large majority of publishing houses. There is a more or less constant flow of correspondence from "permissions" departments requesting authority to quote material printed in government documents. This material, unless previously copyrighted and identified as such, rests in the public domain and can be used freely by the public. As a matter of courtesy and information, "permissions" requests are sent to the agencies originating the material by the Government Printing Office. For textual material appearing in hearings or committee proceedings, requests are sent to the committees developing such material. However, all such material by law is available for whatever use any member of the public wishes to make of it.

Some publishing houses derive substantial profit from reprinting government documents. For example, the Commerce Department annually publishes the *Statistical Abstract of the U.S.* It contains a veritable mountain of statistical information on population, industry, and the economic posture of the country. One company literally stands in line for the first copy of this document and rushes it to its printer. Here the pages are photographed and plates sent to press without alteration. The firm prints a colorful cover for the publication, adds a few pages of review and analysis, plus a dash of political, scientific, sports, and art information, and markets it nationwide. This enterprising publishing house reaps a handsome profit for its energy and ingenuity. If desired, the company could purchase "reproducibles"—either plates or reproduction proofs of this publication, as Title 44 U.S. Code provides for the sale of such material to the public.

In recent years, much controversy has developed over the involvement of private publishers in marketing "red-hot" government reports ahead of the Government Printing Office. Considerable hubbub developed over the report of President Johnson's National Advisory Commission on Civil Disorders, which became a gold mine for one publishing firm. The Commission released a limited number of copies of its report on March 3, 1968. The private publisher had books on newsstands two days later, but the GPO's 700-page book was not placed on sale until April 5, prompting complaints that the private firm had been privileged to receive advance copies of the report. Both the Commission and the publisher vehemently denied this. What actually happened was that final correction and "approval to print" delayed the GPO's issue, while the private firm worked directly from the original release unhampered by last-minute changes by the Commission.

The conflict raised by the report on the Chicago disorders occurring during the 1968 Democratic National Convention was more serious—and different in nature. Dubbed the "Walker Report," for Daniel Walker, the Chicago attorney responsible for its preparation, this report became an overnight bestseller. Originally, it was prepared for printing in sufficient copies for official distribution to the Commission, government agencies, and the news media only. Preliminary estimates of the demand for the report were grossly inadequate. Public interest in the findings was kept at fever pitch by the aftermath of the disorders, as charges of "police brutality," acts of provocation on the part of "hippies" and "yippies," and public statements by political figures exacerbated feelings on all sides.

The Defense Department, to which the Commission was satellited for administrative support, had placed the work of printing the report in a Philadelphia plant under a program contract—a standard annual contract for printing awarded by the Government Printing Office. Soon after production began, it became obvious that the controversial nature of the report would bring thousands of orders from the public, but Commission funds for printing the report were too limited to increase the original order. Consequently, representatives of the Commission decided to approach the Public Printer to ask him to print additional copies of the document for public sale. When GPO officials examined the text and illustrative material, they felt that the explicit language and even more explicit photographs made the additional printing of the document solely for public distribution a matter in which they required guidance from the Joint Committee on Printing. Commission representatives felt that the delay entailed would frustrate the purpose of their request. As an alternative, the

Public Printer agreed to print the material if permitted to insert dashes between the initial and final letters of some of the more objectionable words, explaining that precedent existed in the use of this expedient in the *Congressional Record*. The Commission refused to allow this treatment, declaring that the exact language was necessary to the full understanding of the explosive reaction of protestors and police alike. Time prevented further argument, which became academic in any case when the commercial version hit the streets.

Reports in the news media charged the Public Printer with setting himself up as a censor, or an arbiter of public morals. This, of course, was summarily denied. The U.S. Code states that "The Public Printer shall print additional copies of a Government publication, not confidential in character, required for sale to the public, *subject to regulation by the Joint Committee on Printing*" (italics added). Moreover, in its "Printing and Binding Regulations," the Joint Committee on Printing ignores text material but specifically authorizes the use of illustrations only when they, "are in good taste and do not offend proper sensibilities." The outcome was that private publishers and printers alike enjoyed a publicity field day and as a result sold everything they could put together on the Walker Report for weeks after the Commission publicly released the study. Once again, last-minute corrections to the report further delayed the GPO's version. The Commission reportedly explained that alterations to the text as originally released were vital to the accuracy and completeness of the document.

For many years, the public use of information garnered and prepared with the taxpayer's money has been a burning issue for both advocates and opponents of freedom of information. The Government Printing Office usually winds up as the unwitting malefactor in such cases simply because those involved fail to understand fully that the Government Printing Office is legally bound to print whatever it receives. When a requisition is received from a customer agency, if the printing is certified as being "necessary for the public service," the GPO has little choice except to print it. But the Office is constantly drawn into controversy on the propriety of publication. A typical case in point concerned a rather substantial amount of valuable data accumulated by a science-oriented federal agency, and planned for publication. Because of the costs involved, the agency was disinclined to authorize its immediate printing but was aware of the keen interest of the scientific community in having the information available. A private firm offered to publish the material at its own expense and supply the agency with several hundred copies for the agency's use. In return, the firm wished to market the book commercially. A congressional hearing was scheduled to rule on the merits of this proposition, and, naturally, the Government Printing Office was represented at the meeting. An Eastern senator, after listening patiently to the prospective publisher's testimony, said, "Sir, what you are saying is that if the government makes you a gift of an orchard, you will give the government a basket of apples." This statement succinctly sums up the case of those who object to allowing private firms to profit from federally developed information. *Newsweek* magazine put the issue this way: "Where could a publisher find an author who demands no advance, promises endless productivity, and grinds out one bestseller after another?" It answered its own query with, "the U.S. Government."

The advocates of free use of government-generated material contend that they are in fact performing a public service by making documents available to the public quickly and cheaply. They also suggest that the Government Printing Office cannot meet this demand, nor the price for which the book is sold. In fact, production schedules met by the GPO daily would confound even the largest printing firms. But frequently, the GPO is handicapped by the type of publication ordered by customer agencies. It is bound to produce a document as close to the format requested by the ordering department as possible, provided there is no waste, duplication, neglect, or delay involved. Government style and quality standards do not correspond to those habitually used in, for example, inexpensive pocket books. The government-printed version is thus seldom cheaper than pocket books designed and produced with an eye to manufacturing a product to the absolute minimum standard of quality consistent with anticipated one-time use. Often, however, it is less expensive than commercially produced versions of high quality.

SUPPLIERS TO THE GPO

Printing is by no means the only item on the GPO's shopping list. Printing procurement accounted for nearly $100 million in 1968, but the total procurement activity in that year amounted to $132 million. Of this figure, $26 million went for blank paper and envelopes. The remainder was spent for materials and supplies, subsidiary services, and machinery and equipment. The procurement of materials, supplies, services, machinery and equipment exhibits still another interesting facet of the GPO's relationships with the public—in this case, as a buyer of everything from spiral binding wire to giant web presses.

Whatever the circumstances, the purchase of such items calls for absolute fairness, complete documentation of each transaction, and occasionally the delicacy and discretion of a career diplomat. A wise man once said something to the effect that there was nothing which one person had made that another could not produce less expensively or with less care. The Government Printing Office, like most government agencies, is chained to the federal regulations governing purchases. The overriding objectives of these regulations are the elimination of questionable purchasing practices, favoritism in selecting a particular supplier, and ultimately, the saving of the taxpayer's money. Unfortunately, the fine motives of this body of law do not make government buying any simpler. The key to good procurement rests in precision preparation of clear bidding documents. Of course, this is applicable not only to the Government Printing Office, but to all government purchasing activities. But the Government Printing Office has several unusual problems associated with its procurement, and special care is taken at each step to assure that the craftsmen of the Office are provided with quality materials and equipment. The purchase of supplies and raw materials calls for great care in the preparation of specifications—and an equal amount of care in determining whether these items, once received, meet those specifications.

This function is assumed by the Tests and Technical Control Division in support of the Purchasing Division. For many items used by the Office, federal specifications are available from other sources and, if they apply, are used to bid such items. The General Services Administration's Federal Supply Service, of course, is responsible for preparing specifications, bidding, and purchasing tens-of-thousands of items used by the government. The GPO orders much of this type of supply from regular schedules established by the GSA. Even major items of equipment such as process cameras are obtained from this source, as well as expendable supplies common to graphic arts processes. Films, fixers, and photochemicals are examples. But when the Office has need of items peculiar to its own operation, chemists, metallurgists, and professional specialists in a number of technical fields prepare detailed specifications for their purchase.

Printing inks are typical examples of such items. Aside from ratios of pigment, vehicle, and drying agents, printing inks are much the same. But the variety of colors used in printing is almost without limit. As might be deduced, inks require careful control to assure a "match," not only of the original color requested, but also from batch to batch used during the press run. Normally, commercial color standards are used. The GPO's own "Standard Ink Book" conforms to these selections. Occasionally a disagreement develops over color matching, and, although the ink manufacturing industry is exceptionally cooperative in regard to the problem of color, the situation can become touchy. Proof press tests in the GPO laboratory generally settle the question. But when it cannot be so resolved, a spectrophotometer is used. This scientific referee produces match curves from each sample. Variations of 2 per cent are considered acceptable. In this way, disagreements are settled impartially. If the ink match varies more than the permissible 2 per cent, the supplier replaces the lot. If not, the GPO sends the ink to the pressroom with instructions to use it.

Often, the physical and chemical properties of materials used in the plant demand a high degree of cooperation between the Office and suppliers. For example, an identification card intended for use in Vietnam had to be printed with special fade-and-mildew resistant inks. Exhaustive tests were made by both GPO lab technicians and commercial ink specialists to arrive at the final formulation. In another instance, the White House asked the Government Printing Office to test the inks in the pens with which President Johnson was signing bills into law. In the now-familiar ceremony, the President was using dozens of pens, which he presented to public figures having an interest in the legislation. When it was discovered that the "permanent" ink was far from permanent and was neither waterproof nor fade-resistant, the GPO's Tests and Technical Control unit made suggestions to improve this ink. Now Presidential signatures are truly "permanent."

In other cases where specifications might become so detailed as to be unwieldy, the Government Printing Office sometimes resorts to commercial trade names for products, adding the notation "or equivalent." Technicians regularly monitor product quality furnished in accordance with this type of specification. Manufacturers often are surprised to learn that materials they are supplying under contract fall below minimum standards from time to time. A recent shipment of solvent used on automatic press-washing equipment was found to contain a high concentration of acid. This acid was well on its way toward destroying the metal pumps on presses before the trouble was isolated. The supplier was at first indignant and later shamefaced when confronted with the facts as developed by the GPO's laboratory. It developed that he was using drums previously containing acid that were ineffectively washed before being filled with solvent.

For some time, the postal cards printed by the Government Printing Office have contained an invisible "tag" of phosphorescent ink. This tag triggers sorting and canceling mechanisms in new automatic post office machinery. When trouble reports were sent back to the Government Printing Office about this tagging, technicians discovered that the firm supplying the microscopic phosphors for the ink mixture had furnished a particle size that failed to formulate properly with the ink vehicle. This firm, one of the nation's largest and most highly respected research-oriented companies, scoffed at the idea and decided to run their own test. The GPO's findings were confirmed, the offending material was replaced, and a real problem averted.

In the purchase of equipment, that is, machinery and mechanical or electrical systems intended to produce printing or process graphic arts material at some stage in the manufacturing stream, another aspect of the Government Printing Office's relationships with the public is demonstrated. Buying machinery is naturally subject to the same restriction as buying materials. But because of the spirited competition between graphic-arts equipment manufacturers and the amounts of money involved, much more difficulty is experienced in preparing purchasing documents and satisfactorily concluding purchases.

Specifications for a half-million-dollar perfecting press, for example, are necessarily lengthy and complex. To also write a specification that is broad enough to include all manufacturers' products, and at the same time eliminate those devices which are only marginally able to achieve the desired results, imposes an added burden. Such qualities as reliability, flexibility, and sturdiness are chiefly abstract in character, and yet must be referred to in some fashion in a properly prepared specification. Therefore, the value of a sound specification in permitting the Office to complete a trouble-free transaction is easily understood.

The printing industry has been labeled an industry in transition. What might have satisfied yesterday's needs often is obsolescent when delivered. The Government Printing Office has not been spared this problem. In order to meet its ever-present responsibility to the government to supply printed products at competitive prices and as rapidly and conveniently as possible, it must stay abreast of the rapidly changing technology in the graphic communications industry. New equipment is tumbling from factories and laboratories at an unbelievable rate. Even the best experts are hard pressed to settle on a production mode, equip for this mode of manufacture, and hold to it until the costs of adopting such a system are recovered.

The responsibility for recommending purchases of major items of machinery rests with the GPO's Modernization Committee. This Committee was created to bring the thinking of a number of knowledgeable, experienced production people to bear on prospective acquisitions, and to temper decisions of this group with the professional expertise of engineers, accountants, and technicians. But once the purchase determination is made by the Public Printer acting on recommendations by the Modernization Committee, the problems begin.

Specifications for a half-million-dollar perfecting press, for that they may be general enough to assure true competition and yet specific enough so that the device or system is capable of performing the operation intended. Every manufacturer of equipment designed to perform standard graphic arts operations works very hard to build machinery with exclusive features—features that tend to make his own design safer, faster, simpler, or better. Some of these features are bound to appeal in varying degrees to one or more of the officials involved in the GPO purchase. Moreover, there is a fairly close working arrangement with manufacturers' representatives charged with maintaining or servicing machinery purchased from their firms. When a new purchase is contemplated, these representatives are singularly accommodating with sample specifications. Generally speaking, the Office would have great difficulty composing the complicated engineering criteria for a major item of printing equipment. Months, and even years, might be devoted to such an undertaking. So the examples of specifications furnished by equipment suppliers are helpful in the smooth and orderly purchase of GPO equipment. The co-operation of such suppliers is necessary. But GPO procurement officials must strip these specifications of any proprietary features inhibiting competition between rival manufacturers of similar equipment. Suppliers also painstakingly scrutinize specifications, any part of which might tend to eliminate their firm as a prospective bidder. If something of this sort appears, an immediate appeal is made to the Purchasing Director to have the offending section modified or removed. Occasionally, the complaint is made directly to the Public Printer himself, and sometimes these appeals are carried to members of Congress.

In a number of instances, the Government Printing Office has acted as an unofficial testing activity. Manufacturers vie for a chance to install equipment on a trial basis knowing that acceptance by this busy plant is often tantamount to acceptance by the industry generally. The Government Printing Office endorses no product or equipment, it should be pointed out, nor does it permit advertisements using its name as preferring one device over another.* In one unusual incident, the Office installed a platemaking device to test a manufacturer's claim that his equipment could process plates as fast and as accurately as four or five men. This device, as far as the Government Printing Office or the industry knew, was the only machine that would perform this series of operations. It proved to be everything the maker claimed. Following a lengthy test period, the Office decided to buy the device—only to find that at least one other manufacturer had fabricated a similar piece of equipment. A complaint that the Government Printing Office had not given the other firm an opportunity to demonstrate its equipment forced the Office into the uncomfortable position of having used the original device in line production and now being unable to purchase the device from the company that had developed, built, and supplied it for trial. However, the Office had no alternative but to remove it, prepare general specifications for such a machine, and bid it on the open market.

An even more extraordinary procurement incident occurred a number of years ago that throws additional light on the GPO's relationships with the commercial community. The Office decided to replace a substantial number of its worn-out and obsolete slug-casting machines. Only two firms manufactured these machines. When quotations were received in reply to invitations to bid, the prices were exactly the same. There

* A few years ago, an enterprising dictionary publisher issued radio copy nationwide stating that his volume was the one preferred over all others by the Government Printing Office and that it was therefore considered the style standard for the U.S. Government. A letter to the publisher halted this advertisement and brought an apology to the Government Printing Office.

was no collusion, apparently, only uncommon coincidence. For some unexplained reason, the chief operating official in the unit concerned preferred one brand over another and requested that, in view of the identical prices, shipping charges, and discounts, the Office buy the brand he wished. The howl from the other manufacturer was heard all the way up on Capitol Hill. Charges of favoritism and discrimination filled the air and a full-blown conflict appeared to be developing. The Public Printer settled the matter with the wisdom and finesse of King Solomon: Each manufacturer received an order for half the required machines.

THE GPO AND THE UNIONS

The GPO's relations with employee organizations are of more than passing interest and occupy a substantial amount of management's attention, since the Office must deal with nearly two dozen organizations representing more than three-fourths of its employee complement. Strictly speaking, such relationships are internal matters, but they also have public significance.

When the Office was established in 1861, it inherited the contractual agreements then existing between the workforce of the Wendell plant and the former owners. Organizations or unions representing groups of workers were habitually consulted regarding hiring and firing. Congress, it will be remembered, instructed the Superintendent of Public Printing (later the Public Printer) to "at no time employ more hands than the public work may require." Consequently, when Congress adjourned, the demand for printing dropped and employees were discharged. When Congress returned, printing requirements increased and additional workers were hired. At that time, the Superintendent of Public Printing simply had to advise union representatives that a certain number of vacancies existed.

They in turn would dispatch that number of members to the GPO for employment. These representatives also consulted with GPO officials as to which employees were to be let go when the work decreased. The process worked very well for a time. But agitation for increased wages and shorter hours soon created friction and labor unrest came to the GPO and stayed for nearly a decade.

In 1862, the GPO experienced its first strike. Female press feeders walked out over a wage dispute. The Superintendent of Public Printing acceded to their demands and raised their pay from $5 per week to $6 per week, mainly on the basis of a manpower shortage which existed at that stage of the Civil War. However, when these same press feeders struck again in 1864, the labor shortage had eased somewhat, and their demands were refused. Furthermore, when the leaders of the revolt returned, they found themselves without jobs.

Again in 1862, bookbinders in the GPO struck for higher wages and remained out seven weeks. At issue was the rising cost of living in the Capital. An impasse was reached at the outset of the strike. The Superintendent explained that the Printing Act of 1860 restricted him from paying wages higher than those in local printing shops. The bookbinders on the other hand contended that their hourly wages were only adequate if Congress stayed in session and they were employed a full twelve months. Historically, of course, the legislature adjourned for at least three months each year. During the deadlock members picketed the GPO, Union Station, and many approaches to the city to prevent the importation of strikebreakers. Eventually, the union took their case to the Congress, and a wage increase was ordered.

Other changes were taking place. Daylight Saving and paid holidays appeared in contractual agreements as early as 1863. The Act of 1867 gave the Congressional Printer authority to fix wages without consulting with the Comptroller of the United States. However, in 1877, after Congress discovered rates paid to GPO journeymen were higher than those in the industry, it angrily withdrew this right and returned the authority to the legislature. In 1924, the Kiess Act restored the setting of wages to the Public Printer, and from that time, he has met annually with craft representatives (JCP approval still was necessary before the new rates became effective). Called the scale committees and elected by ballot each year, these groups of representatives have presented wage and other proposals to the Public Printer at annual conferences. The Public Printer reviews the proposals and makes his offer to the scale committee members. They poll the membership to determine whether to accept or reject. Sometimes, there are several meetings before agreement is reached. On occasion, when deadlocks occur, the Joint Committee on Printing is asked to arbitrate.

Since 1948, however, a general agreement among employee groups, the Public Printer, and the Joint Committee on Printing has been in effect. A formula based on the weighted average of the wages paid in twenty-five pre-selected cities has been used to establish GPO scales. Rates on file with the Bureau of Labor Statistics are used for the official computation. By and large, this process has proved satisfactory to all parties, and has greatly simplified the annual haggle over that most sensitive of subjects—wages.

In matters other than wages, the Public Printer is represented by the Division of Personnel, which acts in a labor-management capacity in the GPO. President Kennedy's Executive Order 10988 issued in 1962 redefined the role of employee organizations in government. This order represented a clear departure from the classic and frequently conflicting policies of the government toward unions. Its provisions legitimatized grievance and adverse actions procedures and restated the rights of the employees in connection with his membership in organizations. It also laid down ground rules for three levels of recognition—informal, formal, and exclusive—for employee organizations. In the GPO, this order resulted in the development of one formal, twenty-two exclusive, and several informal types of recognition. Both the Johnson and Nixon administrations continued to refine and support these basic policies.

LIBRARY AND SCHOOL RELATIONSHIPS

The contacts between the Government Printing Office and the public and private educational systems of the nation are numerous but limited in scope, being centered chiefly in school and institutional libraries. This relationship is principally fostered by the Public Documents Division and is keyed to a variety of services available to libraries both designated as depositories and those not having this status. The Division furnishes the same identification and classification for government publications to other institutional libraries which receive government documents from many sources, including depositories, as it does to the depositories themselves. This function results in collections of government documents in such libraries being made more valuable and convenient for library users.

A special notification service is also provided for school and public libraries. This service, now being rendered to nearly 1,500 libraries, keeps them apprised of government publishing activities. Any library that indicates an interest can be placed on a standing magnetic tape list used to circulate information of this type. As part of this service, multiple copies of special flyers, order forms, and brochures are offered to those libraries which wish to redistribute their own clientele.

A number of public and school libraries in cooperation with the Superintendent of Documents have been afforded consigned-agent status and regularly receive government publications on consignment for resale to the public. Two conflicting attitudes on this type of service have tended to keep this program at a modest size. Some librarians feel that the sale of books by libraries is an improper and inappropriate function. They declare that citizens come to their shelves for consultation, study, or borrowing, not purchase, and that selling is inconsistent with the basic library mission. Others refute this position, pointing out that many public libraries now have added "lending-for-a-fee" libraries to their institutions.

No discussion of Public Documents Division's contacts with the public could be complete without touching upon the special relationship that exists between the Superintendent of Documents, representing the Government Printing Office's bookselling and book-distributing function, and the associations of national and state professional librarians. Because of the growing importance of government publications in library systems, the contributions of the federal government to these systems intimately concerns these societies formed to further library science. As a consequence, Documents Division personnel are in great demand at library conclaves and assemblies, and there is a constant exchange of information taking place between the Government Printing Office and the library community.

As a representative of the Public Printer, and as the chief of the Public Documents Division, the Superintendent of Documents is a much-sought-after speaker wherever librarians gather. His expertise in this highly specialized field of library work is constantly in demand. His role, and that of his staff, embraces both the science of documenting and cataloging issues by the government and the means for promoting wider distribution and sale of government publications.

The Federal Depository Library system occupies an important place in the information network. Recent changes in the body of law governing that system have made it even more important. When the Federal Depository Library Act of 1962 embodied new guidelines for the depository program, implementation and interpretation of these guidelines naturally fell upon the shoulders of the Superintendent of Documents. Perhaps the most extensive change, at least for the Superintendent of Documents, was that provision whereby other components of the U.S. Government are required to provide the Superintendent of Documents with certain material. Copies of unclassified publications of public interest or educational value, not produced in the GPO but in other federal printing plants, are involved. Initially, each agency head in the government received a letter from the Public Printer outlining the pertinent parts of the new law and asking that an official in each department or agency, familiar with its publishing program, be selected to work with the Superintendent of Documents. At the very outset, funds for placing this program in operation became a problem. In the 1964 appropriation, Congress disallowed the entire amount intended for its use. To help clarify and interpret this new program, the Public Printer invited seven distinguished librarians to serve as members of an Advisory Committee on Depository Libraries in 1963. Members were chosen from a list submitted by the President of the American Library Association. Since the appointment of this group, the new aspects of the depository library law have been integrated smoothly into the system, helped measurably by restrengthening ties between the Office and the nation's librarians.

To get the depository distribution of non-GPO printed publications started, it was decided to attempt to identify certain of these publications, which came within the criteria established by the Depository Act of 1962. It was necessary to limit the scope of action because of the failure of Congress to appropriate funds to get the program underway. Bureau of the Census and Department of Interior publications were selected for this trial compilation. On the basis of the total number of libraries selecting similar Census and Interior Publications printed by the GPO, a justification was prepared for the 1965 Public Documents Division budget request.

At the House hearings on the Legislative Branch Appropriations for 1965, there was discussion again of the magnitude, scope, and total cost of the program provided by the 1962 law. Responding to a question about possible plans beyond 1965, the Superintendent of Documents explained that this program would be extended to other government departments and agencies in the future provided the means were available. The Chairman of the Subcommittee asked what course of action would be taken "if this depository library situation becomes unwieldy or out of hand." The Superintendent of Documents replied that if experience should prove that the law was incapable of implementation, some modifications would possibly be necessary.

At hearings on the same measure before the Senate Committee on Appropriations, Edmond Low, Librarian of Oklahoma State University, supported the request for $57,000 to conduct the proposed trial program. Low, recognizing the difficulties involved in full-scale operation of the non-GPO portion of the Depository Act, assured the Chairman of the Senate subcommittee that the plan as outlined would be a satisfactory beginning. Public Law 88-454, enacted on August 20, 1964, allowed the requested sum of $57,000 for initiating the program outlined to the committees.

Because the appropriation Act was late and there was much preliminary work to be done before the flow of the material from the two designated agencies could begin, the Public Documents Division postponed until January, 1965, the distribution of the first Census Bureau publications produced outside the Government Printing Office. Once a beginning was made, however, Census Bureau material has continued to reach the Public Documents Division without major incident. By May 1, 1966, more than 650,000 copies of Census Bureau publications were distributed to the depositories. The Public Documents Division also completed surveys on additional series of Interior Department publications, greatly swelling distribution during the remainder of 1966. Annotations, as provided for in the Depository Act of 1962, were prepared by the Interior Department to aid the depositories in making their selections.

Except for funding problems, the progress of this program has been reasonably satisfactory—albeit somewhat piecemeal in character. With time and experience, the distribution of non-GPO publications to depositories should gain momentum, and it is expected will conform to the expressed desires of the Congress.

IMPROVED SERVICES TO THE PUBLIC

In November 1965, President Johnson directed each agency of the federal government to "explore every path in our quest to provide the best possible service for our individual citizens." He placed John W. Macy, Jr., then head of the Civil Service Commission, in charge of this innovative program and instructed each agency to appoint a top staff member to move the program ahead with all possible speed. The committee selected by the Public Printer to undertake this challenging assignment was chaired by the Special Assistant to the Public Printer and consisted of the Purchasing Director, the Deputy Personnel Director, and the Deputy Superintendent of Documents, representing the three principal areas wherein Office services touched the public in general.

The new program in the GPO had a favorable effect on Documents Division sales. For the first time since opening, Saturday bookstore hours were inaugurated in the main bookstore. Approval was obtained to open a GPO bookstore in the State Department. This store became a reality in 1967. At the committee's suggestion, authority also was sought to establish a GPO bookstore in Chicago—the first outside the Washington Metropolitan area. The subsequent expansion of GPO bookstores has already been described in Chapter VI. In

1968, GPO bookstores served 225,000 customers and grossed more than a million dollars in sales.

Under this committee, cooperation with private enterprises such as direct mail organizations, banking houses, radio stations, trade magazine and periodical publishers, and outdoor societies, was intensified for the purpose of promoting government book sales in specialized fields. Results have been very encouraging. Direct mail organizations regularly include flyers in member mailings. National banks, some 14,500 of them, were queried by return postal card asking if they desired to receive informational handouts on income tax matters. More than half responded affirmatively. Radio stations, as a public service, have donated hours of valuable radio time to advertising new publications by the government. Trade magazines were induced to include in their book review sections pertinent new government issues. Outdoor and conservation societies cooperated broadly in promoting documents relating to their goals and aims. Although much of this type of promotion was being carried out before the committee turned its attention to it, the President's directive gave added emphasis to the need for closer ties between government and its citizens.

Another outgrowth of this effort designed to upgrade services to the public is a manual written by the Purchasing Division entitled, *How to Do Business with the GPO*. This booklet explains how commercial suppliers can sell printing, services, and materials to the Government Printing Office. Nearly 10,000 of these brochures have been distributed to printing firms and graphic arts suppliers, many through the Commerce Department–managed Business Opportunity conferences. Through use of this brochure, the bidding base for materials, equipment, and printed products has been noticeably broadened.

This program of improved services has had many salubrious effects upon the Government Printing Office's image and upon the character of services which the Office is called upon to perform. But the ultimate beneficiary was the "public," whether represented by a multimillion-dollar company or an individual inquiring about a government pamphlet.

IX

The Future of the
Government Printing Office

Forecasting things to come is a thorny undertaking. And when an oracle takes a measure of pride in the accuracy of his forecasts, it can become positively hazardous and occasionally embarrassing. But if, as Samuel Johnson said, "The future is purchased by the present," some of the risks are removed. Predicting what is ahead for the GPO is possible with some degree of certainty by careful observation of trends in the printing and publishing field—both inside the government and out.

One of the strongest indicators of tomorrow's tide must be the tremendous growth in demand for reading material and other graphic arts products. Experts have been predicting boom conditions for the printing and publishing industry for more than a decade past. Except for underestimating the magnitude of this boom, they have been consistently correct. The "information explosion," or "print explosion," is now a well-documented phenomenon. The government has contributed part of this detonation, adding to its violence by pumping money and intellect into a broad range of programs, the spin-off of which ultimately is a substantial amount of printing.

Social programs, with their prime objectives a closer association of government with the people, have been big contributors to the government print explosion. Whole new

184

departments and agencies have emerged from this effort. The Department of Housing and Urban Development (HUD) and the Office of Economic Opportunity (OEO) are but two of the newer activities. Each, of course, orders printing from the GPO. Also, whenever a shooting or a cold war is being waged, the effect on the GPO has been more printing. For some time, the military establishment has been the GPO's largest customer. Certainly, population growth and government-sponsored research and development add to the paper deluge.

As one illustration, in June, 1964, the National Bureau of Standards issued a thousand-plus-page hard-bound tome with the descriptive, but hardly imaginative, title of *Handbook of Mathematical Functions.* The first printing was a modest 25,000. Since the book sold at a hardly typical price for a government publication, $6.50, it was not expected to be a hot item for public sale. The Public Documents Division ordered copies, placed them on sale—and was swamped with orders. The second printing—12,500 copies—was ordered in November, 1964. To date, this volume has been through seven printings. In the summer of 1969, the 100,000th copy of this book —perhaps the biggest "sleeper" ever handled by the GPO —was presented to Dr. Lee DuBridge, President Nixon's Science Advisor. Sales are still running strong throughout the world scientific community.

More than fifty pieces of printing have been produced by NASA in connection with its moon-shot research program. Another work, this time the outgrowth of a series of grants for biotoxicological research, demonstrates a relatively new trend in government printing and publishing—high-quality, special-purpose reference volumes. This work, a monumental monograph, *Poisonous and Venomous Marine Animals,* was sponsored by the Deputy Chief of Staff for Research and Development, Department of the Air Force, Office of the Surgeon General, Department of the Army, and the Bureau of Medicine and Surgery, Department of the Navy. It was written by

Dr. Bruce W. Halstead, a premier authority on the subject and a commander in the U.S.N.R. Medical Corps. Dr. Halstead began preparation of this work in 1943 and in 1949 received an initial grant from the National Institutes of Health and the Office of Naval Research. The first direct sponsorship for the monograph was obtained through the School of Aviation Medicine, U.S.A.F. in 1952. Later, upon the recommendation of the Armed Forces Publications Committee and with joint sponsorship of the Armed Forces, printing began in 1963. The monograph is in three volumes, contains more than 3,000 pages, and is sold by the Public Documents Division for $50 a set. About 2,500 sets have been sold. This document abounds with both black-and-white and color plates. According to one expert, it will be "a standard in its field for at least the next seventy-five to one hundred years." Twenty-five years and $2 million went into its preparation, and it represents an enormous contribution to both zoology and medicine.

The publishing mentioned above is only a scant sampling, but it serves to illustrate the innovative character of much government printing and publishing currently being done, a fact which will directly influence the future of this agency. It should be noted that these documents are original in concept, of the greatest significance to a particular discipline, allied to a governmental interest, and produced to a standard of quality not usually associated with government printing.

No less significant than these unusual examples of the Government Printing Office's products in any assessment of what the future holds is the steady and spectacular rise in the public's interest in *all* government documents. From 1954 to 1969, the sale of publications almost doubled. Both in terms of quantity and quality, the ability of the Government Printing Office to fulfill its mission is being challenged.

To meet this challenge, two conditions must be satisfied in the days ahead. First, the Government Printing Office must improve and enlarge the physical structure in which it conducts its activities. And second, it must continue to incorporate the newest technologies in order to remain competitive. Both will shape the future of the Government Printing Office, but of most immediate importance is the crucial shortage of space.

RENOVATION OR RELOCATION

The Government Printing Office must, at minimum, undertake a major renovation of its existing home or, at maximum, relocate to a new facility. Like a repeated pattern in a fabric, the plea for space crops up again and again in the GPO's history. In its first seven years of operation, for example, six separate expansions increased floor space to nearly nine acres from slightly over an acre-and-a-half in the original Wendell plant. But at no time in the century of operation of the Government Printing Office has space become more of an issue than during the administration of James L. Harrison, Public Printer from 1961 to early 1970.

A little history here seems in order.

Shortly after his appointment by President Kennedy, Harrison, in reviewing actions by his predecessor, Raymond Blattenberger, found a study by an in-house committee in 1956 on means for solving the growing space problem in the Government Printing Office. The committee recommended erection of a four-story-and-basement annex on Northwest H Street, which the General Services Administration estimated would cost about $5.25 million. Public Law 87-373, authorizing construction of the annex, was passed in 1961.

When Harrison was questioned in 1962 by the Chairman of the House Appropriation Committee at the annual GPO hearing, he declared that the planned annex was already inadequate considering the rapidly increasing work volume and crowded conditions then present in the plant. Harrison's uneasiness was not without foundation. At that time more than

200,000 square feet of rental warehouse space was being occupied by elements of the Government Printing Office. The
following month, the Legislative Subcommittee of the House
Appropriations Committee indicated that it would act favorably on a suggestion to increase the size of the annex to eight
stories.

This is where the GPO's expansion waters first began to
muddy. Early in 1962, Washington's Redevelopment Land
Agency, moving ponderously toward a start in the Northwest
No. 1 Area, contacted the Office in connection with the GPO's
long-range plans. In discussions with officials of the National
Capital Planning Commission (NCPC) and the Redevelopment Land Agency (RLA), the possibility of the GPO acquiring additional property in its vicinity seemed to offer attractive
alternatives to constructing the planned annex. The prospect
of solving most of the Office's space and materials-handling
problems by expanding not only storage facilities but also
production areas appeared a definite possibility. One aspect
of the already approved addition had cooled the enthusiasm of
space planners. It was planned for the far western end of
Building No. 3. More than 85 per cent of the GPO's daily input of eighteen to twenty carloads of paper was rail delivered.
(Half of this amount went to the huge GSA warehouse complex in Franconia, Virginia—17 miles from the main plant
—and the other half to Building No. 4, *east* of North Capitol
Street.)

The proposed annex was principally for paper storage, but
paper delivered to the top floor of the warehouse would of
necessity have to be transported from GPO's easternmost point
to its westernmost point. After being unloaded, stock would
have to be elevator-dropped four levels to the warehouse sub-
basement, transported by power truck through the under-
ground tunnel connecting buildings Nos. 3 and 4, and then
elevator-lifted to the basement or first level, power-trucked
across the entire length of the main building and again ele-

vator-lifted to an interim storage location in the new annex. Feelers were even extended concerning a bridge across
North Capitol Street in order to permit paper cars to be transported close to using areas in the main production building.
But the Fine Arts Commission turned this idea down summarily on the basis that such a bridge would destroy the imposing vista south from North Capitol Street.

So the meetings with planners from the National Capital
Planning Commission and the Redevelopment Land Agency
opened a channel of thought heretofore considered closed to
the Government Printing Office. In short, the planners informed officials of the Government Printing Office that the redevelopment scheme approved for the Government Printing Office
area contained reservations of three city blocks for public use
—and some of this desirable property could be earmarked for
GPO expansion.

With the alluring prospect of obtaining a sizable tract of
land to the south or the remainder of the land in his own
square, the Public Printer took a close look at the obviously
short-range solution presented by the approved annex and ordered a full study by space planners in his organization. The
study report concluded that while expansion in its present location was an acceptable solution to the GPO's space dilemma, relocation offered the best opportunity to attain the
kind of efficiency the Public Printer was seeking.

Simultaneously, the plan for constructing the annex was
proceeding under its own power. The Bureau of the Budget
confirmed that the scope of PL 87-373 was broad enough to
cover increasing the proposed annex from four stories and
basement to eight stories and basement. But the relocation
recommendation of the Office's space planners had virtually
reversed the thinking on GPO's space problems and, if sanc-
tioned by the Public Printer, would necessitate an official
change of course, not to mention a vast broadening of planning
scope as well as additional financing. Because of the impact

of such a change, Public Printer Harrison decided to seek independent advice from a source outside of government. This advice, it was hoped, would support or refute the in-house recommendation for relocation and give added impetus and direction to planning for the future.

When the Joint Committee on Printing authorized the preliminary engineering study, Harrison asked the GSA, which had already accepted the GPO's transfer of $5.9 million of the $6.4 million annex appropriation, to delay negotiations with prospective architects until a decision could be made on whether to build the annex or to press for relocation. By this time, management was all but convinced that relocation was the best solution to its space problems, and both GSA space planners and the engineers hired for the study were in accord. Expansion in its present location would almost surely aggravate the complicated and costly vertical stock-handling situation, it was felt.

On September 23, 1963, Harrison therefore met with members of the Joint Committee on Printing and presented his relocation proposal. The Committee's reaction was favorable and he was authorized to offer the plan to the other committees of Congress having jurisdiction over such matters. At the meeting, members questioned Harrison sharply on his relocation proposal, principally on the location site. The criteria established were as follows: (1) no more than thirty minutes from the Capitol; (2) tract to be served by rail; and (3) sufficient acreage to satisfy a one-production-level concept. Additionally, it was agreed that the new site should be government owned and located so that overbridge traffic was kept to a minimum.

After conferring with officials of the GSA's Public Buildings Service, it was decided that GSA should present the building prospectus to the Public Works Committees of both houses. Harrison, upon receiving approval from Public Works, was then to take the lead in obtaining funds from the Appropriation committees. It should be noted also that Harrison had, by this time, returned the entire annex appropriation to the Treasury on the strength of his commitment to relocation. Thus, he burned his final bridge on the eight-story-and-basement annex scheme.

In April 1964, both the Senate and House Public Works Committees approved construction of a new Government Printing Office. The price tag was in excess of $46 million. Approval by the Appropriations Committees followed and, in August, Congress passed the Legislative Branch Appropriations Act. The original budget request was for the entire $46,723,000, but since much preliminary work, including choice of a suitable site was yet to be done, only $2.5 million was appropriated, "for necessary expenses, for site selection and general plans and designs of buildings for the Government Printing Office," in the language of the Act.

All was not roses, however, for the proposal became the subject of a mild floor fight in the Senate. Senator William Proxmire attempted to strike the GPO building appropriation from the Act by amendment. Apparently, a hurried campaign of opposition to relocation mounted by Printing Industries of America, Inc., a federation of employing printers, had won over the Wisconsin Senator.

Venerable Carl Hayden, Chairman of the Joint Committee on Printing, in one of his rare floor speeches, probably exposed the real issue when he said:

> The primary objection to the construction of this building seems to come from the printing industry and is based upon their fear that with expanded space the Public Printer will not continue his present policy of contracting government printing to private plants, or at least not to the extent that the private plants now receive government printing.
>
> I would like to point out that the amount of outside purchases of printing, based on billings, compared with printing done by the Government Printing Office has steadily risen.

The Public Printer has assured me that he will continue to buy commercial printing wherever possible.

I assure the Senate, as chairman of the Joint Committee on Printing, which has primary jurisdiction over this subject, that the Public Printer will be required to contract for printing in private commercial plants wherever it is in the best interests of the Government.

Proxmire's amendment was defeated 60 to 19.

More fireworks were in store in the House. Now the problem of a suitable site became a paramount issue in the relocation effort. Both General Services Administration and the National Capital Planning Commission joined the Government Printing Office in the search. Nearly two dozen tracts were investigated. Only three were found to meet the established criteria for construction—two locations in the Bolling-Anacostia Airfield complex, and a portion of the 313-acre National Training School for Boys site. In April, 1955, after National Capital Planning Commission voted unanimously in favor of it, the Joint Committee on Printing approved the southern end of the Bolling-Anacostia location as the site for the new Government Printing Office. This tract was in the Defense Department inventory and efforts to have a portion released ran afoul of the powerful chairman of the House Armed Services Committee, Mendel Rivers. Rivers and the Defense Department had other plans for the former airfield.

Although reluctant to do so, the National Capital Planning Commission in June, adopted a resolution granting eighty-five acres of the National Training School tract for the GPO's building. This tract belonged to the Justice Department's Bureau of Prisons, but through efforts of the Government Printing Office and General Services Administration, it was released to the GSA late in June. The National Capital Planning Commission was not wholly convinced that this large, highly desirable site should contain an employment center such as the GPO, but a majority felt more or less obliged to acquiesce because the members had earlier assured Public Printer Harrison that they could get the Defense Department to release a part of Bolling-Anacostia for the Government Printing Office.

Almost at once, opposition to the GPO's use of the National Training site began to crystallize. Advocates of low-cost housing and community college proponents joined vested printing interests in fighting relocation. Meetings of the National Capital Planning Commission were picketed by all sorts of activists urging that the GPO be prevented from relocating.

National Capital Planning Commission planners, apparently aware that community pressure would ultimately sway the Commission, worked feverishly at schemes to reduce the amount of land allotted for GPO's building. But the GPO and its retained engineers maintained that the economies to be derived from this relocation scheme were largely a result of the one-level production concept, which called for 1.2 million square feet of space on the first level.

Still other forces were at work, and the Commission reversed itself. With no site, the Public Printer had little to support his $46 million construction request. He asked that it be withdrawn and the House Legislative Appropriation Subcommittee acceded. To all intents and purposes, the foes of relocation had triumphed. But as with most real dramas, there is no true beginning or end. Four years earlier, when sites were being studied for the Government Printing Office, a tract of land about four miles from the District line at the intersection of the newly constructed Capital Beltway and U.S. Route 50 had been inspected and found suitable. Two problems prevented any further action on this tract: it was privately owned, and compared with some of the others was considerably farther from the Capitol—although well within the agreed time-distance criterion.

This property now became the focus of attention. The

GSA informed the Public Printer that it was possible to obtain this property through trading land or facilities already government owned. The Penn Central Railroad, which had become involved in the relocation situation during earlier planning for the National Training School site, decided to acquire the beltway tract as a hedge against losing a sizable shipping income from transporting paper and printing for GPO. But trade negotiations soon bogged down on establishing the fair-market value of the parcels involved in the swap.

In March, 1967, Public Printer Harrison met with the Joint Committee on Printing regarding the Beltway site. It was apparent from the outset that the members were now somewhat wary about conferring their approval on this, or any, location. For more than a year, the matter remained static. The GSA was having trouble finalizing trade negotiations with Penn Central. The railroad was keeping an eye on GPO's relocation and was seemingly deliberately stalling to await developments. Each year, the Public Printer hopefully added a request for building funds to his budget and then subsequently was forced to withdraw it because of site complications.

Both the new chairman and the vice chairman (Senator Hayden retired in 1968) of the Joint Committee on Printing were strong supporters of relocation. Apparently Senator B. Everett Jordan's experience as a manufacturer made him cognizant of the advantages of relocation. Representative Sam Friedel's interest was keyed to relocating this installation to his state. But he had other pressures. Many employees residing in Maryland were complaining to him of street violence and loss of personal property in the vicinity of the Government Printing Office. Since the April, 1968 riots, crime had mushroomed in Washington, D.C., and nowhere were citizens more at peril than in the GPO's neighborhood. Around-the-clock operation requiring employees to come and go during the hours of darkness intensified risks for GPO employees.

Thus, relocation to a site where greater employee security was possible became a positive factor in the controversy.

Members of the Joint Committee on Printing opposing the move now sought Mayor Walter Washington's views, hoping to enlist his support. Mayor Washington responded as expected, declaring that removal to the suburbs of the largest employer of skilled and semi-skilled workers in the District of Columbia would be a serious blow to his administration's efforts to maintain the District's employment base. A racial issue also was raised by activists. They suggested that the lower-grade employees, mostly black, would be unable to afford transportation to and from the new site. The more militant mistakenly stated that relocation was primarily motivated by an interest in halting the growth of GPO's black employees (then approximately 47 per cent).

Despite this formidable opposition, on July 31, 1969, the Joint Committee on Printing met and approved the Beltway site. Almost immediately, there was reaction from all sides. The Washington *Star* of August 6, 1969, said:

> To question this decision is certainly not to deny the compelling needs of the GPO—or the deficiencies of its present operation. The existing plant is totally inadequate—a fact that has been recognized for several years. It is understandable, therefore, if the agency is by now sick and tired of being shunted from one proposed location to another, with never a firm decision actually having been made.
>
> But too much procrastination in the past does not justify acting too hastily now. It seems quite likely, on the basis of expert testimony, that the GPO must move from where it is. But we simply do not believe that an adequate new location cannot be found within the District.

One totally unexpected reaction came from the National Capital Planning Commission. Hard on the heels of the news that the Joint Committee on Printing had approved the Beltway site, representatives of the Commission informed the GPO that two rather large sites within the District of Columbia could be made available to the GPO. One was at a previously inspected location called the "Harmony Cemetery" site, rejected earlier on the basis of inadequate size. Now, additional property was available, bringing the total to over sixty acres. The other location was the "coal yard" site fronting on 1st Street, N.E. This 28-acre tract, although tentatively earmarked for Post Office expansion, could be conveyed to the Government Printing Office. Although neither of these sites was wholly government owned (a requirement for the GPO's relocation), partial acquisition was already under way and could be accelerated if necessary. Adjacent to the coal yard site was a full block owned by the D.C. Government, which if added to the tract, would make it approach forty-five acres.

Public Printer Harrison, however, was reluctant to alter his course. Either of these sites would have been attractive to the Office had they appeared prior to approval of the Beltway location—and had been of acceptable size. The prospect of still another request for sanctioning a relocation site, this time because of developments after the fact, seemed perilous indeed. Harrison's action upon receiving the Beltway site okay was to request restoration of the GPO's planning funds by one of the congressional appropriations committees. The committees were currently considering his request and the knowledge that the Public Printer was studying a new site in the District of Columbia would hardly encourage favorable action on allotting some $4.5 million for site and building design in the upcoming legislative appropriations. Of course, should this attempt fail, these funds could be included in the regular deficiency appropriation or in the supplemental appropriation.

This remains the status of the GPO's building relocation as of this writing. Looking ahead, it appears that only time remains before the Government Printing Office moves or expands in place. The National Visitors' Center to be built at the Union Station location will attract a great deal more motor traffic into an already overburdened area. Added to this is the prospect of a sports arena on, or adjacent to, the present GPO site, a transportation center expected to accommodate bus and taxi terminals, and tracts allocated to private commercial development, all in the immediate vicinity of the Government Printing Office.

Continuing to operate in this crowded, traffic-choked, prime location is unthinkable for a large quasi-industrial operation such as the Government Printing Office. As one urban planner explained, "It is the poorest possible utilization of a high-prestige location and, moreover, it is economically absurd to manufacture printing on some of the costliest land in our nation's Capital—it's like having a privy on the White House lawn." Regardless of the final outcome, GPO's space problems will have to be resolved—if not by relocation, then by addition and remodeling.

BURGEONING BUSINESS—AND COMPUTERS

If the Government Printing Office's future solution to its space dilemma is shrouded in uncertainty, its solution to the problem of a burgeoning business volume is not. Whether in a new home or a renovated one, faster and more efficient equipment must be incorporated in the production stream. The GPO, as any manufacturer of printed products, must look to technical innovation to cope with shorter schedules, increased quantities, and higher quality. Modern governments' printing needs can best be expressed in terms of speed. Months and even years may be consumed in preparation of a manuscript. But once authorization to proceed is received, printing, which constitutes a major part of program implementation, cannot be delayed. As one might suspect, the chief time-consumer in the printing process is composition—the conversion of manuscript copy to some finished graphic form. A book page such as this that you are reading can be set into type in about fifteen minutes by a competent Linotype operator. But the composing process includes proofreading and correction and verification as well. Each page of type, after initial setting, spends many additional hours in the composing room complex. When the department, or author, also reads galley proofs, makes corrections, and revises each galley—checks page proofs and inserts corrections—more hours are needed to produce a "clean" page ready for press. Consequently, technological emphasis has been concentrated largely upon shortening and simplifying the composing process. In recent years, many devices closely related to typewriters have been marketed as expedient means for producing camera copy, thus bypassing hot-metal composition. The manufacturer's goal is machine-composed copy of good quality, which in many instances can be produced by noncraft personnel. A wide range of machines producing this type of composition, familiarly known as "cold type," have found acceptance in the industry.

The proliferation of ADP equipment within the federal establishment has brought further refinements. Readout devices that print the results of computer data manipulation produce a new kind of copy. This material is being sent to the Government Printing Office as camera-ready copy, which is inexpensive to produce and, more often than not, the byproduct of a primary computer assignment, such as list maintenance, inventory control work, or accounting tasks. As each generation of computers has become more and more sophisticated and programing skills within government have grown, the Office has found that between 20 and 30 per cent of its total copy input is in computer-printout form.

Unfortunately, much of the time and cost advantage of this sort of copy preparation is dissipated. Printout copy consists of monospaced block letters with fixed spacing between lines and appears on marginally-punched continuous forms stock.

Because the character is transformed from the matrix to the paper by striking through an inked or carboned ribbon, quality is largely a function of ribbon perfection and is subject to inconsistencies in the mechanical striking system as well.

At the order of the Joint Committee on Printing in 1962, Public Printer Harrison instituted a research and development program designed to study and recommend a solution to the problems stemming from the reproduction of material produced by high-speed printers on ADP equipment.

A position was created for an Electronic Printing Research Officer and a GPO/Departmental Electronic Printing Committee was formed. The Committee's findings confirmed the fact that computer-generated copy, characterized by all capital letters and wide line-spacing, resulted in excessive waste of paper, presswork, and binding, and produced substandard printing. The Committee happily did not stop there, but went on to suggest a solution. It proposed a high-speed electronic phototypesetting device operating from magnetic tapes which would produce a fully-formatted page of hard copy or negative material and also prepared the basic specifications for such a device. Conceived along the lines of what was then an ultra-sophisticated system, far in advance of the current state of the art, general specifications were sent to sixty-three firms inviting them to submit bids. Only six responded with proposals, and, after careful study, the Committee found that only one met the special requirements of the system. An award was made to the Mergenthaler Linotype Company for two machines at a bid price of about $2 million. Mergenthaler, an old-line graphic arts manufacturer, had teamed with CBS Laboratories on this project and divided the contract. Mergenthaler was to furnish the software while CBS, which had already developed a system possessing many of the desired operational characteristics, took the responsibility for the hardware.

The outcome exceeded everyone's expectations. Much later, Senator Hayden, then Chairman of the Joint Committee on

Printing, pushed the *COMPOSE* button on the Linotron 1010, and in a matter of seconds this system composed and proofed a birthday greeting to him. (The date was October 2, 1967, and Hayden was 90 years old.) But the interim between concept and realization was alive with problems and delays. The radically new system was a product of much innovative research. As delivered, it used magnetic tapes as an input source. These tapes contain not only manuscript data but also typographic instructions and system commands. The information merge is done by off-line computer.

When the Linotron system is actuated, data and control characters are fed to a control buffer from the tape reader. Control signals establish type size and grid selection. The position of the first data character is contained in the tape code, and when this is decoded by control circuitry, an electronic gate opens and allows this character through in video signal form. This signal is sent to a display CR tube and precisely positioned. When the character appears on the display tube, it is photographed through a fixed-focus optical system onto film. The same process is repeated until an entire page is composed. At this time, a film transport advances fresh film, storing the first page in a casette, and another page is begun.

The system composes at up to 1,000-characters-per-second, varying in speed with the point size of the type being set. It is capable of generating, displaying, and positioning any symbol, in random order, which appears on one of the four glass character grids in the machine. Each grid, about the size of a slice of bread, contains 256 alphanumeric characters, giving the system 1020 characters available in ½ second (grids change automatically upon commands on the control tapes). It also possesses the ability to provide paper proofs on demand for system checking, and it has an accessory for slide projection of graphics. In what is called its "proof mode," it can compose at twice its normal speed. In this mode, however, the quality of the output is sufficient only for proofreading—not reproduction.

The importance of this breakthrough in electronic photo-composing cannot be overstated—especially as concerns government printing. The Linotron is an extraordinarily efficient device. When operating from properly programed magnetic tapes, it supplies error-free, high-quality reproducibles at a fraction of the cost of a conventional page. A note of caution is necessary, however. The economies derived from the use of this system spring from a variety of sources. First, and perhaps of singular import, is the cost of establishing a raw data base. At this time, data must be placed on magnetic tape by manual keystroking of some sort, although optical scanning is proving feasible for certain types of material. If magnetic tapes must be prepared by manual keyboarding solely for photocomposer use, there is little advantage over conventional keyboarding. If, however, a computer, and there are now more than 4,000 in government, already contains information, any part of which is desired for printing, it can be retrieved for input to a photocomposing system. As an example, the National Library of Medicine indexes about 25,000 issues of biomedical journals annually—nearly a quarter of a million articles. A high-speed computer system called MEDLARS (Medical Literature Analysis and Retrieval System) is used to store these citations. Upon demand, MEDLARS will search and answer complex biomedical questions as well as prepare bibliographies of journals and extracts of articles. Basically, the system is intended to respond to demand searches and to provide a printed product directly from computer memory holdings. So printing —one objective—shares the costs of manual input of information with the concommitant objective of demand search responses. The principal printed product of MEDLARS is a monthly bibliography *Index Medicus*. This volume is widely used throughout the world as a medical literature reference. MEDLARS employs a high-speed computer phototypesetter referred to as GRACE (Graphic Arts Composing Equipment). This device operates independently of the computer at approximately 18,000 characters per minute and produces hard copy ready for paste-up and camera.

High speed, computer-oriented composing systems are but one answer. However significant, composing speed only moves the job from manuscript to typeform. The product must be placed on the press in some form and printed, then bound and finished. But the shadow of an ever-advancing technology in these subsequent operations can already be seen. The main effort today and in the foreseeable future is not merely automation, but toward a fully integrated printing system.

Presses that in the past merely transferred images to paper are now establishing salients into domains heretofore strictly associated with finishing. We already have presses which "perfect" (print both sides of the sheets), fold, and trim. It is just a matter of time until more complicated finishing operations are added to press lines. To carry this concept further, greater standardization of printed product is needed. Nowhere does standardization have a better chance for success than in government. Uniformity of sizes, formats, and materials has been advanced through regulation by the Joint Committee on Printing. In years to come, the Government Printing Office will benefit from any increased emphasis on standardizing government work.

A fully-integrated graphic communications system, however, goes decidedly further. It is expected that it would include gathering and processing information, as well as displaying, editing, printing, and delivering it. The *Congressional Record*, for example, has been the object of any number of suggestions, bordering on the integrated communications system concept. One suggestion envisages a data transmission line carrying verbatim proceedings from the floor of Congress directly to the GPO. Another would employ facsimile transmission, a refinement which would enable the printer setting type to insert revisions to their floor statements made by members. Still another would tie keystroking by the Recorders of Debate directly, or through a buffer storage system, to a computer. With this idea, the speed and data manipulation features of the computer could be used to great advantage to print out copy, or to provide programed tape for driving a photocomposer.

At the present time, the loss of congressional control as well as a lack of graphic flexibility have barred any serious consideration of these suggestions. But the cost-saving and rapid-response prospects are so alluring that a system in some similar form is almost inevitable for the future.

So, in contemplating what changes will come in the days ahead, the author feels that a new physical plant and some rather startling equipment innovations are certain. In addition, a general upgrading in the quality and appearance of government publications can be expected. In government publishing, a strong current is running, outdistancing the natural and traditional conservatism of the departments and agencies. The use of process color work, which is expensive, is growing. Typographic inertia, or opposition to new design forms, is on the wane. Greater public concern for what its government is doing is restructuring the attitudes and approaches of federal administrators toward telling their stories in print.

For example, for the past five years the annual report of the Secretary of Interior has been not only beautifully written, designed, and printed, but has sold strongly through the Public Documents Division. Even the titles of these reports spark the imagination: 1965—*Quest for Quality;* 1966—*Population Challenge;* 1967—*The Third Wave;* 1968—*Man; An Endangered Specie;* and 1969—*It's Your World.* Compare the nearly 130,000 copies of *Quest for Quality* sold to the public with the handful of the Secretary's reports printed a decade ago! The Agriculture Yearbook is perhaps an even more dramatically illustrative example. In 1895, this document sold a total of forty-nine copies for the entire year. The Yearbook for 1965, *Consumers All,* sold in excess of 106,000 copies— and at $2.75 per copy. Above everything else, the Apollo missions have found the heart of the public market. More than 3.5 million lithographs of the moon mission have been sold through GPO's Public Documents Division.

All elements needed to give shape to the Government Printing Office of the future are now present. Demand for printing by the government agencies is trending toward an all-time high. Increased public interest in what the Government publishes has driven public documents sales to new peaks. The Government Printing Office must respond.

Internally, there will probably be a major reorganization with the traditional compartmentalization of operations disappearing. Simplification of workflow must be achieved. Instead of five divisions, prepress, press, and finishing would suffice as far as production-oriented groupings are concerned. Of course, planning would remain, and also shipping, which would include an expanded distribution operation.

It is also possible that the Public Documents operation will be separated from the main Office, although at the moment the intimate association between the two tends to militate against this. But even today, establishment of regional Documents sales and distribution centers are being seriously considered. The deluge of mail orders has almost reached the saturation point. Regional distribution and sales offices and warehouses would measurably shorten the time required to process orders and effect distribution within geographic areas.

The Government Printing Office might be significantly smaller in physical size in years hence. Streamlined organizational structure and dispersal make such an eventuality possible. The question of whether the Government's printing needs are best served by one large office has never been fully resolved. Advocates of the regional office concept for both production and Documents sales and distribution point out that situating a number of smaller plants in strategic locations throughout the country not only would provide a quicker response to agency requirements but would save shipping costs, broaden the base of commercial suppliers, and ease the problem of recruiting labor. Since most of the federal departments are represented in our major metropolitan centers, this concept has some merit. Except for an undeniable loss of control and some duplication of staff and equipment, it has few disadvantages. As presently conceived, the Public Printer would still exercise authority over such regional plants. The buying of printing is now somewhat decentralized as we have seen with procurement offices in a number of cities. The same is true of GPO's printing operations through its Field Service Offices, although on a very reduced scale compared with the total printing effort. So the framework for dispersal already exists. The main Office would serve the needs of Congress and departmental needs within the area in which the main Office is located. Heretofore, because of the substantial investment in the buildings and equipment, full utilization of the facility was needed to invoke efficient and economical operation. As needs grow and the necessity for expansion of the central office arrives, it would appear only practical that some of the production capacity of the central Office be diverted to small regional plants.

Of course, this is all speculation. The concept of concentration versus dispersal runs in cycles. Currently, the advantage appears to lie with concentration—that is, one major office serving the principal needs of the government for printing and binding. However, it is obvious that soon thinking may soon turn to decentralization in order to cope with the burgeoning requirements of the government itself and the public. Only time will tell.

Appendix I
Careers at the GPO

Career positions in the Government Printing Office fall into two broad categories. The first can generally be classified as professional or quasiprofessional positions common to many agencies of the U.S. Government and not associated especially with the printing mission of the GPO.

To be eligible for these programs it is necessary that applicants qualify in the Federal Service Entrance Examination or other appropriate examinations, pass the required physical examination, and be a citizen of or owe allegiance to the United States.

Career positions are in such fields as personnel management, general administration, procurement and supply, electronic data processing, accounting, and library science.

Personnel Management. Specialized training in employee relations, employment, classification, and training. Opportunities for rotational training and on-the-job assignments designed to give full orientation in all areas of personnel management.

General Administration. Selected rotational assignments to give familiarity in such diversified areas as procurement, inventory, distribution, customer service, and sales planning in the Public Documents Division.

Procurement and Supply. Broad-based trainee program located in the Purchasing Division. Trainees given full orientation in such skills as procurement, contract administration, marketing, and supply management.

Data Processing. Intensive training utilizing the newest and most modern civilian electronic data processing equipment in the Washington, D.C., area.

Accounting. Opportunities for specialized experience in systems accounting, budget accounting, cost accounting, and auditing.

Library Science. Positions located in public Documents Division, which maintains an ongoing supply of approximately 2 million publications.

GPO administrative-management training programs are designed to develop a select group of persons who have demonstrated the potential to absorb higher-graded responsibilities in the administrative-management functions. These programs provide participants with an over-all view of the functions of administration, management, and the mission of the Government Printing Office with emphasis in a specialized career development program in the area to which assigned. The objective is to produce a professional with a thorough understanding of the duties and operations of the assigned divisions.

The flexibility of these programs not only allows concentration for the target position, but sufficient diversity to allow the "trainee" to grow professionally through extracurricular activities. Trainees participate in courses presented at the Government Printing Office in work-related areas and also receive courses given on an interagency or nongovernmental basis. They are encouraged to enroll in classes at local universities in various leadership, management, or other skills related to their assigned duties and join and participate in the activities of professional associations and societies in order to accelerate their growth and keep abreast with changing trends. These programs provide the trainee with rotational assignments in order to gain a broad background in the specific duties of supervisory and staff personnel.

The second group of positions are more or less peculiar to the special mission of the GPO. Most are craft or trade oriented and terminate at journeyman levels. There are exceptions to this since a high percentage of supervisory and managerial positions possess craft background prerequisites.

In recent years, career ladders have been established for those already employed in the Office that can lead to journeyman status and above. Three avenues are open to journeyman positions in the GPO:

(1) Appointment as a journeyman from established Civil Service registers.
(2) Appointment as an apprentice.
(3) In-house training programs.

The first requires certification by the Civil Service Commission after examination of experience qualifications. Applicants are rated on a scale of 100 based on the extent and quality of their experience and training relevant to the duties of the position. Appointment as an apprentice is based on scores obtained on an examination administered nationally by the Civil Service Commission. The apprentice program is a four-year course designed to train unskilled candidates to become journeyman craftsmen in more than a half dozen occupations. Both classroom and on-the-job training is given.

There are two sets of training programs: those in the Production Divisions, and those in the Engineering Division. These programs are open to all employees of the GPO. Before an employee can start in one of these programs, he must have worked at the Office for six months. He must also pass a written test given by the Office. One test is given for those who want training for jobs in the Production divisions and a separate one for those who want training in the Engineering Division. Each test is given once a year. Information about how to apply is posted on GPO bulletin boards well ahead of time. Although most of these programs consist of four years of on-the-job training and lead to journeyman status, several last for a shorter period and lead to lower level jobs.

Listed below are the craft areas in which our employees are trained:

I
TRAINING PROGRAMS IN
PRODUCTION DIVISION

Journeyman Positions
Bookbinder
Linotype Machinist
Cylinder Pressman

Monotype Machinist
Offset Platemaker-Stripper
Offset Stripper
Offset Pressman

Nonjourneyman Positions
Card Reproducer
Junior Offset Press Assistant
Monotype Casterman
Slide Bank Operative
Matrix Keeper
Spool Deskman

II
TRAINING PROGRAMS IN
ENGINEERING DIVISION

Journeyman Positions
Blacksmith
Carpenter
Electrician
Masonry Mechanic
Painter
Sheet Metal Worker
Stationary Engineer

Appendix II

Laws and Regulations Governing Public Printing

Following are such extracts of laws and regulations as appear pertinent to the subject material presented in this book. The complete body of law covering Public Printing and Binding may be found in the United States Code, title 44.

[Extracts from United States Code, title 44]

§ 103. Joint Committee on Printing: remedial powers

The Joint Committee on Printing may use any measures it considers necessary to remedy neglect, delay, duplication, or waste in the public printing and binding and the distribution of Government publications.

§ 501. Government printing, binding, and blank-book work to be done at the Government Printing Office

All printing, binding, and blank-book work for Congress, the Executive Office, the Judiciary, other than the Supreme Court of the United States, and every executive department, independent office and establishment of the Government, shall be done at the Government Printing Office, except—

(1) classes of work the Joint Committee on Printing considers to be urgent or necessary to have done elsewhere; and

(2) printing in field printing plants operated by an execu-

tive department, independent office or establishment, and the procurement of printing by an executive department, independent office or establishment from allotments for contract field printing, if approved by the Joint Committee on Printing.

Printing or binding may be done at the Government Printing Office only when authorized by law.

§ 502. Procurement of printing, binding, and blank-book work by Public Printer

Printing, binding, and blank-book work authorized by law, which the Public Printer is not able or equipped to do at the Government Printing Office, may be produced elsewhere under contracts made by him with the approval of the Joint Committee on Printing.

GOVERNMENT PRINTING AND BINDING REGULATIONS OF THE JOINT COMMITTEE ON PRINTING

(All references to these Regulations must cite number and paragraph)

Resolved by the Joint Committee on Printing, under authority of sections 103, 501, and 502, title 44, United States Code, That, except as otherwise provided herein, from and after March 1, 1969, the following shall supersede and repeal all regulations heretofore promulgated by the committee which are inconsistent herewith.

Title I: Definitions

1. Printing.—The term "printing" as used in these regulations shall be construed to include and apply to the processes of composition, platemaking, presswork, and binding; the equipment as classified in paragraph 8 and used in such processes; and the end items produced by such processes and equipment. (Composition shall include typesetting or final copy prepared by any method used as a substitute for typesetting when such material is procured commercially or produced in authorized printing plants and is to be used in the production of printing or a printing plate.)

2. Duplicating.—The term "duplicating" as used in these regulations means that material produced by use of (a) equipment listed in column 2 of paragraph 8, and (b) stencils, masters, and plates which are to be used on single unit duplicating equipment not larger than 11 by 17 inches and which have a maximum image of 10¾ by 14¼ inches: *Provided,* That not to exceed 5,000 production units shall be produced of any page and that items consisting of multiple pages will not exceed 25,000 production units in the aggregate.

3. Department.—The term "department," as used in these regulations, means any executive or military department or independent agency of the Government.

4. Printing Plant.—The term "printing plant," as used in these regulations, means any plant which produces "printing" as defined in paragraph 1, owned or operated wholly or in part by the Government or at Government expense, and shall include all such plants located on property owned or controlled by the Government. No printing plant shall be operated without prior authorization of the Joint Committee on Printing. Work done by such plants shall not include any items which are determined to be commercially procurable. No plant shall be moved from the building in which it was authorized for operation, or disestablished, without prior authority of the committee.

5. Government Printing Office Regional Printing Procurement Office.—This term means any office, established by the Public Printer in accordance with Joint Committee on Printing authorization, which shall procure Federal printing needs which are determined to be commercially procurable and which originate or are for distribution within its region.

6. Federal Printing.—This term means all printing as defined in paragraph 1 for the use of all departments, irrespective of the place of production or procurement origin or ultimate end-use.

Determination as to where Federal printing is to be requisitioned shall be made by the head of each department through a central service, as defined in paragraph 30, in accordance with the collective provisions provided in paragraphs 4, 5, 28, and 46.

7–1. Production Unit.—A production unit means one sheet, size 8 by 10½ inches, one side only, one color.

7–2. All production from presses of whatever size shall be computed on the basis of the unit size of press multiplied by the number of impressions obtained from the individual press concerned. For example.

	Units		*Units*
11 by 17 inches or less (10¾ x 14″ maximum image)	1	22 by 29 inches	6
		22 by 34 inches	8
11 by 17 inches or less, tandem (10¾ x 14″ maximum image)	2	25 by 38 inches	10
11 by 17 inches	2	34 by 44 inches	16
14 by 20 inches	2	45 by 48 inches	24
11 by 17 inches, tandem	4	42 by 58 inches	28
17 by 22 inches	4	48 by 54 inches	30

[*Title II* omitted.]

Title III: General Provisions

13. Advertisements, Commercial.—Except as provided in paragraphs 14, 15, and 16, no Government publication or other Government printed matter, prepared or produced with either appropriated or nonappropriated funds or identified with an activity of the Government, shall contain any advertisement inserted by or for any private individual, firm, or corporation; or contain material which implies in any manner that the Government endorses or favors any specific commercial product, commodity, or service.

14. Art Signatures.—When the size of signatures on freehand art is out of proportion or relation to the design, the copy is unacceptable and shall not be printed unless the signature is removed or sufficiently reduced in size. Signatures of technical illustrators, designers, typographers, or layout artists shall not be printed.

15. Courtesy Credit Lines.—Courtesy credit lines for uncopyrighted materials contributed or loaned by nongovernmental parties shall be subordinate in size of type to that of both text and legends for illustrations. When all materials have come from a single nongovernmental source, credit lines shall be given only in an un-displayed paragraph. Credit lines shall not be given for:

(*a*) Materials purchased by a department.

(*b*) Nongovernment designers, typographers, or layout artists.

(*c*) Government art directors, designers, typographers, layout artists, or photographers.

16. Copyright Notices.—Copyright notices shall be subordinated in size of type to that of both text and legends for illustrations. When privately copyrighted material is reprinted in a Government publication, notice of copyright is essential in order that the public not be misled.

17–1. Color Printing.—The Committee recognizes that printing in two or more colors generally increases costs. Consequently, it is the responsibility of the head of any department, independent office or establishment of the Government to assure that all multicolor printing shall contribute demonstrable value toward achieving a greater fulfillment of the ultimate end-purpose of whatever printed item in which it is included.

17–2. Demonstrably valuable multicolor printing, for the purpose of these regulations, includes the following categories:

(*a*) Maps and technical diagrams where additional color is necessary for clarity.

(*b*) Object identification (medical specimens, diseases, plants, flags, uniforms, etc.).

(*c*) Safety programs, fire prevention, saving bonds programs, and competitive areas of personnel recruiting.

(*d*) Areas wherein clearly identifiable savings in costs can be soundly predicated on multicolor use.

(*e*) Printing for programs required by law, whose relative success or failure is in direct ratio to the degree of public response, and where that response can be logically attributable to the number of colors planned and the manner in which they are proposed to be used.

Color for promotional or motivational purposes such as programs concerning public health, safety, consumer benefits; or to encourage utilization of Government facilities such as programs for social security, medicare, and certain areas of need for veterans would come within this category.

17–3. Multicolor printing which does not meet the demonstrably valuable contribution requirement of these regulations, includes but is not exclusively limited to the following categories:

(*a*) Printed items wherein additional color is used primarily for decorative effect.

(*b*) Printed items where additional color is used primarily in lieu of effective layout and design.

(*c*) Printed items where additional color is used excessively, i.e., four colors when two or three will fulfill the need; three colors when two are adequate; two colors when one—with or without reverse treatment—is adequate.

(*d*) Printed items wherein the inclusion of multicolor does not reflect careful, competent advance planning which recognizes the contribution the use of color is expected to make to the ultimate end-purpose.

18. Illustrations.—Illustrations are to be used in Government printed matter only when they:

(*a*) Relate entirely to the transaction of public business, and are in the public interest.

(*b*) Related directly to the subject matter and are necessary to explain the text.

(*c*) Do not serve to aggrandize any individual.

(*d*) Are in good taste and do not offend proper sensibilities.

(*e*) Are restricted to the minimum size necessary to accomplish their purpose.

(*f*) Illustrate employees actually engaged in an act or service related to their official duties.

19. Authors' Names on Covers.—Personal names shall not be printed on the covers of publications for the purpose of identifying authorship, unless otherwise authorized by the Joint Committee on Printing. This restriction, however, does not apply to identifying authorship on backstrips (spines), self-covers, or title pages.

20. Cards: Calling, Greeting.—Printing or engraving of calling or greeting cards is considered to be personal rather than official and shall not be done at Government expense.

21. Blank Books.—Blank books not available through General Services Administration but regularly carried in stock by Commercial dealers and which require no printing and/or binding operation after receipt of order may be procured without obtaining a waiver from the Government Printing Office: *Provided,* That no order or orders for each type of blank book exceeds $500 in any one year.

22–1. Calendars, Date: Desk and Wall.—Standardized Government desk and wall calendars are the only calendars which departments are authorized to obtain at Government expense, and shall be ordered from the General Services Administration.

22–2. Style, size, and format of the standardized wall calendar, to be procured from the Government Printing Office, shall be subject to approval of the Joint Committee on Printing.

Schedule and appointment sheets are not considered to be calendars.

23. Certificate of Necessity.—Section 1103, title 44, United States Code:

> When a department, the Supreme Court, the Court of Claims, or the Library of Congress requires printing or binding to be done, it shall certify that it is necessary for the public service . . .

24–1. Correspondence and Liaison With Committee.—All official correspondence for the consideration of the Joint Committee on Printing is to be signed by the head of the department or an official designated by him. The committee shall be notified in writing by the head of the department of any official so designated.

In order to insure prompt delivery, all official correspondence should be addressed as follows:

> *Chairman, Joint Committee on Printing*
> *United States Senate Post Office*
> *Washington, D.C. 20510*

24–2. All matters pertaining to printing, binding, and the distribution of printed matter shall be referred to the committee by and through one designated source in each department.

25. Form and Style of Work for Departments.—The head of each department shall cause printing and binding for general use to be standardized. With respect to printing which is requisitioned from the Government Printing Office, attention is again directed to section 1105, title 44, United States Code, which provides that—

> The Public Printer shall determine the form and style in which the printing or binding ordered by a department is executed, and the material and the size of type used, having proper regard to economy, workmanship, and the purposes for which the work is needed.

The Government Printing Office Style Manual, approved by the Joint Committee on Printing, was specifically compiled and published to meet the requirements of this law. It is the opinion of the committee that deviations therefrom generally constitute a waste in public printing and binding.

26–1. Forms, Standard, Procurement of.—Standard forms approved by the Bureau of the Budget, the General Accounting Office, or other responsible agency shall be obtained from the General Services Administration, unless otherwise authorized by the Joint Committee on Printing.

26–2. The committee recognizes that as a substitute for overprinting of standard forms, the filling in of variable processing data on a preprinted master or a die-impressed stencil can provide definite economies and therefore authorizes the General Services Administration to furnish such masters and stencils where economies can be demonstrated.

27–1. Journals, Magazines, Periodicals, and Similar Publications.—The committee invites attention to section 1108, title 44, United States Code, relating to periodicals which reads as follows:

> The head of an executive department, independent agency or establishment of the Government, with the approval of the Director of the Bureau of the Budget, may use from the appropriations available for printing and binding such sums as are necessary for the printing of journals, magazines, periodicals, and similar publications he certifies in writing to be necessary in the transaction of the public business required by law of the department, office, or establishment. There may be printed, in addition to those necessary for the public business, not to exceed two thousand copies for free

distribution by the issuing department, office, or establishment. The Public Printer, subject to regulation by the Joint Committee on Printing, shall print additional copies required for sale to the public by the Superintendent of Documents; but the printing of these additional copies may not interfere with the prompt execution of printing for the Government.

27–2. The term "journals, magazines, periodicals, and similar publications," as used in above section, shall be construed as not applying to strictly administrative reports, memoranda, and similar materials, or to strictly statistical materials, and information required exclusively for the official use of the issuing office or service in the transaction of its routine business. Such information shall be construed as being required exclusively for the use of the issuing office or service in the transaction of its routine business if not more than 2,000 copies, or not more than 10 per cent of the total quantity printed, whichever is lesser, are for free distribution to other than the issuing department, office, or establishment, its official established auxiliary organizations, and other individuals and organizations required to be kept informed in the transaction of the routine business of the department, office, or establishment.

28. Legal Requirements.—Sections 501 and 502, title 44, United States Code:

SEC. 501. All printing, binding, and blank-book work for Congress, the Executive Office, the Judiciary, other than the Supreme Court of the United States, and every executive department, independent office and establishment of the Government, shall be done at the Government Printing Office, except—

(1) classes of work the Joint Committee on Printing considers to be urgent or necessary to have done elsewhere; and

(2) printing in field printing plants operated by an executive department, independent office or establishment, and the procurement of printing by an executive department, independent office or establishment from allotments for contract field printing, if approved by the Joint Committee on Printing.

Printing or binding may be done at the Government Printing Office only when authorized by law.

SEC. 502. Printing, binding, and blank-book work authorized by law, which the Public Printer is not able or equipped to do at the Government Printing Office, may be produced elsewhere under contracts made by him with the approval of the Joint Committee on Printing.

29. Legality and Necessity.—No printing, binding, or blank-book work shall be done at the Government Printing Office or at any other printing or binding office, plant, or school of the Government unless authorized by law. (See secs. 501 and 1123, title 44, U.S.C.) All printed matter issued shall be devoted to the work which the branch or officer of the Government issuing the same is required by law to undertake, and shall not contain matter which is unnecessary in the transaction of the public business or matter relating to work which any other branch of the Government service is authorized to perform. (See secs. 1102, 1113, and 1118, title 44, U.S.C.)

30. Central Service.—Heads of departments shall maintain under their direct supervision a central service with responsibility for the conduct of a coordinated program controlling the development of materials to be printed, and the procurement, production, and distribution of printed matter. Also, the committee strongly urges that the central service maintain equal responsibility and control of duplicated matter.

31. Mailing Lists.—All departments shall make necessary revisions in their mailing lists at least once each year in order to eliminate waste in Government funds caused by publications being improperly addressed or mailed to persons no longer desiring them. It is the judgment of the Joint Committee on Printing that the use of titles on mailing lists in lieu of names will reduce the cost of list maintenance.

32. Mailing: Self-Mailer Technique.—The penalty or postage indicia and mailing address shall be imprinted directly upon printed materials rather than using separate envelopes for mailing whenever such technique will prove feasible and economical, and in accordance with existing postal regulations.

33. Neglect, Delay, Duplication, or Waste.—The attention of the committee should be promptly called to "any neglect, delay, duplication, or waste in the public printing and binding and the distribution of Government publications."

34–1. Paper, Standardization of.—The committee invites attention to section 509, title 44, United States Code, relating to standards of paper, which reads as follows:

The Joint Committee on Printing shall fix upon standards of paper for the different descriptions of public printing and binding, and the Public

Printer, under their direction, shall advertise in six newspapers or trade journals, published in different cities, for sealed proposals to furnish the Government with paper, as specified in the schedule to be furnished applicants by the Public Printer, setting forth in detail the quality and quantities required for the public printing. The Public Printer shall furnish samples of the standard of papers fixed upon to applicants who desire to bid.

34–2. The "Government Paper Specification Standards" establishes specification standards of paper for the public printing and binding for the U.S. Government. Unless otherwise authorized by the Joint Committee on Printing, these specifications and standards are mandatory for use by the departments of the Government in the preparation of procurement documents for paper stocks and in specifying paper stocks to be used in printing, binding, or duplicating. It is the opinion of the committee that types, grades, or weights, other than those given under these standards generally constitute waste in public printing, and it is directed that the procurement or use of such paper types, grades, or weights, for printing, binding, or duplicating be discontinued.

34–3. Semiannual and annual contracts for paper, in general, are not in the best interests of the Government. Such procurement practices should be used only when savings in costs are clearly demonstrable.

34–4. The Public Printer is authorized and directed to furnish at cost to the departments such copies of these standards, and standard samples, as they may require in the transaction of the public business.

35–1. Printing Requirements Resulting From Contracts for Equipment and Services.—The Joint Committee on Printing does not intend that contractors shall become prime sources of printing for departments or agencies. Therefore, the inclusion of printing, as defined in paragraph 1, within contracts for the manufacture and/or operation of equipment and for services such as architectural, engineering, and research, is prohibited unless authorized by the Joint Committee on Printing.

35–2. This regulation does not preclude the procurement of writing, editing, preparation of manuscript copy, or preparation of related illustrative material as a part of contracts; or incidental printing, e.g., forms and instructional materials to be used by the contractor, as may be required to respond to the terms of a contract.

36–1. Printing Requirements Resulting From Grants.—The Joint Committee on Printing does not intend that grantees shall become prime sources of printing for the use of departments and agencies. Therefore, the inclusion of printing, as defined in paragraph 1, within grants is prohibited unless authorized by the Joint Committee on Printing.

36–2. This regulation does not preclude—
  (*a*) The issuance of grants by any department or agency for the support of nongovernment publications, provided such grants were issued pursuant to an authorization of law and were not made primarily or substantially for the purpose of having material printed for the use of any department or agency.
  (*b*) The publication of findings by grantees within the terms of their grants provided that such publication is not primarily or substantially for the purpose of having such findings printed for the use of a department or agency.
  (*c*) The initiation by departments and agencies of the procurement of writing, editing, preparation of manuscript copy, or preparation of related illustrative material, from grantees; or the internal printing requirements of the grantee required to respond to the terms of the grant. However, the printing of such material must be accomplished in accordance with printing laws and regulations.

36–3. For the purposes of this paragraph, a requirement for a grantee to provide in excess of 5,000 production units of only one page, or 25,000 production units in the aggregate of multiple pages of his findings for the use of a department or agency will be deemed to be printing primarily or substantially for a department or agency.

37. Private or Commercial Work.—No work of a private or commercial nature may be accomplished at any Government plant even though the Government is reimbursed therefor. (See secs. 1102 and 1113, title 44, U.S.C.)

38. Publications, Allocation of.—No department of the Government shall allocate publications to the credit of any Member of Congress unless such allocation is specifically provided for by law.

39–1. Publications, Free Distribution of.—Departments shall not make free distribution of any publication to any private individual or private organization in quantities exceeding 50 copies without prior approval of the Joint Committee on Printing. This quantity limitation shall not apply when the production cost of the publications to be distributed is less than $50.

39–2. Requests for committee approval shall list the name of the publication, the name of the person or organization desiring the same, and the number of copies desired.

39–3. This restriction includes the free distribution in bulk of any material to private individuals or organizations for redistribution to names on their mailing lists. Committee approval is not required when the initiative for distribution through nongovernmental facilities is taken by departments. (See also sec. 4154, title 39, U.S.C., supp. 5.)

40. Publications, Identification of.—All documents and publications printed at Government expense shall have printed thereon the name of the branch, bureau, department, or office of the Government issuing the same and the date of issuance. If copies are intended primarily for sale, the selling price and where obtainable shall also be shown.

41. Publications, Sale of by Superintendent of Documents.— The Superintendent of Documents will sell only those publications printed by the Government Printing Office or ordered printed through the Government Printing Office or the Government Printing Office Regional Printing Procurement Offices. This restriction on sale shall not affect the continued Catalog listing by the Superintendent of Documents of publications which are not printed by or ordered printed through the Government Printing Office. Nothing in this paragraph shall be construed as modifying or repealing provisions of sections 1702, 1711, and 1720 of title 44, United States Code.

42. Responsibility for Application and Enforcement of Regulations.—The head of each department is responsible for the application and enforcement of these regulations and other applicable regulations and legislative provisions.

43–1. Stationery, Embossed.—The Public Printer may furnish, upon requisition, to the President of the United States, members of his Cabinet, and the Department of State (for diplomatic correspondence exclusively), such quantities of embossed stationery as may be necessary for official use. The Comptroller General, the Librarian of Congress, the Public Printer, the head of each permanent commission, independent establishment or board, and the Judges of the United States Courts may requisition embossed noteheads or letterheads not to exceed 5,000 copies in the aggregate, and envelopes therefor in any one fiscal year: *Provided,* That greater quantities may be furnished upon the approval of the Joint Committee on Printing. The Public Printer shall not honor requests from any Government activity for embossing second sheets or other than standard-size envelopes. No embossed stationery other than listed above shall be produced or procured at Government expense unless authorized by the Joint Committee on Printing.

43–2. The provisions apply also to thermographic printing.

44. Stationery, Personalized.—The printing of names of officers or officials of the executive or judicial branches of the Government on official stationery and preprinted mastheads may be accomplished only after approval by the Joint Committee on Printing. Addresses and telephone numbers should be omitted in order to allow greatest distribution and prevent the creation of "frozen" stocks frequently caused by changes. The committee directs that no personalized second sheets shall be produced or procured at Government expense.

45. Stationery: Sizes, Quality, Weight, Printing Thereon, etc.— The committee directs attention to the Federal Property Management Regulation which prescribes standards (sizes, grades and weights of paper, and colors of ink and paper) to be used for printing stationery and envelopes for official Government correspondence.

46–1. Waiver, Purchase of Printing by.—Section 504, title 44, United States Code:

The Joint Committee on Printing may permit the Public Printer to authorize an executive department, independent office, or establishment of the Government to purchase direct for its use such printing, binding, and blank-book work, otherwise authorized by law, as the Government Printing Office is not able or suitably equipped to execute or as may be more economically or in the better interest of the Government executed elsewhere.

46–2. Pursuant to the above, the Public Printer is permitted to return to any department of the Government any written requisition for printing, binding, and blank-book work, otherwise authorized by law, as in his opinion he is neither able nor suitably equipped to execute or which may be more economically, or in the better interest of the Government, procured elsewhere than at the Government Printing Office or the Government Printing Office Regional Printing Procurement Offices; and in all such instances is hereby permitted to authorize such Government activity to procure the work direct from other sources. Such waiver, when granted, shall not be construed as an exemption from the provisions of these regulations. Upon all such returned requisitions the Public Printer shall endorse a statement that the action taken is in accordance with the provision of section 504, title 44, United States Code.

46–3. No department requisitioning printing from the Government Printing Office or the Government Printing Office Regional Printing Procurement Offices shall anticipate the release of any requisition for direct procurement, until so advised by the Public Printer.

[*Title IV* omitted.]

Title V: Authorized Federal Plants

55. Plants Authorized To Do Printing.—The plants hereinafter named are authorized to produce printing, as defined in paragraph 1, in accordance with the provisions of paragraphs 4, 5, and 6 of these regulations. All departments shall submit reports and inventories promptly, as required by paragraphs 47 to 54, inclusive, of title IV.

ALPHABETICAL PLANT LISTING BY DEPARTMENTS

ADMINISTRATIVE OFFICE OF THE U.S. COURTS:
Washington, D.C.

AGRICULTURE, DEPARTMENT OF:
      Office of Plant and Operations (Washington, D.C.)

  AGRICULTURE STABILIZATION AND CONSERVATION SERVICE:
  New Orleans, La.

  FOREST SERVICE:

Asheville, N.C.	Berkeley, Calif.	San Francisco, Calif.
Atlanta, Ga.	Madison, Wisc.	Upper Darby, Pa.
	Missoula, Mont.	

  SOIL CONSERVATION SERVICE:

| Fort Worth, Tex. | Hyattsville, Md. | Portland, Oreg. |
| | Lincoln, Nebr. | |

AIR FORCE, DEPARTMENT OF THE:
  Aeronautical Chart and Information Center (St. Louis, Mo.)
  Andrews Air Force Base (Camp Springs, Md.)
  Arnold Engineering Development Center (Tullahoma, Tenn.)
  Barksdale Air Force Base (Shreveport, La.)
  Edwards Air Force Base (Muroc, Calif.)
  Eglin Air Force Base (Valparaiso, Fla.)
  Ent Air Force Base (Colorado Springs, Colo.)
  Griffis Air Force Base (Rome, N.Y.)
  Gunter Air Force Base (Montgomery, Ala.)
  Hill Air Force Base (Ogden, Utah)
  Holloman Air Force Base (Alamogordo, N. Mex.)
  Keesler Air Force Base (Biloxi, Miss.)
  Kelly Air Force Base (San Antonio, Tex.):
    San Antonio Air Materiel Area
    United States Air Force Security Service
  L. G. Hanscom Field (Bedford, Mass.)
  Langley Air Force Base (Hampton, Va.)
  McClellan Air Force Base (Sacramento, Calif.)
  March Air Force Base (Riverside, Calif.)
  Norton Air Force Base (San Bernardino, Calif.)
  Offutt Air Force Base (Omaha, Nebr.)
  Patrick Air Force Base (Cocoa Beach, Fla.)
  Robins Air Force Base (Macon, Ga.)
  Scott Air Force Base (Belleville, Ill.)
  Secretary of the Air Force (Washington, D.C.)

Sheppard Air Force Base (Wichita Falls, Tex.)
Space and Missile Organization (Inglewood, Calif.)
Tinker Air Force Base (Oklahoma City, Okla.)
United States Air Force Academy (Colorado Springs, Colo.)
United States Air Forces in Europe (Wiesbaden, Germany)
Vandenberg Air Force Base (Lompoc, Calif.)
Westover Air Force Base (Chicopee Falls, Mass.)
Wright-Patterson Air Force Base (Dayton, Ohio)

ARMY, DEPARTMENT OF THE:
Aberdeen, Md. (Proving Ground)
Albuquerque, N. Mex.:
Sandia Base
U.S. Army Engineer District
Brooklyn, N.Y. (Military Ocean Terminal)
Camp Keyes, Augusta, Maine (National Guard Bureau)
Carlisle Barracks, Pa. (U.S. Army War College)
Chambersburg, Pa. (Letterkenny Army Depot)
Chicago, Ill.:
Fifth U.S. Army Headquarters
U.S. Army Engineer District
U.S. Army Support Command
Corozal, C.Z. (U.S. Army Forces, Southern Command)
Detroit, Mich.:
U.S. Army Engineer District
U.S. Army Engineer District, Lake Survey
Dover, N.J. (Picatinny Arsenal)
Edgewood Arsenal, Md.
Fort Belvoir, Va.:
Department of Topography
U.S. Army Engineer Center
Fort Benjamin Harrison, Ind.
Fort Benning, Ga. (U.S. Army Infantry School)
Fort Bliss, Tex. (U.S. Air Defense Center)
Fort Bragg, N.C. (XVIII Airborne Corps and Fort Bragg)
Fort Detrick, Md.
Fort Douglas, Utah (Desert Test Center)
Fort Eustis, Va. (U.S. Army Transportation Center and Fort Eustis)
Fort George G. Meade, Md. (First U.S. Army Headquarters)
Fort Gordon, Ga. (U.S. Army School/Training Center)
Fort Holabird, Md. (U.S. Army Intelligence Center and Fort
Holabird)
Fort Huachuca, Ariz. (U.S. Army Electronic Proving Ground)
Fort Knox, Ky. (U.S. Army Armor School)
Fort Leavenworth, Kans.:
Disciplinary Barracks

U.S. Army Command General Staff College
Fort Lee, Va. (U.S. Army Quartermaster Center and Fort Lee)
Fort Leonard Wood, Mo.
Fort McPherson, Ga. (Third U.S. Army Headquarters)
Fort Monmouth, N.J. (U.S. Army Electronics Command)
Fort Monroe, Va. (U.S. Continental Army Command)
Fort Richardson, Alaska (U.S. Army, Alaska)
Fort Riley, Kans.
Fort Rucker, Ala. (U.S. Army Aviation School)
Fort Sill, Okla. (U.S. Army Artillery and Missile Center)
Galveston, Tex. (U.S. Army Engineer District)
Gravelly Point, Va. (Chief of Engineers)
Huntington, West Va. (U.S. Army Engineer District)
Jacksonville, Fla. (U.S. Army Engineer District)
Joliet, Ill. (Army Ammunition Plant)
Kansas City, Mo. (U.S. Army Engineer District)
Kawasaki City, Japan (U.S. Army, Japan)
Las Cruces, N. Mex. (White Sands Missile Range)
Lathrop, Calif. (Sharpe Army Depot)
Leghorn, Italy (U.S. Army Engineer Division, Mediterranean)
Lexington, Ky. (Lexington-Blue Grass Army Depot)
Little Rock, Ark. (U.S. Army Engineer District)
Long Island City, N.Y. (U.S. Army Pictorial Center)
Los Angeles, Calif. (U.S. Army Engineer District)
Louisville, Ky. (U.S. Army Engineer District)
Merrit Island, Fla. (Canaveral U.S. Army Engineer District)
Mobile, Ala. (U.S. Army Engineer District)
Monterery, Presidio of, Calif. (Defense Language Institute)
Murnau, Germany (U.S. Army School Command, Europe)
Nashville, Tenn. (U.S. Army Engineer District)
Natick, Mass. (Natick Laboratories)
New Cumberland, Pa. (Army Depot)
Norfolk, Va. (U.S. Army Engineer District)
Oakland, Calif. (Army Base)
Omaha, Nebr. (U.S. Army Engineer District)
Pasadena, Calif., U.S. Army Southwest Procurement Agency
Philadelphia, Pa.:
    Frankford Arsenal
    U.S. Army Electronics Material Agency
    U.S. Army Engineer District
Pittsburgh, Pa. (U.S. Army Engineer District)
Portland, Oreg. (U.S. Army Engineer District)
Pueblo, Colo. (Army Depot)
Redstone Arsenal, Ala.
Rock Island, Ill. (Arsenal)
Roedelheim, Germany (AG Support Center, Europe)

Sacramento, Calif.:
Army Depot
U.S. Army Engineer District
St. Louis, Mo. (U.S. Army Aviation Systems Command)
San Antonio, Tex. (Army Map Service, San Antonio Field Office)
San Francisco, Calif.:
Sixth U.S. Army Headquarters
U.S. Army Engineer District
Savanna, Ill. (Army Depot)
Savannah, Ga. (U.S. Army Engineer District)
Seattle, Wash. (U.S. Army Engineer District)
Seoul, Korea (U.S. Army Engineer District, Far East)
Texarkana, Tex. (Red River Army Depot)
Tobyhanna, Pa. (Army Depot)
Tulsa, Okla. (U.S. Army Engineer District)
Vicksburg, Miss. (U.S. Army Engineer Waterways Experiment
Station)
Walla Walla, Wash. (U.S. Army Engineer District)
Waltham, Mass. (New England U.S. Army Engineer Division)
Warren, Mich. (U.S. Army Tank Automotive Command)
Washington, D.C.:
Armed Forces Institute of Pathology
Army Map Service
Finance and Accounts Office, U.S. Army
National War College
Watertown, Mass. (U.S. Army Materials Research Agency)
West Point, N.Y. (U.S. Military Academy)
Yuma, Ariz (Proving Ground)

ATOMIC ENERGY COMMISSION:

Aiken, S.C.
Albuquerque, N. Mex.:
Atomic Energy Commission
Sandia Corporation
Ames, Iowa
Berkeley, Calif.
Boulder, Colo.
Chicago, Ill.
Cincinnati, Ohio
Germantown, Md.
Grand Junction, Colo.
Idaho Falls, Idaho
Kansas City, Mo.
Los Alamos, N. Mex. (University
of California)
Mercury, Nev.
Miamisburg, Ohio
Oak Ridge, Tenn.
Oak Ridge, Tenn. (Union Carbide
Nuclear Co.)
Paducah, Ky.
Pittsburgh, Pa.
Portsmouth, Ohio
Richland, Wash.
Schenectady, N.Y.
Upton, N.Y.

BUREAU OF THE BUDGET:*
Washington, D.C.

* Now the Office of Management and Budget.

CANAL ZONE GOVERNMENT:
La Boca, C.Z.

CIVIL AERONAUTICS BOARD:
Washington, D.C.

CIVIL SERVICE COMMISSION:
Atlanta, Ga.   Philadelphia, Pa.   Washington, D.C.
                      Seattle, Wash.

COMMERCE, DEPARTMENT OF:
Office of Publications (Washington, D.C.)

CENSUS, BUREAU OF THE:	ENVIRONMENTAL SCIENCE SERVICES
Jeffersonville, Ind.	ADMINISTRATION:
MARITIME ADMINISTRATION:	Asheville, N.C.
Kings Point, Long	Washington, D.C.
Island, N.Y.	Boulder, Colo.

DEFENSE INTELLIGENCE AGENCY:
Arlington Hall, Va.

DEFENSE SUPPLY AGENCY:
Alexandria, Va.   Memphis, Tenn.   Philadelphia, Pa.
Battle Creek, Mich.   New York, N.Y.   Richmond, Va.

FEDERAL COMMUNICATIONS COMMISSION:
Washington, D.C.

FEDERAL HOME LOAN BANK BOARD:
Washington, D.C.

FEDERAL POWER COMMISSION:
Washington, D.C.

FEDERAL TRADE COMMISSION:
Washington, D.C.

GENERAL ACCOUNTING OFFICE:
Washington, D.C.

GENERAL SERVICES ADMINISTRATION:
Atlanta, Ga.   Juneau, Alaska
Atlanta, Ga. (Branch Plant)   Kansas City, Mo.
Billings, Mont.   New York, N.Y.
Boston, Mass.   St. Louis, Mo.
Cincinnati, Ohio   Salt Lake City, Utah
Dallas, Tex.   San Francisco, Calif.
Fort Worth, Tex.   Washington, D.C.

GOVERNMENT PRINTING OFFICE:
Chicago, Ill.—Main Post Office Building, 433 West Van Buren
Street

Denver, Colo.—Denver Federal Center, Bldg. 52
New York, N.Y.—Post Office Building, Morgan Annex, 341 Ninth
    Avenue
San Francisco, Calif.—49 Fourth Street
Seattle, Wash.—2430 Fourth Avenue South
Washington, D.C.—Washington Navy Yard

HEALTH, EDUCATION, AND WELFARE, DEPARTMENT OF:
Atlanta, Ga.   Lexington, Ky.
Bethesda, Md. (National Institutes of Health)   Washington, D.C.
        Woodlawn, Md. (Social Security Administration)

HOUSING AND URBAN DEVELOPMENT, DEPARTMENT OF:
Washington, D.C.

INTERIOR, DEPARTMENT OF THE:
    Geological Survey Map Plant (Washington, D.C.)
    Main Plant (Washington, D.C.)
    BONNEVILLE POWER ADMINISTRATION, Portland, Oreg.
    BUREAU OF INDIAN AFFAIRS (School Printing Courses):
    Chilocco School, Chilocco, Okla.
    Haskell Institute, Lawrence, Kans.
    Phoenix School, Phoenix, Ariz.
    BUREAU OF MINES:
    Pittsburgh, Pa.
    BUREAU OF RECLAMATION:
    Boise, Idaho   Boulder City, Nev.

INTERSTATE COMMERCE COMMISSION:
Washington, D.C.

JUSTICE, DEPARTMENT OF:
    Administrative Division (Washington, D.C.)
    FEDERAL BUREAU OF INVESTIGATION (Washington, D.C.)
    FEDERAL PRISON INDUSTRIES, INC.:
    Lompoc, Calif.   Marion, Ill.   Sandstone, Minn.

LABOR, DEPARTMENT OF:
Washington, D.C.

LIBRARY OF CONGRESS:
Washington, D.C.

NATIONAL AERONAUTICS AND SPACE
ADMINISTRATION:
Cleveland, Ohio   Kennedy Space   Sandusky, Ohio
Edwards, Calif.   Center, Fla.   (Cleveland branch
Greenbelt, Md.   Moffet Field, Calif.   plant)
Hampton, Va.   New Orleans, La.   Wallops Island, Va.
Houston, Tex.   Pasadena, Calif.   Washington, D.C.

NATIONAL LABOR RELATIONS BOARD:
Washington, D.C.

NATIONAL SECURITY AGENCY:
Fort George G. Meade, Md.

NAVY, DEPARTMENT OF THE:
Annapolis, Md. (Branch NDW Publications and Printing Service Office)
Argentia, Newfoundland (Naval Station)
Bellevue, D.C. (Naval Research Laboratory)
Boston, Mass. (1ND Publications and Printing Service Office)
Bremerton, Wash. (13ND Publications and Printing Service Office)
Brooklyn, N.Y. (3ND Publications and Printing Service Office)
Camp Lejeune, N.C. (Marine Corps Base)
Charleston, S.C. (6ND Publications and Printing Service Office)
China Lake, Calif. (Naval Ordnance Test Station)
Cleveland, Ohio (Navy Finance Center)
Corpus Christi, Tex. (Branch 8ND Publications and Printing Service Office)
Crane, Ind. (Naval Ammunition Depot)
Cumberland, Md. (Allegany Ballistics Laboratory)
Dahlgren, Va. (Naval Weapons Laboratory)
Great Lakes, Ill. (9ND Publications and Printing Service Office)
Guam, Marianas Islands (Branch 14ND Publications and Printing Service Office)
Guantánamo Bay, Cuba (Branch 10ND Publications and Printing Service Office)
Indian Head, Md. (Naval Propellant Plant)
Jacksonville, Fla.:
  Branch 6ND Publications and Printing Service Office
  Fleet Intelligence Center, Europe
Keflavik, Iceland (Naval Station)
Key West, Fla. (Branch 6ND Publications and Printing Service Office)
Kodiak, Alaska
London, England (U.S. Naval Activities, United Kingdom)
Louisville, Ky. (Naval Ordnance Plant)
McAlester, Okla. (Naval Ammunition Depot)
Mechanicsburg, Pa. (Naval Supply Depot)
Monterey, Calif. (Naval Postgraduate School)
Naples, Italy (NAVEUR Publications and Printing Service Office)
New Orleans, La. (8ND Publications and Printing Service Office)
Newport, R.I.:
  Branch 1ND Publications and Printing Service Office
  Commander, Destroyer Force Atlantic

Norfolk, Va.:
  Commander in Chief Atlantic Fleet
  5ND Publications and Printing Service Office
Oahu, Hawaii (Naval Ammunition Depot)
Oakland, Calif. (12ND Publications and Printing Service Office)
Okinawa, Ryukyu Islands
Orlando, Fla. (Branch 6ND Publications and Printing Service Office)
Panama City, Fla. (Navy Mine Defense Laboratory)
Patuxent River, Md. (Naval Air Test Center)
Pearl Harbor, Hawaii:
  Fleet Intelligence Center, Pacific
  14ND Publications and Printing Service Office
Pensacola, Fla. (CNATRA Publications and Printing Service Office)
Philadelphia, Pa.:
  Naval Supply Depot (4ND Publications and Printing Service Office)
  U.S. Naval Base (Branch 4ND Publications and Printing Service Office)
Point Mugu, Calif. (Branch 11ND Publications and Printing Service Office)
Portsmouth, N.H.:
  Naval Shipyard (Branch 1ND Publications and Printing Service Office)
  Retraining Command (Branch 1ND Publications and Printing Service Office)
Portsmouth, Va. (Branch 5ND Publications and Printing Service Office)
Quantico, Va. (Marine Corps Schools)
Quonset Point, R.I. (Naval Air Station)
Rota, Spain (Branch NAVEUR Publications and Printing Service Office)
San Diego, Calif. (11ND Publications and Printing Service Office)
San Juan, P.R. (10ND Publications and Printing Service Office)
Subic Bay, Philippine Islands (Branch 14ND Publications and Printing Service Office)
Suitland, Md. (Naval Reconnaissance and Technical Support Center)
Suitland, Md. (Oceanographic Office)
Vallejo, Calif., Mare Island Naval Shipyard (Branch 12ND Publications and Printing Service Office)
Washington, D.C. (Defense Printing Service)
White Oak, Md. (Naval Ordnance Laboratory)

POST OFFICE, DEPARTMENT OF THE:
  Washington, D.C.

RAILROAD RETIREMENT BOARD:
Chicago, Ill.

SECURITIES AND EXCHANGE COMMISSION:
Washington, D.C.

SELECTIVE SERVICE SYSTEM:
Washington, D.C.

SMALL BUSINESS ADMINISTRATION:
Washington, D.C.

SMITHSONIAN INSTITUTION:
Cambridge, Mass.

STATE, DEPARTMENT OF:
Washington D.C.

TRANSPORTATION, DEPARTMENT OF:
Office of the Secretary (Washington, D.C.)
COAST GUARD, U.S. (GOVERNORS ISLAND, N.Y.)
FEDERAL AVIATION ADMINISTRATION:

Anchorage, Alaska	Fort Worth, Tex.	Los Angeles, Calif.
Atlantic City, N.J.	Jamaica, Long Island, N.Y.	Oklahoma City, Okla.

TREASURY, DEPARTMENT OF THE:
Office of Administrative Services (Washington, D.C.)
BUREAU OF CUSTOMS:

New York, N.Y.	Washington, D.C.

INTERNAL REVENUE SERVICE:

Atlanta, Ga.	New York, N.Y.	San Francisco, Calif.
Chicago, Ill.	Philadelphia, Pa.	Washington, D.C.

PUBLIC DEBT, BUREAU OF THE (Washington, D.C.)
U.S. SAVINGS BOND DIVISION (Chicago, Ill.)

U.S. INFORMATION AGENCY:
Washington, D.C.

U.S. TARIFF COMMISSION:
Washington, D.C.

VETERANS ADMINISTRATION:
Arlington, Va.

Appendix III

Heads of Public Printing, 1852–1970

SUPERINTENDENTS OF PUBLIC PRINTING

John T. Towers, September 1, 1852–December 6, 1853
A. G. Seaman, December 7, 1853–December, 1857
George W. Bowman, December, 1857–May 12, 1859
John Heart, May 13, 1859–March 4, 1861

GPO SUPERINTENDENTS OF PUBLIC PRINTING

John D. Defrees, March 23, 1861–August 31, 1866
Cornelius Wendell, September 1, 1866–February 28, 1867
John D. Defrees, March 1, 1867–April 14, 1869

CONGRESSIONAL PRINTER

Almon M. Clapp, April 15, 1869–July 31, 1876

PUBLIC PRINTERS

Almon M. Clapp, August 1, 1876–May 30, 1877
John D. Defrees, June 1, 1877–April 14, 1882
Sterling P. Rounds, April 15, 1882–September 12, 1886
Thomas E. Benedict, September 13, 1886–May 6, 1889
Frank W. Palmer, May 7, 1889–May 2, 1894

Thomas E. Benedict, May 3, 1894–March 30, 1897
Frank W. Palmer, March 31, 1897–September 8, 1905
O. J. Ricketts (Acting), September 9, 1905–November 27, 1905
Charles A. Stillings, November 28, 1905–February 5, 1908
William S. Rossiter (Acting), February 6, 1908–June 7, 1908
Capt. Henry T. Brian (Acting), June 8, 1908–June 9, 1908
John S. Leech, June 9, 1908–November 30, 1908
Samuel B. Donnelly, December 1, 1908–June 20, 1913
Cornelius Ford, June 20, 1913–April 4, 1921
George H. Carter, April 5, 1921–July 1, 1934
Augustus E. Giegengack, July 2, 1934–March 15, 1948
John J. Deviny (Acting), March 16, 1948–May 5, 1948
John J. Deviny, May 6, 1948–February 28, 1953
Philip L. Cole (Acting), March 1, 1953–April 27, 1953
Raymond Blattenberger, April 28, 1953–January 31, 1961
John M. Wilson (Acting), February 1, 1961–March 4, 1961
Felix E. Cristofane (Acting), March 7, 1961–March 17, 1961
James L. Harrison, March 17, 1961–March 31, 1970
Adolphus Nichols Spence II, April 1, 1970–

Bibliography

Annual Reports of the Public Printers of the U.S. Government Printing Office—1861–1968.

ECKMAN, JAMES. *The Heritage of the Printer.* Philadelphia, Pa.: North American Publishing Company, 1965.

ELLIS, JOHN B. *Sights and Secrets of the National Capital.* New York: U.S. Publishing Company, 1869.

KERR, R. W. *History of the Government Printing Office for a Century.* Lancaster, Pa.: Inquirer Printing and Publishing Company, 1881.

MERRITT, LEROY CHARLES. *The U.S. Government as Publisher.* Chicago, Ill.: University of Chicago Press, 1943.

MORISON, SAMUEL ELIOT. *The Oxford History of the American People.* New York: Oxford University Press, 1965.

OSWALD, JOHN CLYDE. *Printing in the Americas.* Port Washington, N.Y.: Kennikat Press, Inc., 1965.

Public Printing in Peace and War. Washington, D.C., U.S.G.P.O., 1947.

SCHMECKEBIER, LAWRENCE F. *The GPO, Its History, Activities and Organization.* Baltimore, Maryland: The Johns Hopkins Press, 1925.

SCHMECKEBIER, LAWRENCE F., and EASTIN, ROY B. *Government Publications and Their Use.* Washington, D.C.: Brookings Institution, 1961.

THOMAS, ISAIAH. *History of Printing in America.* Albany, N.Y.: American Antiquarian Society, 1874.

Index

Other volumes published in the Praeger Library of U.S.
Government Departments and Agencies are